THE UNRAVELING

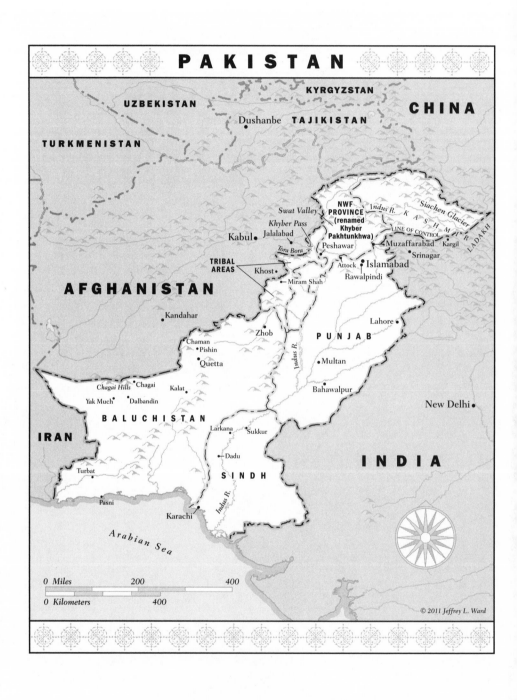

THE
UNRAVELING

PAKISTAN
in the Age of Jihad

JOHN R. SCHMIDT

Farrar, Straus and Giroux New York

FARRAR, STRAUS AND GIROUX
18 West 18th Street, New York 10011

Copyright © 2011 by John R. Schmidt
Map copyright © 2011 by Jeffrey L. Ward
All rights reserved
Distributed in Canada by D&M Publishers, Inc.
Printed in the United States of America
First edition, 2011

Library of Congress Cataloging-in-Publication Data
Schmidt, John R., 1948–
    The unraveling : Pakistan in the age of jihad / John R. Schmidt.— 1st ed.
        p.   cm.
    Includes bibliographical references and index.
    ISBN 978-0-374-28043-7 (hardcover : alk. paper)
    1. Pakistan—Politics and government—1988–   2. Political culture—Pakistan.
3. Pakistan—Foreign relations.   4. Pakistan—Social conditions.   5. Feudalism—
Political aspects—Pakistan.   6. Political leadership—Pakistan.   7. Pakistan. Army.
8. Islamic fundamentalism—Pakistan.   9. Jihad—Political aspects—Pakistan.
10. Terrorism—Government policy—Pakistan.   I. Title.

DS389.S37 2011
954.9105'3—dc23

                                                            2011016162

Designed by Abby Kagan

www.fsgbooks.com

10   9   8   7   6   5   4   3   2   1

For Meg, Graham, and Gordon

Contents

THE UNRAVELING

Introduction

MARCH 25, 2000, ISLAMABAD

It is almost a full eighteen months before 9/11. President Clinton has agreed to make a brief five-hour stopover in Pakistan at the end of a long South Asian trip. The visit is politically controversial because it could be seen as legitimizing the rule of Pervez Musharraf, who had come to power in a military coup the previous October. But Pakistan, armed with nuclear weapons and using jihadist groups to fight a proxy war with India in the disputed province of Kashmir, is simply too important to ignore. The Secret Service, responsible for protecting the president, has its own reasons for opposing the trip. They are concerned about the possibility that Al Qaeda, the jihadist group responsible for bombing the U.S. embassies in Kenya and Tanzania eighteen months earlier, may attempt to assassinate the president. Al Qaeda is based in neighboring Afghanistan, and its head, Osama bin Laden, is an honored guest of the Taliban, the emerging victor of the Afghan civil war, whose strongest supporter just happens be the government of Pakistan.

Despite these Secret Service concerns, the president decides to go through with the trip and the moment of his arrival is at hand. In the bright morning sunshine, the glimmer of an aircraft swings into view. It is not the famous Boeing 747 Air Force One but a considerably smaller 737 decked out in the unmistakable blue-and-white livery of the U.S. government. It lands and taxis to a stop in front of the small reviewing stand, but no president alights. Its passengers turn out to be members of the traveling press corps. Soon another, even smaller, plane appears on the horizon. It is a business jet also bearing U.S. government markings. Landing, it rolls to a stop behind the 737. A few officials emerge, but the president is not among them. A short while later, another aircraft appears, similar in size to the business jet but with no markings to betray its country of origin. It taxis to a stop near the previous plane. A few more officials alight, but once again, no president. More time passes and, finally, yet another small business jet glides into view. A carbon copy of the previous plane, it is totally unmarked. It taxis to a spot hidden from view behind the 737. More minutes pass. Suddenly, the door to the plane swings open and a familiar visage emerges into the glaring sunlight. The president of the United States has finally landed.

FEBRUARY 21, 2002, KARACHI

Daniel Pearl, South Asia correspondent for *The Wall Street Journal*, vanishes on his way to meet with a well-known Muslim cleric in the sprawling southern port city of Karachi. Several days later his employer receives an e-mail showing Pearl in chains, a gun pointed at his head. His captors say he will be executed unless the United States releases Pakistani prisoners held at Guantánamo Bay. In a nod to patriotic Pakistani sensibilities, they also call for the handing over of F-16 aircraft originally purchased in the 1980s but never delivered due to U.S. sanctions against the Pakistani nuclear program. An intensive manhunt is launched, but no trace of Pearl is found. As Pearl's captors well know, Karachi, a vast urban melting pot of twelve million people, devoid of greenery and replete with slums, is an easy place to hide. It is also no stranger to violence, having witnessed decades of street fighting and ethnic and religious warfare, punctuated by occasional attacks against foreigners, including the ambush and murder of two U.S. diplomats in 1995 on their way to work.

Daniel Pearl will suffer a similar fate. On February 21, unknown persons deliver a videotape to the U.S. consulate in Karachi. It lasts three and a half minutes and begins with footage of Pearl relating the details of his Jewish heritage and repeating the demands of his captors. It ends with images of Pearl lying shirtless on a barren floor with his throat cut, already apparently dead. One of his captors then severs the head from his lifeless body, holding it up to the camera as the demands of the captors are flashed one more time on the screen. Five years later, Khalid Sheikh Mohammed, the number three ranking person in Al Qaeda and mastermind of 9/11, will boast to his U.S. captors at Guantánamo that he was the person who performed the grisly deed.

DECEMBER 27, 2007, RAWALPINDI

Benazir Bhutto waves to tumultuous crowds while standing in the open sunroof of an SUV as she leaves a rally in the northern Punjab city of Rawalpindi. She had returned to Pakistan only two months earlier as part of an elaborate deal with President Musharraf to end her eight years of exile and to participate once again in national elections. On arriving in Karachi, her motorcade had been greeted by thousands of adoring supporters eager to welcome her back to her homeland. But their joy and hers had been cut short by the work of attempted assassins, who exploded two large bombs at the front of her procession, sparing her but killing more than 140 others, amid great carnage and pandemonium.

Now she is tempting fate again, campaigning out in the open despite numerous warnings that her life remains in peril. As her SUV moves through a sea of parting humanity, shots ring out, followed by the loud retort of a bomb. Shocked by the percussive effect, Bhutto flies backward and down, the back of her head slamming against the back of the open hatch, fracturing her skull. She is rushed to a nearby hospital, but it is too late. The two-time prime minister Benazir Bhutto, at that moment the most popular politician in Pakistan, is dead. Recriminations begin almost immediately, as Bhutto supporters blame the government for failing to provide adequate security. Claims and counterclaims of responsibility for the assassination are traded back and forth. CIA Director Michael Hayden delivers the U.S. verdict a month later. He lays blame for the assassination squarely at the doorstep of Baitullah Mehsud, leader of the Pakistani Taliban. Enmeshed in a struggle with the

Pakistan army for control of the hardscrabble tribal area of South Waziristan on the Afghan frontier, and closely allied with Al Qaeda, Mehsud had decided to fight back with acts of terrorism inside urban
Pakistan. Benazir Bhutto had just become his most prominent victim.

NOVEMBER 26, 2008, MUMBAI

Ten clean-shaven, well-groomed young men, smartly dressed in black
T-shirts and cargo pants, stride purposefully from the dock area of
Mumbai through the streets of the gigantic Indian metropolis. Split-
ting up, they make their way, some by taxi, others by foot, to several
different venues around the city. Two, including Ajmal Kasab, visit the
central railroad terminus, calmly spraying the main passenger hall
with fire from their AK-47s, killing more than fifty. Other targets include a hospital, a popular café, and two large hotels, the Oberoi and
the Taj Mahal. An obscure Jewish center, which can only have been a
planned target, is also attacked and its residents taken hostage and
later killed. By the time the carnage comes to an end with the final
storming of the Taj Mahal by Indian commandos more than sixty hours
after the attacks had begun, more than 160 people lay dead, several of
them Western tourists. Dead alongside the victims was a peace process between India and Pakistan that had been launched almost five
years before. For, as the sole survivor Kasab soon makes clear to his
captors, he and his fellow young men came from Pakistan.

They were sent by the Lashkar-e-Taiba, a jihadist group whose opu-
lent headquarters lies a few miles from the Punjab capital of Lahore.
This group was formed sometime at the beginning of the 1990s with
the support and possibly at the instigation of the Pakistan army intelligence service, ISI. Its primary mission was to infiltrate Kashmir in support of a local Muslim insurrection against Indian rule that had recently
erupted in the disputed territory. The Lashkar had quickly become notorious for its brazen assaults against Indian occupation forces in the
heavily Muslim Kashmir valley (or Vale of Kashmir, as it is more formally known) and for terrorist spectaculars inside India itself. Embarrassed by the Mumbai attacks, and clearly on the defensive, the
Pakistani authorities deny involvement in the attacks but promise to
cooperate in the investigation. Although they eventually bring charges

against the mastermind of the attacks and several of his accomplices, they make no move against the organization as a whole and seem determined to protect its leader, Hafiz Saeed.

MARCH 3, 2009, LAHORE

The Sri Lankan national cricket team is on its way to Lahore cricket ground to take part in a match with its Pakistani counterpart. Cricket is the national pastime of Pakistan and the only major sport it plays on the international stage. The Pakistanis are grateful that the Sri Lankans have come to Pakistan because they are the only world cricketing power that remains willing to do so. In order to assuage Sri Lankan concerns about terrorism, the Pakistani authorities had promised to provide the kind of security usually deployed only for visiting heads of state. As the bus carrying the Sri Lankan team passes through Liberty Square on its final approach to the stadium, it suddenly runs into a hail of machine gun fire. The stunned cricket players hit the floor as shrapnel explodes around them. Their quick-thinking bus driver floors his vehicle and manages to force his way through to the nearby cricket ground. Although seven team members suffer minor injuries, everyone on the bus miraculously survives. The match umpires traveling in a minivan immediately behind are not so fortunate. Their driver is killed and one of the umpires critically wounded. Security cameras mounted at the scene later reveal several of the twelve assailants standing out in the open methodically firing their weapons, unchallenged by police or other security personnel. Six of the policemen escorting the convoy were already dead. After thirty minutes of firing, their ammunition spent, all twelve terrorists manage to slip away unscathed.

Early suspicion falls on the Lashkar-e-Taiba, since the attack bears the hallmarks of previous Lashkar operations, including the Mumbai massacre three months earlier. Observers speculate it may have been intended as a shot across the bow designed to demonstrate the damage the Lashkar could cause if the government decided to move against it. Suspicion later shifts to an emerging, still shadowy group called the Punjabi Taliban. As more information continues to emerge, it begins to take shape as a loose-knit consortium of jihadist and sectarian groups or their splintered offspring, who have gradually turned against the Pakistani state. As their name implies, the Punjabi Taliban enjoy close ties to the Pakistani Taliban of the tribal areas. But unlike the former, who hail from the ethnic Pashtun periphery of northwestern Pakistan, the Punjabi variety draw their recruits from the Punjab heartland, particularly from the Seraiki belt in the south of the province, a majority Sunni region dominated by unpopular Shiite landlords. Unlike the Lashkar-e-Taiba, which is still prepared to cooperate with the state, the Punjabi Taliban seek only its destruction. Seven months later they will be blamed for carrying out an even more brazen attack against the headquarters of the Pakistan army in Rawalpindi.

This is the story of how such things came to happen in a country that was conceived amid great hopes and expectations as a homeland for South Asian Muslims by a Western business-suited lawyer of decidedly secular ambitions named Mohammed Ali Jinnah. It is the story of how this country became instead a monument to poor government and home to an increasingly toxic witches' brew of radical Islamist groups, which have declared war against Western civilization and come to threaten the foundations of Pakistan itself. It is also the story of how a self-absorbed feudal political class disposed to kick serious problems down the road, and a powerful army in love with its image and bewitched by its obsession with India thought they could use radical Islamic forces to advance Pakistani foreign policy goals without having to pay a steep price for it and were proved wrong. This is a cautionary tale, and my primary purpose in telling it is to explain how Pakistan, thanks to selfish leadership, poor judgment, unconscionable hubris, and a modicum of bad luck, ended up becoming the most dangerous place on earth. Although my focus remains firmly fixed on the people who have ruled over Pakistan, they are not the only players in this drama. India and the United States, through their own mistakes and miscalculations, have also contributed mightily to the current calamity. This, as we shall see, is a story without heroes.

The myriad problems that plague Pakistan today can be traced back to the founding of the state. That is where this story begins. I explore the early history of Pakistan from its creation in the partition of the British Raj in 1947 through the first twenty-five years of its existence. This is how long it took for the feudal civilian politicians, who together with the army now dominate Pakistan politically, to rise to the apex of power. As we shall see, the predominantly Muslim lands that became Pakistan existed on the periphery of the Raj and were relative backwaters. Under British rule they had been dominated politically and economically by wealthy landowners who ruled over large estates and were popularly known as feudals. But these worthies played little role in governing the country at its creation. Its first rulers were politicians from the All India Muslim League, who had led the fight for a separate Pakistani state but who hailed from the major urban centers of India such as New Delhi, Bombay, and Calcutta. With no political constituency in the lands they now governed, these outsiders had little interest in putting their leadership to the vote. As a result, Pakistan was starved for democracy from the very beginning.

This might not have mattered so much for our story had it not been for Kashmir. The struggle between India and Pakistan for control of this overwhelmingly Muslim territory created bad blood between the two neighbors from the outset. Among Pakistanis it fostered a visceral enmity that has become a defining characteristic of their state and is indisputably the primary driver behind their cultivation of radical Islamist forces for state ends. The Kashmir dispute also convinced the early rulers of Pakistan that they needed to maintain a large and powerful army. Within a decade it had become so powerful that it was able to sweep aside the founding Muslim League leadership. The army ruled for more than a decade before its disastrous defeat in the war for Bangladesh independence forced it to turn power back over to the civilians. By this time the original Muslim Leaguers were long gone, replaced by the feudal landlords who had dominated the region prior to partition and who would bring with them their own distinctive brand of politics. They have shared and alternated in power with the army ever since.

In the pages that follow I take a close look at these two groups. These are the people whose actions first led to the rise of jihadist forces in their country and whose decisions continue to shape the course of events there. It is impossible to fully understand why the Pakistanis behave as they do, in their dealings with radical Islam and much else besides, without understanding the motivations and habits of behavior that drive these two groups.

The civilian political class practices a form of politics directly derived from the underlying feudal culture of the region. Political parties in Pakistan are coalitions of patronage networks whose pursuit of power is aimed at gaining access to state resources, which can then be shared among their members. Civilian rulers tend to be so narrowly focused on satisfying their patronage networks that they find it difficult or impossible to address the systemic problems that plague their country. Rather than confront serious problems, they leave them to fester and worsen over time. This has not only produced chronically bad government but also directly aided the spread of radical Islam.

The army has tended to reinforce this behavior, although its primary fixation has been on India, which, despite everything, it continues to regard as the most serious threat to the Pakistani state. The army is by far the most professional organization in Pakistan. Unlike the feudal political establishment, it is a highly selective meritocracy and its officers regard themselves as an elite. It was their decision, supported by their feudal cousins, to nurture jihadist groups as low-cost weapons of war against India. As we shall see, it was their folly to believe they could control them.

No understanding of Pakistan can be complete without examining the role of religion. Mohammed Ali Jinnah, the driving force behind the founding of the state, conceived of Pakistan as a homeland for South Asian Muslims. Although his vision was a secular one, the role of Islam has been contentious from the outset. Judged solely by the headlines, it might appear that Pakistan is overrun with wild-eyed Muslim fundamentalists bearing a grudge. But nothing could be farther from the truth. The majority of Pakistanis are followers of a colorful brand of Sunni Islam that is among the most tolerant and nonthreatening in the entire Muslim world. It is, in fact, the dominant form of Islam throughout most of South Asia and is deeply embedded in the feudal culture of the region. What is true, however, is that the two largest minority sects of Sunni Islam in Pakistan are fundamentalist in nature. It is from these sects that the major jihadist and sectarian groups in Pakistan have sprung. There is also a sizable Shiite minority, historically well integrated into the country's feudal culture and politics. Jinnah, revered by Pakistanis as the Quaid-e-Azam (Great Leader) of his nation, was a Shiite.

Religious political parties exist in Pakistan but have never done well at the polls. Most Pakistanis, in keeping with the underlying feudal culture of the region, vote for the mainstream feudal parties. But the religious parties have been a relentless pressure group pushing to

Islamicize Pakistani society from its very beginning. They eventually found a kindred spirit in the army dictator Zia ul-Haq, who tried to reconstitute Pakistan along Islamic fundamentalist lines, roiling sectarian waters and laying the groundwork for much of the violence that was to follow. It was under Zia that the first real stirrings of radical Islam emerged. The venue was Afghanistan, in the crucible of the Cold War, when the Pakistanis, spurred on and financed by the United States, decided to use exiled Afghan religious groups to help contest the Soviet invasion of their troubled neighbor. This decade-long effort, begun in 1979, attracted Islamic radicals from around the world, Osama bin Laden among them, and succeeded in driving the Soviets out of Afghanistan, but not without serious consequences for Pakistan. Galvanized by the anti-Soviet crusade, the first Pakistani jihadist and sectarian groups came into being at this time, fed by a rapidly expanding number of radical mosques and madrassas. Some sent their members off to fight against the Soviets, while others stayed home to do battle with Shiite extremists, who had themselves become radicalized by the recent revolution in Iran.

It might have ended there, as the Soviets were leaving Afghanistan, had the Pakistanis decided to rein them in, but fate saw fit to intervene. For just as the last Soviet soldier was stepping across the Friendship Bridge, the Muslim population of Kashmir was rising in a popular insurrection against Indian rule. Flattered by their success against the Soviets in Afghanistan, the Pakistanis made the fateful decision to employ the very same tactics in Kashmir. They began infiltrating forces into the Kashmir valley to support the insurrection. Many were local Kashmiris who had fled across the Line of Control into Pakistan in search of training and support. But the Pakistanis also encouraged their veterans of the anti-Soviet jihad to transfer their efforts to this new theater of conflict. Perhaps not surprisingly, the very first Pakistani jihadist group ever formed, the Harakat-ul-Mujahideen, was the first such group to be employed in Kashmir. Not content to stop here, the Pakistanis encouraged the creation of new groups to join the gathering jihad. The perpetrator of the Mumbai massacre, the Lashkar-e-Taiba, was formed at this time, followed several years later by the Jaish-e-Mohammed, a successor organization to the Harakat-ul-Mujahideen. The steady rise in jihadist infiltration during the first decade of the insurrection forced India to pour more and more of its own security forces into the Kashmir valley. By some accounts this eventually peaked at half a million men, a commitment rivaling the size of the U.S. effort in Vietnam.

The Pakistanis would revisit this precedent five years later, in 1994, in the midst of the civil war that erupted following the Soviet departure from Afghanistan. The Pakistanis, unhappy with the Afghan faction they were supporting at the time, decided to shift their backing to an emerging group of dynamic young Afghan religious zealots, many of whom had studied at Pakistani madrassas during the Soviet occupation. These former religious students would call themselves the Taliban. Many Pakistanis from the tribal areas and neighboring Northwest Frontier Province (NWFP) also joined their ranks. Thanks to popular disgust with the petty warlords who dominated southern Afghanistan, and with considerable Pakistani support, their progress proved spectacular. Within two years, they had taken control of the Afghan capital of Kabul. Within four years, they had managed to seize 80 percent of the country.

Surveying the fruits of their labors a decade after the last Soviet left Afghanistan, the Pakistanis were justifiably pleased. They had succeeded in tying the Indian army down in Kashmir and had reason to hope their jihadist proxies might prevail there just as they had against the Soviets in Afghanistan. There were equal grounds for satisfaction with developments in Afghanistan, where their Taliban clients seemed to constitute an inexorably rising tide. But this moment of seeming triumph proved to be as brief as it was illusory, for the Pakistani strategy of using radical Islamists to advance their foreign policy agenda was already beginning to unravel. In Kashmir, the Lashkar-e-Taiba and Jaish-e-Mohammed began to show a penchant for carrying out spectacular terrorist attacks against civilian targets. These culminated in the December 2001 assault on the Indian parliament in New Delhi and the May 2002 massacre of families of Indian soldiers serving in Kashmir, events that catapulted Pakistan and India to the brink of war. In Afghanistan, meanwhile, the Taliban decided to extend sanctuary to Osama bin Laden, whose Al Qaeda operatives would go on to blow up two U.S. embassies in East Africa in August 1998 and come close to sinking the U.S. destroyer *Cole* two years later. Pakistani entreaties that the Taliban leader Mullah Omar hand over bin Laden would fall on deaf ears.

I arrived in Pakistan the day before the East Africa bombings and departed three years later, just two months before 9/11. A career Foreign Service officer, I was assigned to the U.S. embassy in Islamabad as the political counselor. It was my job, along with the officers on my staff, to report to Washington on political developments in Pakistan. Since the United States did not have an embassy in Kabul at that time, we were also responsible for covering events in Afghanistan. It was a turbulent time in Pakistani history, featuring the army coup that brought Pervez Musharraf to power and a near war with India over the army's seizure of Indian border posts at Kargil on the Line of Control in Kashmir. These were high-profile, front-page events, but the most profound and enduring concern I experienced during those three years was over the rise of radical Islam. It was not just that the Pakistanis were using radical Islamic groups in Afghanistan and Kashmir as instruments of foreign policy. These groups were also gaining a strong foothold inside Pakistan itself. Since the favored jihadists recruited from the same radical mosques and madrassas that served as feeder organizations for violent sectarian groups, the Pakistanis were inclined to leave all of them alone. In parts of the country they had already begun to extend their influence into their local communities. The word *Talibanization* entered the lexicon. The Pakistanis, I felt, were playing with fire. It would explode in their faces on 9/11.

I take a close look at the disastrous impact that 9/11 had on Pakistani fortunes. Forced to choose between their Taliban allies and a very angry United States, the Pakistanis opted to support the latter and then watched as U.S.-led forces proceeded to drive the Taliban and their Al Qaeda guests onto Pakistani soil. As we shall see, subsequent Pakistani efforts to support the United States by helping track down senior Al Qaeda officials won them early praise from Washington but converted bin Laden and his followers into enemies. To make matters worse, many Pakistani jihadists, angered by Pakistani support for the United States, decided to throw in their lot with Al Qaeda and turn against the state. Matters deteriorated even further when, under U.S. pressure, the reluctant Pakistanis sent forces into their remote tribal areas to hunt for Al Qaeda militants. This action, beginning in early 2004, brought them into armed conflict with local Pakistani groups that had been sheltering Al Qaeda. These groups quickly coalesced into what came to be called the Pakistani Taliban and made their own war on the state. But the Pakistanis left the Afghan Taliban forces encamped on their territory strictly alone as a hedge against a future Afghanistan they feared would be dominated by their mortal enemy, India.

Shaken by the violent Pakistani Taliban pushback, the Pakistanis tried to deal their way out by inking a series of cease-fire agreements with the renegade forces. This earned them only a short respite, thanks to the storming of Lal Masjid in the summer of 2007, an event that claimed more than one hundred lives and was comparable to 9/11 in its impact on Pakistan. Lal Masjid was a radical mosque and madrassa complex in the heart of Islamabad whose inhabitants had been responsible for a wave of kidnappings and vigilante attacks. The Pakistani decision, after months of dithering, to finally storm the complex created a violent backlash within the radical Islamic community. The Pakistani Taliban resumed their attacks on Pakistani forces and succeeded in fending off subsequent army efforts to drive them from their strongholds. The army failed due largely to its unwillingness to commit adequate forces to the endeavor, prompted by concern over domestic opposition to fighting fellow Pakistanis and reluctance to move forces from its Indian frontier. The Pakistani Taliban eventually brought almost all the tribal areas under their sway, as well as the beautiful Swat Valley, the number one outdoor tourist destination in Pakistan, located in the NWFP only a hundred miles from Islamabad. Worse still, the Pakistani Taliban and their Al Qaeda mentors launched a devastating terrorism campaign inside urban Pakistan itself that would soon number among its victims Benazir Bhutto, the former, and likely future, prime minister of Pakistan.

I bring the story up to the present day, beginning with the notorious Mumbai massacre in November 2008, an attack carried out by the Lashkar-e-Taiba, by this time the only major Pakistani jihadist group that had not yet turned against the state. Mumbai would bring a sudden, violent end to the promising peace process between Pakistan and India that had begun five years earlier. The Indians charged that the Pakistanis themselves were behind the attack, an accusation that gained credence in light of Pakistan's subsequent refusal to crack down on the Lashkar. But this refusal can just as easily be explained by a Pakistani desire to keep this, the most formidable of all Pakistani jihadist groups, from turning against the state. The problem in deciding where the truth lies, here as in so much else having to do with Pakistani involvement with radical Islamists, is the lack of definitive evidence. This is why it is so important to understand Pakistani motives and develop some appreciation of how and why decision makers act as they do. Whatever the truth behind Mumbai, it is hard to see how it served Pakistani interests.

Pakistani fortunes, in fact, reached their lowest ebb in the immediate aftermath of Mumbai, when Pakistani Taliban forces in the Swat Valley reneged on yet another peace agreement and moved into the neighboring district of Buner, a mere sixty miles from Islamabad. This turned out to be the watershed event that finally galvanized the Pakistanis to action. With domestic opinion finally on their side, this time they sent a much larger force into the region, amounting to almost a third of the regular army, first into Swat and then into the tribal areas. They succeeded in driving the major Pakistani Taliban forces out of their primary strongholds but failed to completely defeat them. As a result, the domestic terrorism campaign in urban Pakistan continued, marked by the emergence of a new player on the scene, the Punjabi Taliban, closely allied to their namesakes in the tribal areas and Swat. Nor would the Pakistanis succeed in satisfying a United States that found itself increasingly beleaguered by the resurgence of Taliban forces in neighboring Afghanistan. Although the Pakistanis acquiesced reluctantly in U.S. drone attacks against Afghan Taliban targets in the tribal areas, they steadfastly refused to undertake operations against them themselves, stubbornly clinging to the hope they might someday be able to use them to prevent India from gaining a foothold in Afghanistan once U.S. forces departed the region.

The situation in Afghanistan, where divergent Pakistani, U.S., and Indian interests all collide, highlights the fact that this is not simply a story about Pakistan and the choices it has made. It is also a story about India, whose founding fathers could not resist the temptation to wrest Kashmir away from Pakistan at partition, despite the fact that it was a heavily Muslim area with historically close ties to Punjab. This landgrab earned it the enduring enmity of its Muslim neighbor, resulting in permanent confrontation, several wars and periodic military clashes, the long-running insurgency in Kashmir, terrorist spectaculars such as Mumbai, and a nuclear face-off that could someday lay waste to all its major cities. Pakistani animosity toward India has been the primary driver behind its use of radical Islamic groups for state ends. Even today, Pakistan's policy toward Afghanistan and, specifically, its continuing willingness to allow Afghan Taliban forces to use Pakistani territory to attack U.S. forces in Afghanistan, is driven in no small measure by concerns over the substantial Indian presence there. Yet India accepts no responsibility for this state of affairs, choosing to portray itself exclusively as a victim. It indignantly turns away all outside efforts to help resolve its disputes with its hostile neighbor, despite the fact that its policies in Afghanistan and Kashmir directly affect important U.S. interests.

This is also a story about the United States, whose relations with Pakistan over the years have been decidedly bipolar. The United States has been both a close friend and a hectoring adversary depending on the foreign policy flavor of the moment. This has perplexed and dismayed the Pakistanis, who tend to be more constant in both their friendships and their feuds. They remember all too well how the United States imposed sanctions on Pakistan for its nuclear program only eighteen months after partnering with them to drive the last Soviet soldier out of Afghanistan. As the Pakistanis turned increasingly to jihadists for help in pursuing foreign policy goals, U.S. attention shifted elsewhere. By the time the bombings of the U.S. embassies in East Africa demonstrated the folly of this neglect, the United States found itself with limited options. Even today, U.S. ability to put pressure on Pakistan to do more against the Afghan Taliban is limited by the dependence of its forces in Afghanistan on overland supply routes through Pakistan. U.S. options are also limited by Washington's long-standing unwillingness to bring pressure to bear on India. U.S. soldiers are dying in Afghanistan in part because India has established a substantial presence there, this despite the fact it has no convincing strategic interests in the country other than to threaten Pakistan on its western frontier. The killing of Osama bin Laden just as I was putting the finishing touches on this book pays sad testimony to the increasingly acrimonious nature of relations between the United States and its ostensible Pakistani ally. The operation, which was conducted by U.S. special forces operating without Pakistani knowledge or consent deep inside Pakistani territory, deeply embarrassed the Pakistanis. Abbottabad, the relatively small city where bin Laden met his final end, lies barely thirty miles north of Islamabad and serves as home to the Pakistan Military Academy, the Pakistani counterpart to West Point.

The fact that Osama bin Laden was killed not far from the Pakistani political capital in a city known for its association with the Pakistan army seems somehow fitting. For this is ultimately a story about

Pakistan and the choices it has made, which have dismayed the world and threaten to bring the country to the brink of destruction. Pakistan today is awash in radical Islamic groups, at war with some and reluctant to move against others, out of fear for the consequences of doing so or because it still hopes to use them in its forlorn struggle with India. How is this story going to end? This is the question I set for myself in the penultimate chapter. Will the Pakistanis be able to resist the forces of radical Islam pressing in on them, or are they destined to succumb to the radical Islamic threat? In attempting to answer this question, I examine the impact that events in Afghanistan, the continuing presence of Al Qaeda in the region even after the death of bin Laden, and relations with the United States are likely to have on Pakistani fortunes. I consider whether the Pakistani Taliban can be completely crushed and, if not, whether their growing cooperation with jihadist forces in the Punjab heartland of Pakistan represents an existential threat to the state. I also consider prospects for another Mumbai and whether the Lashkar-e-Taiba will someday turn against the Pakistanis. Since it is one thing to assert that Pakistan will fall to jihadist forces and quite another to describe convincingly how it might happen, I attempt to sketch out what I regard as the most plausible scenario.

I bring this story of Pakistan in the age of jihad to its conclusion by considering what would happen if jihadist forces actually did come to power in Pakistan. My intention is to illustrate how much is at stake here. Pakistan is a nuclear-armed state. If jihadists succeed in seizing power in Islamabad, they will inherit an arsenal that today numbers approximately one hundred nuclear warheads. There has been a good deal of debate in recent years about whether Iran could be deterred if it developed nuclear weapons. But what about a Pakistan governed by jihadists? Given the widely held belief among radical Islamists that martyrdom in the pursuit of jihad guarantees them entry into paradise, is it reasonable to believe that they could be deterred? Could the United States, or India, for that matter, afford to risk finding out, or would they feel the need to strike first? And if they did decide to strike first, what would the impact be on Pakistan itself? Could it survive such an onslaught, or would this precipitate the final unraveling of the Pakistani state? These are just some of the questions I explore in considering this, the darkest of all Pakistani scenarios. Let us hope it never comes to that.

1. An Improbable State

Pakistan is an improbable country. The forefathers of the people who now dominate it politically and militarily were bystanders in the movement to create the Pakistani state. The people actually responsible for its creation were outsiders. Mohammed Ali Jinnah, leader of the Muslim League and founder of the nation, was a Bombay lawyer who wanted a separate homeland for the subcontinent's Muslims because he feared they would become a political underclass in a unified India dominated by Hindus. His vision was secular, not religious, similar to the one that drove the founding of Israel as a place where Jews could live free from persecution. It had not always been this way. Early in his political career, Jinnah had been a member of the Congress Party of Gandhi and Nehru, and had worked with them in pursuing Indian independence from Britain. But he had moved on to join the Muslim League and parted final company with his former colleagues because of their conflicting views on the status of Muslims in an independent India. Jinnah believed that Muslims constituted a distinctive community—he used the term *nation*—entitled to parallel status with the Hindu majority, while Congress insisted on a unitary state with no special status accorded on religious grounds. These differences proved unbridgeable, and at a mass meeting of the Muslim League in Lahore in 1940, Jinnah appeared to take matters one step further, calling not simply for special status for Muslims in an independent India but also for some sort of division along communal lines.

Here matters stood until the end of World War II. At that time, a Britain vastly weakened by the war began moving the subcontinent rapidly toward independence. In the negotiations that ensued, Jinnah played his cards very close to the vest. Some historians have argued that he did not really favor a separate Muslim state at all but preferred a form of confederation in which a Muslim component composed of the Muslim majority provinces of the British Raj would share power at the center as an equal partner with a similarly constituted Hindu entity. Central to his conception was the status of Punjab and Bengal. These were far and away the most populous and politically important of the Muslim-majority provinces, although the majority in each case was a slender one. Jinnah wanted them included in the Muslim entity, not simply because of their Muslim majorities but also because, unlike the other Muslim-majority provinces, they had substantial Hindu populations. This Hindu presence in the Muslim entity would help ensure fair treatment for the significant Muslim minority destined to remain behind in the Hindu-majority provinces. Jinnah adamantly opposed any suggestions that Punjab and Bengal, due to their balanced populations, themselves be partitioned along communal lines, arguing that this would result in "a mutilated and moth-eaten" Muslim entity whose very viability would be in question.

Congress, for its part, would have none of this. It was unprepared to grant equal status to a Muslim population that was outnumbered by the Hindu community four to one, and it insisted that an independent India have a strong central government representing all Indians regardless of religious affiliation. If push came to shove and the British decided to inflict a separate Muslim entity on them, they demanded that Punjab and Bengal also be partitioned. Forced to choose between these incompatible demands, the British tried to steer a middle course. Rather than give Congress the undivided unitary state it wanted, they decided to partition the Raj along communal lines. Jinnah ended up with his Muslim entity, but as a completely independent state, not the equal pillar of a confederated India that would have given him a platform to speak on behalf of all Indian Muslims. Equally troubling for Jinnah, the British acquiesced in Congress's insistence that Punjab and Bengal themselves be partitioned, leaving Jinnah with his "mutilated and moth-eaten" state. It would consist of what was left of these two partitioned provinces, along with three other indisputably Muslim majority provinces, all of which were located on the western periphery of the Raj: Sindh, the Northwest Frontier Province, and Baluchistan. Pakistan, such as it was, had been born.

Contrary to most expectations, which proved to be naive, partition turned out to be a bloody affair. This was particularly true in the Punjab, where Hindus and Sikhs living in the Pakistani west fled eastward, while Muslims living in the Indian east fled west. Along the way each group was set upon by the other in thousands of separate encounters that claimed hundreds of thousands of lives. The Pakistani state that resulted from the division of British India consisted of western and eastern halves separated by a thousand miles of Indian territory. As Jinnah both knew and lamented, both halves had existed on the extreme periphery of the Raj and were relative backwaters. The area that became West Pakistan and was to later morph into the Pakistan of today following the breakaway of Bangladesh was a latecomer to British India. The Punjab, which despite having been cut in two formed the heart of West Pakistan and was by far its most populous province, had been an integral part of the Moghul empire. Its capital, Lahore, is the site of some of the greatest monuments of Moghul architecture. When the empire began to crumble in the early part of the eighteenth century, the Punjab fell under a succession of lesser rulers, eventually becoming the centerpiece of a Sikh empire formed in the early nineteenth century. The other areas that constituted West Pakistan—Sindh, Baluchistan, and the Northwest Frontier Province—suffered similar fates, significant portions of the latter also falling under Sikh control.

The British move into the region took place in the middle of the nineteenth century, many decades, and in some cases more than a century, after they had brought the heartland areas of the subcontinent under their control. Their motive for coming was not strictly territorial gain but rather to use these territories as a barrier against Russian penetration into the region, as part of what became known as the Great Game. Sindh was taken over in 1843. Punjab and large parts of what came to be known as the Northwest Frontier Province were wrested from the Sikhs in 1849. Most of Baluchistan was incorporated during the following decade. British passage into the region was not always easy. The British fought two bloody wars with the Sikhs.

Attempts to conquer Afghanistan failed utterly, and the entire British garrison of Kabul suffered annihilation at the hands of Pashtun tribal warriors during a horrific retreat from the Afghan capital in 1842.

Britain's desire to use these territories primarily as a buffer against Russian expansion was reflected in the way they were governed. Although the region was heavily garrisoned as a hedge against Russian penetration, the British footprint was considerably lighter here than elsewhere in the Raj. In the Punjab, the British left the landed Muslim feudal aristocracy, which had managed to weather the era of Sikh rule relatively intact, essentially in charge of their own affairs. At the beginning of the twentieth century, its western border areas, populated largely by Pashtuns, along with additional territory extracted from Afghanistan, were consolidated into the Northwest Frontier Province, adding yet another layer of buffer. As a final buffer, the British had established the frontier tribal areas to the west of the NWFP between the Raj and Afghan territory, whose ruler was obliged to agree to a border between the two that became known as the Durand Line. The Baluch lands were similarly left to manage their own affairs, while for the better part of a century Sindh, as something of an exception, was governed from neighboring Bombay.

This heavily garrisoned, largely self-governing buffer on the western extremity of the Raj was far from the political ferment in the center of British rule that would lead in time to independence and partition. Unlike Bengal, where the Muslim League of Mohammed Ali Jinnah had a substantial following, the areas that were destined to become West Pakistan were dominated by local notables. In Punjab and Sindh, the Muslim leadership was drawn from the rural agricultural elites popularly known as "feudals." Their politics, based on patron-client relationships that had long dominated the region, were alien to the urban-centered Muslim League, with its own single-minded fixation on promoting Muslim civil and political rights. In Punjab, feudal landlords running under the banner of the local Unionist Party drubbed Muslim League candidates in the 1937 provincial elections held by the British under the recently enacted Government of India Act. The results were similar in Sindh. The leaders of the Muslim League had no idea how to play at feudal politics and would never learn. Nonetheless, with independence looming at the end of World War II, they managed to co-opt these local worthies, who swept into office in the

1946 provincial elections under a Muslim League banner, while campaigning in the same old feudal way.

The men who would actually govern the new nation were not from there. Mohammed Ali Jinnah was born in Karachi but had been educated at the Inns of Court in London and made his career in Bombay. Most of the Muslim League leadership came from similar backgrounds, hailing from the great population centers of northern and western India, such as New Delhi, Calcutta, and Bombay. This was where their natural political constituency and potential vote banks lay. But relatively few of their political supporters chose to follow them into the new country. Most were either too poor to afford the long journey or unwilling to risk starting over in a new and foreign land. Fully one-third of the Muslim population of British India, numbering thirty-five million people, remained behind. The great majority of the more than six million Muslims who did move west made the much shorter journey from eastern to western Punjab in the bloody population exchange that occurred at the time of partition. Only a relatively small number, comprising only 3 percent of the population of the new state, migrated from the urban heartland of British India into the nascent state, most of them settling in the new capital of Karachi.

These mohajirs (Arabic for "emigrant"), as they came to be called, were outsiders from the start. The one advantage they possessed, and it was considerable, was their predominance in the upper reaches of the Muslim League and in the civil service. So long as Mohammed Ali Jinnah dominated the political landscape, their sparse numbers and outsider status made little difference. But Jinnah was already wasting away from tuberculosis when independence came, looking the part of a cadaver long before he became one. His death barely a year after partition left a vacuum that his political heirs, none of whom enjoyed anything approaching his stature, found increasingly difficult to fill. The assassination of his trusted deputy and anointed successor, Liaquat Ali Khan, three years later, left relative nonentities in charge of the government of Pakistan. Names such as Khawaja Nazimuddin, Ghulam Mohammed, and Iskander Mirza do not echo down the corridors of history, even within Pakistan itself. Overwhelmed by the difficulties inherent in building a new nation from scratch, and with no experience in managing the affairs of state, the surviving Muslim Leaguers turned increasingly to senior civil servants, many of them also mohajirs, who had opted for Pakistan at independence after serving in the British colonial administration. With no natural political constituency on Pakistani soil, neither group had any real interest in putting their hold on power to the vote.

A constituent assembly, tasked with promulgating a constitution, did exist, peopled in West Pakistan by many of the same feudal landlords who had flocked to the Muslim League banner during the 1946 provincial elections. But it was largely ignored and in 1954 summarily dismissed. In fact, no constitution would emerge until 1956, almost a decade after independence, when a reconstituted assembly finally managed the deed. The closest the first parliamentary Pakistanis had come previously to agreeing on one was in the Objectives Resolution passed in 1949, which takes up less than half a page. This suited the mohajir politicians and civil servants who dominated the executive branch of government, since it enabled them to run the country more or less as they saw fit. But whether they realized it at the time or not, their command of the highest offices of government was a rapidly wasting asset, since they had neither the personal stature nor the political base to maintain it. The mohajirs were already doomed to devolve into a purely regional political force centered on Karachi, led by former student radicals with a penchant for street fighting. But the instrument of their demise would not be the disputatious feudal landlords who had filled the West Pakistan seats in the original constituent assembly. Their rise to political power would have to await the ascent of the Sindhi landlord Zulfiqar Ali Bhutto in the aftermath of the breakaway of Bangladesh. But that event still lay more than a decade in the future.

The instrument that ended the mohajir grip on power and hastened the final disintegration of the original Muslim League was the Pakistan army. Unlike the mohajirs, the army was largely an indigenous force. Punjabi soldiers from the so-called army triangle of Rawalpindi, Attock, and Jhelum in northern Punjab had dominated the ranks of the Indian army under British rule. At the time of partition, however, the newly constituted Pakistan army was sufficiently bereft of senior officers that Jinnah asked British officers to stay on to fill out the senior ranks. The first two army chiefs were British; the third was Ayub Khan, who would become the first military dictator of Pakistan. It was Ayub, educated in the British way at Sandhurst and dismayed at the squabbling of the politicians and government officials around him, who moved in to fill the gap left by the mohajir decline. But he might never have had the chance had it not been for the dispute with India over control of Kashmir that broke out at the time of partition.

Jammu and Kashmir, to give it its full name, was a princely state with an overwhelmingly Muslim population ruled over by a Hindu maharaja. There were hundreds of such entities under the Raj, each nominally sovereign but in fact fully subordinate to British rule. At the time of independence, the British preserved this fiction of special status by giving each princely sovereign the right to opt for either India or Pakistan. In almost every instance this posed no threat to the basic principle guiding partition that Muslim majority areas would pass to Pakistan and majority Hindu areas to India. But there were three exceptions. Two princely states, those of Hyderabad and Junagadh, had heavily Hindu majority populations but were ruled by Muslims. The third was Kashmir. The Muslim ruler of Junagadh opted for Pakistan but was forced to flee under Indian pressure. His Hyderabad counterpart temporized for a year before an Indian invasion obliged him to accede to India, thus bringing this largest of princely states under Indian control. But events in Kashmir were to play out somewhat differently.

The ruler of Kashmir was a Hindu by the name of Hari Singh. The Muslim heartland of the princely state, centered on the beautiful Vale of Kashmir, had been in Hindu hands for only a century. Singh's enterprising great-grandfather Gulab, who was ruler of the much smaller majority Hindu state of Jammu just to the south of Kashmir, had agreed to indemnify the British for the costs they had incurred in fighting the First Sikh War in return for British help in securing the throne of Kashmir. The Vale at this time was still a part of the Sikh empire the British had just defeated and was headed by an appointed Muslim governor. The British, eager for the cash, sent a force of ten thousand men into the area, removed the governor, and installed Gulab Singh on the throne.

Thanks to this event, a seemingly minor incident in the annals of the Great Game, Hari Singh had to choose between Pakistan and India as the time of partition drew near. He proceeded cautiously, negotiating a standstill agreement with the nascent Pakistani government, giving Pakistan responsibility for maintaining Kashmir's postal and communications systems. Such agreements generally served as precursors to accession, and this led the Pakistanis, who regarded Kashmir with its heavy Muslim majority as theirs by right, to believe that events were moving in their direction. But at this point, unanticipated developments intervened. Muslims in the Poonch area of Kashmir suddenly rose in what appears to have been a spontaneous insurrection against taxes recently imposed by the local Hindu authorities. The new Pakistani government, fearing this might upset the applecart, decided to take Kashmir by force, hastily arranging to send Pashtun irregulars from the NWFP into the princely state. As this unruly ragtag army marched toward the Kashmiri capital of Srinagar, a panicked Hari Singh called on the Indians for support. They obliged in return for his signature on the Instrument of Accession to India and immediately began flying Indian troops into Srinagar airport.

These forces succeeded in stopping the Pashtuns in their tracks and eventually began pushing them back. Regular Pakistan army forces soon entered the fray but were able to produce only a stalemate. After more than a year of fighting between the two increasingly exhausted fledgling armies, the two sides agreed to a cease-fire. The main prize, the heavily Muslim Vale of Kashmir, remained in Indian hands. Pakistan had to content itself with a narrow sliver of Kashmiri territory to the southwest, which it named Azad (free) Kashmir, as well as a large but sparsely settled area in the Karakorum mountains to the north. But the issue of who should finally rule Kashmir was far from settled. Pakistan and India agreed to refer the matter to the UN, which mandated a plebiscite. The chief sticking point was the requirement that Pakistan remove its forces from the areas under its control. The Pakistanis refused out of fear that India would move its own forces into them, which the Indians strongly implied they had the right to do. As a result, no plebiscite was ever held.

Both sides have continued to maintain their own separate claims to the princely state. India asserts that all of Jammu and Kashmir passed into Indian possession once Hari Singh signed the Instrument of Accession. Pakistan claims that UN involvement and the fact that India had at one time agreed in principle to a plebiscite demonstrate that this cannot be so. But Pakistani claims go beyond legal niceties. They argue that, since the basic principle underlying partition was that majority Muslim areas should become part of Pakistan, Kashmir is by right theirs. They point to Indian hypocrisy in incorporating the Hindu-majority princely states of Hyderabad and Junagadh despite their Muslim rulers, while denying Pakistan the same right in Kashmir. As far as most Pakistanis are concerned, the Indian seizure of Kashmir was a landgrab pure and simple, and they have never been able to reconcile themselves to the unfairness of it. Regardless of who is right or wrong, legally or morally, the fact of the matter is that the Kashmir dispute poisoned relations between Pakistan and India from the very beginning. The fact that India delayed, and in some cases reneged on, transferring some of the material and financial assets owed to Pakistan under the terms of the partition agreement did not help matters. Most Pakistanis concluded that India could not be trusted and suspected that it did not really accept the legitimacy of a separate Muslim state. Consequently, they would need to remain vigilant and cultivate a powerful army.

From that time forward, a disproportionate share of scarce Pakistani resources began to flow to the army. Ayub Khan, the first native Pakistani chief of army staff, soon took his place beside the civilian successors of Jinnah and Liaquat at the apex of political power. Like Jinnah and the other early leaders of the Pakistan movement, Ayub was a man of secular tastes and ambitions. Despite his Sandhurst education and its preachment that the military should stay out of politics, he grew increasingly frustrated with what he saw as the selfish and shortsighted behavior of his civilian colleagues. His memoirs are replete with descriptions of their venality. His disgust only increased when squabbling politicians from West and East Pakistan proved unable to agree on a formula for national elections under the terms of the 1956 constitution they had recently approved. He must also have noticed that, although his civilian colleagues carried impressive political titles such as president and prime minister, they had no popular political following. And he, moreover, had all the guns. In October 1958, he conspired with the president, Iskander Mirza, who was a civil servant, not a politician, to declare martial law. Only three weeks later, Ayub had Mirza dumped and seized the reins of power for himself. The army had made it all the way to the top and would never stray far from it again.

Ayub governed as a pro-Western, pro-business leader who shared the largely secular views of the mohajir class he had brushed aside. His secular orientation was sufficiently strong that at one point he even tried to drop the word *Islamic* from the official title of the state. His distaste for politicians was reflected in a new constitution he pushed through creating a political system he called Basic Democracies, in which direct elections were held at only the lowest, most local units of government. Pervez Musharraf, a general of similar disposition, would institute a similar scheme for similar reasons some forty years later. Ayub also remembered the Pakistani claim to Kashmir and managed to involve Pakistan in another war with India over it. Events in the former princely state since the first war ended had precipitated increasing disenchantment with Indian rule. At first, Sheikh Abdullah, the unchallenged leader of the Kashmir Muslim community, had worked cooperatively with the Indian authorities. Called the Lion of Kashmir, he had been a friend of Nehru's and was sympathetic to the Congress Party. His land redistribution program had made him wildly popular among his Muslim constituents, and he managed to secure virtually full autonomy for Kashmir under Article 370 of the Indian Constitution. By 1953, however, this began to strike him as too little. Overly impressed, perhaps, by his own star power, he began moving toward advocacy of full independence, proposing that this be one of the options included in any future plebiscite, in addition to the Pakistan-or-India choice set out in the UN mandate. Alarmed by this turn of events, the Indian government helped engineer his removal by ambitious subordinates and he was subsequently imprisoned as a security threat.

There matters stood for another decade. In late 1963, the most venerated religious relic in Kashmir, a strand of hair reputed to be from the beard of the Prophet Mohammed, disappeared from its shrine in a Srinagar mosque. This provoked mass demonstrations by angry Muslims in the Kashmir valley as well as attacks against Hindus, in Kashmir and other parts of India. A panicked Indian government released Sheikh Abdullah in an effort to calm the waters and even allowed him to travel to Pakistan for discussions with Ayub aimed at defusing the crisis. The relic was eventually returned to its shrine, but an unrepentant Abdullah continued to stoke unrest, prompting the Indians to return him to prison in May 1965. The Pakistanis, meanwhile, drew conclusions from these events that would soon lead to war. Ayub and his army colleagues had been encouraged by the trouncing India had suffered at the hands of China in their 1962 border war and impressed by their own prowess in besting Indian forces in skirmishes in the disputed Rann of Kutch border area early in 1965. They conceived the idea of sending irregular forces into Kashmir to foment a general Muslim uprising. The young Pakistani foreign minister, Zulfiqar Ali Bhutto, was one of the biggest supporters of the plan. The idea was not a new one. During the previous decade, the Pakistan army had begun studying low-intensity guerrilla warfare as a possible weapon to use against India in Kashmir. They had gotten their inspiration from studying a number of successful insurgencies elsewhere. Algeria, Yugoslavia, North Korea, and, especially, China headed the list.

But the gambit, launched in August 1965, was a flop. Many of the infiltrators were intercepted on their way in and the rest failed miserably in their efforts to spark a Muslim insurrection. A follow-up attack by regular Pakistan army forces made little headway, and the Pakistanis were caught napping when Indian forces invaded Pakistan farther to the south near the Punjabi capital of Lahore. The result was a political debacle for Ayub, who was forced to accept a punitive cease-fire after the United States imposed an arms embargo that left Pakistani forces critically short of spare parts. The 1965 war marked the second time Pakistan and India had fought over Kashmir and it was also the second time that Pakistan had sent irregular forces into the disputed territory, following in the footsteps of the ragtag Pashtuns they had used in 1947. But its particular importance for our story lies in the fact that it seems to have been the first time Pakistanis used the term *mujahideen* to refer to irregular forces fighting for a Pakistani cause.

This attribution, which seems to have originated with Bhutto, is significant because of its religious connotations. In Islamic parlance, mujahideen are warriors seeking to spread the cause of Islam through jihad, or holy war. But this does not really fit the events of 1965. There is no evidence that the irregular forces that infiltrated Kashmir harbored radical Islamic views or were otherwise driven by Islamic ideology, any more than the secular Ayub himself was. By most accounts, the infiltrators were Kashmiris who had ended up living on the Pakistani side of the original cease-fire line and were motivated not by religious zeal but by a more secular desire to reunite their homeland and liberate their fellow Kashmiris from Indian rule. In referring to them as mujahideen, Pakistani officials may have been trying to wrap them in the Islamic equivalent of the flag, suggesting that even at this relatively early date, jihadist motivations were regarded as virtuous and praiseworthy, even by Pakistanis such as Ayub and Bhutto, who were decidedly secular in their own management of the affairs of state. It also provided them with deniability by creating the impression that these were religiously motivated individuals acting according to their own lights.

Although the 1965 war dealt Ayub a politically fatal blow, it electrified the career of Zulfiqar Ali Bhutto, who argued that Pakistan should have fought on no matter what. He would resign as foreign minister the following year, and a year later form the Pakistan Peoples Party (PPP). The other major casualty of the 1965 war was the already imperiled relationship between West and East Pakistan. These two entities had been strange bedfellows from the beginning, separated by the entire breadth of India, with little in common beyond the fact of their Muslim majorities. Preindependence Bengal had been one of the founding territories of the British Raj and its dominant city, Calcutta, had served as the British capital until 1911. Jinnah had wanted Calcutta badly, proclaiming at one point that without it Pakistan would be like a man without a heart. But the British had given it to India, along with the western half of Bengal, even while conceding that the remainder, centered on Dacca, was little more than a "rural slum." This attitude carried over into the new Pakistani state, where political power quickly gravitated westward. In part, this reflected the closer cultural affinities between the northern and western areas of India, from which the mohajirs had come, and the neighboring areas of Punjab and Sindh, which lay immediately to the west. It also reflected the overwhelming predominance of West Pakistanis in the army and in the growing civil service bureaucracy that emerged after independence. Even in a purely Pakistani context, East Pakistan was regarded as a backwater.

This did not go unnoticed by the Bengalis. They were unhappy early on at the refusal of the ruling mohajir elite in Karachi to accord Bengali the status of an official language alongside Urdu. This had led to strikes and violent demonstrations in Dacca in 1952. A new political party, the Awami League, had emerged in 1950 to represent Bengali interests and had quickly consigned the local Muslim League to oblivion. But it had been unable to substantially improve the lot of the East Pakistanis, who failed to benefit from the economic development and strong economic growth that characterized the Ayub era. During the 1965 war with India over Kashmir, East Pakistan was left virtually undefended, a fact not lost on its inhabitants. This proved to be a watershed event that stoked growing Bengali desires to manage their own affairs. These desires were given full expression a year later when the Awami League leader, Sheikh Mujib, promulgated his Six Points, calling for the granting of complete autonomy to the East. This event was to set the stage for the final unraveling of the original Pakistani state.

Beset from all sides, a sick and dispirited Ayub Khan resigned in 1968, and his Basic Democracies scheme collapsed almost immediately thereafter. His replacement, a nondescript general named Yahya Khan, attempted to calm the situation in East Pakistan by steering the country toward its first nationwide elections. He also decided that the distribution of seats in the new national assembly would be based on population. This represented a potential opportunity for the Bengalis since East Pakistan at the time had a slightly larger population than West. Since the first major task of the assembly would be to formulate a new constitution to replace the discredited Ayub version, a good deal was riding on the outcome. Despite the East Pakistani advantage in seats, Yahya and the West Pakistani politicians contesting the election, now dominated by Zulfiqar Ali Bhutto, expected mixed results that would favor neither East nor West. But when the elections were finally held at the end of 1970, the Awami League of Sheikh Mujib ended up winning all but two of the seats contested in Bengal, giving it an absolute majority in the new assembly.

At this the West balked. Yahya, egged on by Bhutto, refused to convene the new body without assurances from Mujib that he would not seek to insert his Six Points into the new constitution. This Mujib was not prepared to do, and events quickly deteriorated from there, leading to open revolt in the East and a bloody crackdown by the Pakistan army, which drove millions of East Pakistanis across the border into India. Beset with refugees and sensing an opportunity to mortally wound its troublesome foe, the Indians decided to intervene. In the ensuing conflict, the third between the two countries since partition, the Indians made short work of the isolated Pakistan army forces in

Bengal, forcing the entire garrison of more than ninety thousand to surrender. They also managed to fight off a hastily assembled Pakistani assault in Kashmir aimed at drawing Indian forces away from the east. As a result of these events, the new nation of Bangladesh came into being. The Pakistan army found itself discredited for the very first time, and Yahya was forced to resign, both as army chief and leader of Pakistan. Into this vacuum stepped the leading civilian politician in the newly downsized nation, Zulfiqar Ali Bhutto.

Bhutto, whose PPP had dominated the election results in the West, was the first member of the indigenous landed feudal aristocracy to reach the apex of political power in Pakistan. He entered government through the foreign ministry and moved up quickly to head several ministries before becoming foreign minister. His rise to prominence symbolized that of his class as a whole, as his mentor, Ayub, turned increasingly to native West Pakistanis for political support during his years in office. Many had joined the Convention Muslim League party that Ayub established as a pro-army successor to the moribund original. Although Bhutto was a feudal, he was also a man of his times. Where Ayub had been pro-business, Bhutto was a third-world socialist. Where Ayub had been pro-American, Bhutto was pro-Chinese and proceeded to lead Pakistan into the Non-Aligned Movement. Charismatic and ruthless by turns, he was as authoritarian in temperament as any military dictator. He consciously tried to marginalize or subordinate the other centers of power in the newly downsized country but discovered to his chagrin that he could not easily function without them. He reorganized and downgraded the civil service, firing many of its senior members, but discovered he needed bureaucrats to manage the industries and financial institutions he had insisted on nationalizing. He tried to cut the recently humiliated army even further down to size by forming his own paramilitary force, but he found he needed army soldiers to put down a separatist rebellion in Baluchistan, an intervention that helped to restore both its confidence and its power. In 1972, he made the fateful decision to pursue a nuclear weapons program in order to keep pace with India. And while his socialist populism and mania for nationalization earned him the support of the poor and dispossessed, it dealt the Pakistani economy a blow from which it has never recovered.

In national elections held in 1977, six years after Bhutto came to power, his PPP won a victory far too overwhelming to be credible. This sparked a large and violent protest movement that spanned the political opposition and persuaded the army it needed to intervene. Bhutto was removed from power, imprisoned, and later hanged on a conveniently found murder charge. The instrument of his downfall was the ungrateful Zia ul-Haq, whom Bhutto had made army chief by jumping him over several more senior officers. Bhutto had reputedly appointed him because of his fawning behavior, which proved to be a fatal mistake. While Zia would take Pakistan in a decidedly different direction, Bhutto nonetheless left behind a substantial legacy of his own. Although his socialist policies proved anachronistic, he had already begun moving in directions more consistent with his feudal heritage. Beset by mounting opposition elsewhere, he fell back on the support of fellow landlords, who benefited from cheap loans provided by the newly nationalized banks. As in other third-world countries, the nationalization of industry brought substantial resources directly under government control, providing a rich source of political patronage, a commodity whose pursuit would become the cornerstone of Pakistani political life.

But Bhutto's most important legacy was not a policy or a program but the ascendency of his own socioeconomic class. His tenure represented the rise to power of the traditional landowning gentry of Punjab and Sindh, accompanied by a newly moneyed urban industrialist class whose leaders would absorb and espouse the very same feudal politics. His own party would shrug off his antiquated socialism under the leadership of his daughter, Benazir Bhutto, and take its place at the center of Pakistani politics, alongside the party of the Lahore industrialist Nawaz Sharif, who would appropriate the name Muslim League. But his Muslim League was not the party of Mohammed Ali Jinnah. That party and the Pakistan it once dominated were no more. The new Pakistan that was emerging was not the grand homeland for subcontinent Muslims that Jinnah had intended, but a strictly regional variation that would be dominated politically by two groups of players who were already firmly rooted in its soil.

One was a civilian political class consisting of wealthy landowners and their industrialist counterparts, who would pursue a distinctive form of politics derived directly from their feudal past. The other group, the army, whose leaders sprang from considerably more modest roots, would seek to keep their civilian betters on a short leash, while pursuing their self-anointed destiny as defenders of the nation against what they imagined to be an ever-present Indian threat. Rich in ambition but lacking in judgment, these two groups would carry Pakistan into the age of jihad.

2. The Feudals and the Army

In the preface to his study on feudal culture in Pakistan, the social anthropologist Stephen Lyon relates the story of a rural landowner named Malik Asif. It is a bright sunny day in the Attock district of Punjab bordering the Indus River. With no other commitments to detain him, he decides to hold one of his periodic morning audiences for local villagers. On this particular morning, two people have come to see him. One is an old sharecropper named Baba Raheem who used to farm land for Asif's father when Malik was a boy and who now works for Asif's uncle. He has come to ask Malik Asif for help in filling out a complicated form that his son must submit in order to apply for an identity card. This is something Baba Raheem and his son cannot possibly do on their own because they are illiterate. Baba Raheem has come to Malik Asif because his current employer, Malik Asif's uncle, is angry at him for having refused to work some land and is punishing him by not helping. Baba Raheem hopes that Malik Asif will help him in appreciation for the many long years of loyal service he provided to his father.

The other man is a neighboring landowner by the name of Zahir Khan. His uncle, who lives in another district some distance away, has asked him to help one of his local villagers find work as a sharecropper. Zahir Khan is unable to help his uncle by hiring the man himself since he has no spare land to farm. But he has heard that Malik Asif is looking for someone to farm several acres of his land. He has decided to seek his help while at the same time doing him a favor, a gesture he hopes will also enable him to discharge the familial obligation he feels toward his uncle. He has no idea whether the man his uncle has recommended is any good at farming. If he turns out to be good at it, Malik Asif will be grateful. If not, little will be lost since Malik Asif needs someone badly and most sharecroppers are not very good at farming in any event.

Malik Asif seems prepared to help Baba Raheem, despite the fact his uncle might not appreciate the gesture, because he does feel strong bonds of loyalty toward him due to his long years of association with his family. He also decides to take on the sharecropper recommended by Zahir Khan. He understands perfectly well that the man may not work out, but he needs someone to work his spare land and welcomes the opportunity to do a favor for his landlord neighbor.

Lyon uses this real-life vignette to illustrate some of the bonds of reciprocal obligation that lie at the heart of Pakistani feudal culture. Members of Pakistani feudal society are enmeshed in networks of obligations whose precise natures are defined by the various roles they fill within the overall social structure. Although Malik Asif is superior in status to Baba Raheem, he nonetheless feels ties of obligation to him. Zahir Shah, by contrast, is his equal in station, but each man feels positively disposed to seek favors from, and grant favors to, the other. In seeking to do a favor for Malik Asif, Zahir Shah has not only given his neighbor a reason to repay it at a later date but also discharged the obligation he felt to his uncle, who will thereby incur an obligation to help him. This granting of favors and incurring of obligations is one of the cornerstones of Pakistani feudal society.

Malik Asif, like his fellow landowners, sits at the top of a local network of reciprocal expectations and obligations. His sharecroppers are obligated to provide him with a certain percentage of their crops as payment for the right to farm his land. He, in turn, is obligated to provide them with the food and other necessities they are unable to provide for themselves and to help them out in special times of need. Although this patron-client relationship between landowner and sharecropper is a vital one in feudal Pakistani society, it is far from the only one. Each landowner is also enmeshed in a broader network of familial ties. He is a father to sons who owe fealty and loyalty to him. Within his own generation, he fits into a pecking order consisting of younger and older brothers and cousins. He also looks upward to his own father, uncles, grandfathers, and great uncles, all of whom are tied together in an even broader patrilineal clan association known in Pakistan as a *biraderi*. Members of a biraderi are linked to one another by their own distinctive network of reciprocal expectations and obligations, which include patterns of mutual cooperation and support and occasionally rivalry and competition. As the example of Malik Asif and Zahir Shah illustrates, such networks extend beyond farm and family to include neighboring landlords and important figures in their village community. These various interlocking networks together constitute the basic fabric of rural Pakistani life.

Power relationships are a key element in this fabric. Although a landowner is bound by ties of obligation to his sharecroppers, he is more powerful than they are and exercises control over them. Power and status also vary within nuclear families and more broadly within biraderis. Fathers and uncles have more influence and exercise more power than sons and nephews. Often a senior member of a biraderi will be acknowledged as the overall head of the clan. It is also true that some landowners are more powerful than their neighbors and enjoy greater status in their communities. The power and status that accrue to a landowner are not solely a function of how much land he inherits from his father, but depend on his ability to protect his holdings from the depredations of others and to extend them even farther. From time immemorial the most successful landlords have enjoyed great prestige and influence extending far beyond the relatively narrow confines of their own home territories.

It does not take a great deal of imagination to envision how such a culture would adapt to the demands of electoral politics. A biraderi would be likely to support members of its own clan in local elections and form associations with neighboring biraderis to support candidates for elections at the larger district level. Malik Asif and Zahir Shah may be not only acquaintances prepared to do favors for each other but also political allies. Political alliances at the regional and national levels represent ever larger assemblages of biraderi networks culminating in the formation of political parties. As a strictly practical matter, political parties do not crystallize from the bottom up but from the top down, with a Zulfiqar Ali Bhutto or a Nawaz Sharif reaching out to regional and local factional leaders, who sit on top of their own regional and local networks. This is not a new phenomenon. As noted in chapter 1, feudal landlords drubbed the Muslim League in regional elections held in Punjab in 1937. They competed under the banner of the Unionist Party and were able to exploit their biraderi and other associational networks to outmaneuver their befuddled opponents.

It was these very same feudal networks that abandoned the Unionist Party for the Muslim League several years later when it became clear that a homeland for subcontinent Muslims was likely to emerge from the coming partition of the Raj. Competing under a Muslim League banner in the regional elections held in 1946, they swept to victory and ended up forming the great bulk of the West Pakistani representation in the constituent assembly established after independence. Although they were dominated politically during the first two decades of Pakistan's existence, first by the mohajir class and then by the army, they finally emerged on top when Zulfiqar Ali Bhutto came to power following the breakaway of Bangladesh. Even though Bhutto was later supplanted by another military dictator, the feudal political class was by then entrenched as the civilian alternative to army rule. The politics that would emerge under Benazir Bhutto and her great rival, Nawaz Sharif, after the death of Zia would be feudal in character and even the army would find itself drawn inexorably into it.

The mainstream political parties in Pakistan can best be viewed as patronage networks, whose primary goal in seeking political office is to gain access to state resources, which can then be used to distribute patronage among their members. Two parties have come to dominate civilian Pakistani politics since the death of Zulfiqar Ali Bhutto. The PPP he established is one of them, led by his daughter Benazir until her own assassination in December 2007. The other is the Pakistan Muslim League (PML) of Nawaz Sharif. Nawaz rose to prominence during the rule of Zia ul-Haq, who made him chief minister of the Punjab, the highest executive position in the province. There is actually a certain commonality in the origins of the two parties since both were founded by the civilian protégés of military dictators. The chief difference is that Bhutto founded the PPP after having parted ways with Ayub, while Nawaz formed the PML with army encouragement, although an army general would later remove him in a coup.

Not unlike Malik Asif in his village, Nawaz Sharif and Asif Zardari, who succeeded his wife, Benazir Bhutto, as leader of the PPP, sit on top of vast networks of reciprocal expectations and obligations. Beneath them are powerful patrons in their own right who have given these party leaders their political support and expect repayment in kind. These men, and sometimes women, command regional networks that constitute the essential building blocks of each party, whose own component parts extend down to the biraderi level and the individual landowner and his sharecroppers. But Pakistani political parties are not now, nor have they ever been, an exclusively rural phenomenon. Feudal politics have long since penetrated the cities and towns, and the wealthy industrialists who have risen to prominence in recent decades have fully internalized the feudal way of doing business. Nawaz Sharif is himself an example, having inherited a substantial industrial empire from his father based on textiles and iron foundries. So too is Chaudhry Shujaat, who leads his own breakaway faction of the PML, formed after Nawaz Sharif was ousted by the army chief, Pervez Musharraf, in the 1999 coup. Their patronage networks reach down into the factories and shops of urban Pakistan as well as into the rural countryside.

Electoral politics are inherently competitive. In the feudal political system that has evolved in Pakistan, political parties and individual candidates attract support by promising to do a better job of delivering the spoils of office than the competition, even if, at the most basic level, this means little more than helping a tenant farmer or factory worker pay an overdue electricity bill. Much like Malik Asif in his village, many politicians host regular open house sessions where their constituents can come to ask for help. Most candidates for national and provincial office can count on the support of one or more patronage networks, which the Pakistanis like to call vote banks. These typically center on a particular party, such that any candidate from that party can count on support from the members of the party vote bank. Since feudal party politics in Pakistan tend toward dynasticism, major parties are typically associated with and dominated by a particular family. The PPP is dominated by the Bhutto family. It was so heavily associated with the person of Benazir Bhutto at the time of her assassination that some observers doubted its ability to survive her death. It did so by making her widower, Asif Zardari, and their nineteen-year-old son, Bilawal, at the time a university student in Britain, joint heads

of the party. Zardari was elevated even though he had long been a figure of popular derision for a corrupt acquisitiveness that had earned
him the nickname Mr. Ten Percent.

Similarly, the Nawaz Sharif wing of the PML (popularly known as
the PML-N; the N is for Nawaz) is completely dominated by Nawaz
and his younger brother Shahbaz. Their faction went into decline
when they were both exiled to Saudi Arabia following the Musharraf
coup but quickly revived when they were allowed to return in late
2007. While they were in exile, their leadership of the party was temporarily undercut by a breakaway faction (known as the PML-Q; the
Q is for Quaid-l-Azam, that is, Jinnah) of party notables led by Chaudhry
Shujaat, who made the decision to support the new army government following the coup. The popularity of the Chaudhry wing itself
waned with the declining popularity of Musharraf, and a number of its
supporters, together with their patronage networks, returned to the
Nawaz fold when the Sharifs returned. Although each of the major
parties has its hard core of unshakable support, the breakaway of the
Chaudhry wing demonstrates the tactical nature of Pakistani politics.
Political networks and individual politicians not infrequently change
their loyalties based on their tactical assessment of where their best
interests lie.

This is much easier to do in a political system based on patronage
because the basic calculations are not ideological but are narrowly
focused on self-interest. Although loyalty clearly counts for something
in a feudal system, political leaders and individual politicians are ultimately motivated by considerations of electability and the relative
likelihood of gaining access to state resources. The problem of party
switching is sufficiently serious that Nawaz Sharif, during his second
term as prime minister, used his overwhelming parliamentary majority
to pass a constitutional amendment forbidding members of the national and provincial assemblies from switching sides. This is not to
say there are no ideological differences between the major parties.
The PPP continues to pay lip service to its socialist origins, although in
practice this simply means it tends to be somewhat more progressive
on social and religious issues. Members of the Nawaz and Chaudhry
wings of the PML tend to be more conservative in their social and
religious attitudes and, until Nawaz ran afoul of it, more closely supportive of and linked to the army.

Pakistani politics are notoriously cutthroat, with the mainstream parties locked in a perpetual struggle to undermine one another in the competition for access to political patronage. Parties out of power represent anything but a loyal opposition, regardless of their composition. They have no interest in waiting five years for their next chance at the patronage feeding trough and behave accordingly. Parties in power, on the other hand, are equally unprepared to leave their defeated opponents in peace. It has become a favored tactic over the years to pursue corruption charges against them. The Ehtesab Bureau established by Nawaz Sharif at the beginning of his second term as prime minister was particularly notorious in this regard. A senior PML politician confessed to me during this period that he thought the number one political problem in Pakistan was the inability of Pakistani governments to behave as if they might someday be in opposition.

Despite the competitive, and frequently combative, nature of Pakistani politics, one thing all politicians seem to agree on is the need to preserve the prerequisites of their socioeconomic class. This is reflected most clearly in their united resistance, regardless of party affiliation, to paying income taxes. Feudal landlords have led the way, steadfastly opposing any attempt to impose taxes on agricultural income. Despite the fact that agriculture is responsible for 22 percent of Pakistan's gross domestic product, it generates only 1 percent of its tax revenue. I had the opportunity to discuss this state of affairs with a wealthy Punjabi landowner who was also a politician and former government minister. She pointed out that she and her fellow landowners had an obligation to provide a safety net for the sharecroppers who worked their lands. Because they had to take care of so many people, they simply could not afford to pay taxes. Part of her argument was undoubtedly correct. As noted earlier, furnishing food and other necessities and providing assistance in times of need are arguably the most important reciprocal obligations assumed by landlords in feudal Pakistani society.

But, at its core, the argument is specious. The feudal landlords who dominate much of Pakistani politics are not struggling to get by, even in hard economic times. They may provide their sharecroppers with the basic staples of life, but they do not provide them or their children with critical social services such as access to education. In Pakistan, as elsewhere, that is supposed to be a job for the state. But the state has not been very good at it. As we saw at the beginning of this chapter, Baba Raheem and his son were both illiterate. This is why the elder Raheem needed help from Malik Asif in the first place. Unfortunately, Baba Raheem and his son are hardly exceptional, particularly in rural society. Only 57 percent of Pakistanis can read or write, not surprising given the fact that Pakistan spends only 2 percent of its gross national product on education, the lowest in a region that includes Nepal and Bangladesh. A large part of the reason for this is that feudal landowners do not pay taxes on their income, leaving the state with insufficient funds to finance public education. This is not simply a failing of the landlord class, however. Pakistani industrialists have embraced the feudal resistance to paying taxes just as they have embraced feudal politics. Pervez Musharraf complained a year after seizing power that only 1 percent of Pakistanis paid any income tax at all. More recent estimates put the figure at 2 percent. Even the U.S. secretary of state, Hillary Clinton, in a visit to Pakistan in the fall of 2009, felt compelled to note that the ratio of taxes to gross domestic product was among the lowest in the world.

These are not just interesting facts; they have real consequences. Pakistan's gross underinvestment in education at all levels is a key reason it lacks competitiveness in the world economy. Pakistan had no counterparts to the five technology institutes in India established by Nehru whose graduates helped propel that country to the forefront of the information technology revolution. Forty percent of the Pakistani workforce continues to work on the land, and its export economy remains heavily dependent on the production of low-quality textiles that compete poorly in the global marketplace. There is no sign on the horizon of the kind of economic breakout that propelled South Korea forward a generation ago or is propelling China and India forward today. I vividly remember a conversation I had with a senior Pakistani diplomat several years ago. He was criticizing India for having two economies, a successful high-tech one that catered to the English-speaking elite, and an underfunded economy that delivered a miserable existence to everyone else. I remember thinking at the time that that was one more successful economy than Pakistan had. Yet despite its sorry economic state today, fifty years ago per capita income in Pakistan equaled that of South Korea and far outdistanced that of China. The lack of funding for public education has not only helped cripple Pakistan economically but also directly encouraged the rise of religious madrassas.

But it is not just that feudal politicians are selfish. They are so narrowly focused on tending to their patronage networks and maximizing their short-term self-interest that they find it difficult or impossible to address long-term systemic problems. Once a political party or coalition emerges victorious in an election, the most urgent task facing its leadership is not to fix the education system but to begin distributing the spoils of office. Faction leaders and senior party patrons expect to be rewarded with government positions appropriate to their station, beginning with the most senior ministerial positions in the cabinet. This process works its way down the food chain of governmental offices until all the positions available through patronage have been filled. (Asif Zardari at one time had sixty ministers in his cabinet.) Government officials are then able to use the influence and access to resources that come with their positions to advantage both themselves and the members of their patronage networks.

Lyon provides two examples that vividly demonstrate how this process works. One concerns a midlevel civil servant who wishes to secure a posting closer to his home district. His brother and uncles are well connected politically and he asks them for help. They agree to put the request to the PML-N provincial assemblyman who represents their Punjab district. He is predisposed to grant them this favor since they are influential members of his local patronage network and were instrumental in his recent election. His constraint is that he has no direct power in the matter since civil service transfers are a provenance of the national government. What he does have is membership in good standing in the patronage network of Chaudhry Shujaat, who at this particular moment is interior minister in the Nawaz Sharif cabinet. By trading on his ties to this national leader, he is able to get the civil servant transferred closer to home, even though this requires transferring a more senior and better-qualified civil servant out of the position.

The other example involves a successful businessman, born in Pakistan but currently a U.S. resident, who is coming back to Pakistan for a visit. Like many Pakistanis who have left the country and made good, he is returning with an impressive number of suitcases, each containing expensive presents for various family members and friends. One of

his prospective beneficiaries, a boyhood acquaintance, is eager to ensure that the businessman will not have to suffer the depredations of
Pakistani customs officials, who are notorious for confiscating gifts as
bribes. He contacts his local provincial assemblyman, who is related to
him by marriage, and asks him to help. The assemblyman belongs to a
patronage network led by a well-known national cabinet minister, who
arranges to have his personal assistant meet the incoming businessman
at the airport. After using his relationship to the cabinet minister to
clear the way with the airport authorities, the assistant escorts the businessman directly off the plane and into the airport VIP lounge. He
takes his passport, gets it stamped, and returns several minutes later
with the businessman's unopened luggage, taking his leave only after
personally escorting the happy visitor to the parking lot.

Just how ingrained such behavior has become in Pakistani political
culture can be seen from my own experience. I was preparing to return to Washington after my three years as political counselor at the
U.S. embassy in Islamabad. The major political parties frequently hold
farewell receptions for departing senior U.S. diplomats, and Chaudhry
Shujaat hosted one for me at his Islamabad residence. This was almost
two years after the coup that deposed Nawaz Sharif, and Shujaat was
by then the leader of the PML-Q, closely allied with Pervez Musharraf, and arguably the most powerful politician in Pakistan. I happened
to let slip that my family and I would be stopping in Hong Kong for
a few days on our way back to the States. Although I strongly doubt
Chaudhry Shujaat viewed me as a member of his patronage network,
he replied immediately that he had good Pakistani contacts in Hong
Kong who would meet us at the airport, see to our luggage, and drive
us to our hotel. I thanked him for his kindness but told him as politely
as I could that this would not be necessary since we had already made
other arrangements. After the reception, I asked my Pakistani political
assistant to contact Shujaat to reemphasize the point. He agreed to do
so but replied with some bemusement that it would do no good. He
was right. As soon as my family and I cleared immigration in Hong
Kong, we found three well-dressed Pakistani men waiting for us. They
introduced themselves, escorted us to a comfortable waiting room,
politely but firmly asked us for our baggage stubs, returned several
minutes later with our luggage, and escorted us and our bags to the
parking lot.

Although Pakistani politicians are masterly in the art of dispensing patronage, they have great difficulty providing effective governance. With their attention firmly but narrowly focused on satisfying the needs of their patronage networks, there is little left over for the nation as a whole. Policies aimed at a nationwide audience tend to be populist in nature, such as government subsidies on imported commodities including food and petroleum, or Nawaz Sharif's so-called Yellow Taxi scheme, which made low-cost small business loans available to people who were unlikely to pay them back. Politicians tend to prefer such measures because they are both highly visible and have immediate payoffs. More systemic, longer-term solutions to urgent national problems not only threaten vested feudal interests, as in the case of income taxes, but also play out over far too long a time frame to appeal to politicians whose touchstone is the short-term dispensing of political patronage.

It requires little imagination to see where such policies lead. They lead to the poorhouse. Nations whose economies are uncompetitive in the global marketplace yet dependent on imported fuel and other vital commodities, and whose governments pay out more than they take in, are bound to be chronically broke. Pakistani governments have repeatedly found themselves forced to borrow money from the IMF and other international lenders. They have done this so frequently and for so long that servicing their international debt now consumes a third of the Pakistani federal budget, more than twice the amount spent on the second largest budgetary item, which in Pakistan, of course, is national defense. The sad fact of the matter is that Pakistani governments cannot come close to balancing their books even though they massively underfund public education and other social sector services.

Rather than alter the selfish and shortsighted behaviors that have led them to this pretty pass, Pakistani governments have become experts in the art of manipulating the IMF and other international creditors. In order to get the money they need to see them through the crisis of the moment, they frequently agree to tough terms. These typically include solemn promises to tax agricultural income and end government subsidies of basic commodities. After receiving their first tranche of funds, however, they often simply walk away from the agreement and return to their bad old ways. Alternatively, they make no real effort to meet the targets they accepted and instead seek to renegotiate more liberal terms, which the IMF almost always agrees to do. These stratagems have provided successive governments with the funds they need to avoid defaulting on their loans but without having to implement any serious or long-lasting reforms. The Pakistanis have been able to get away with such behavior because the IMF and other creditors are unwilling to risk the consequences of a Pakistani financial collapse. Pakistani governments not only know this, they depend on it.

This tendency to kick serious problems down the road has become a defining characteristic of feudal politics in Pakistan. This is not only a natural default setting for a political system based on the dispensing of political patronage; it is also reinforced by what has proved to be the ephemeral nature of civilian Pakistani governments. Since the return to electoral politics following the death of Zia in 1988, no civilian government has served out its full term of office. Knowing this, politicians waste no time taking their turn at the patronage feeding trough. The pattern has become a familiar one. A new government is elected and takes office amid widespread hopes that maybe this time things will be different. But each government proves as feudal as its predecessor, focused single-mindedly on servicing its patronage networks. The economy fails to improve, and another financial crisis inevitably looms. The government now finds itself increasingly unpopular but is too much a victim of the patronage imperatives that drive it to be able to change its ways. Its patronage networks begin to hemorrhage. The political opposition begins clamoring for blood. The press is appalled at such manifest incompetence, and ordinary Pakistanis want to throw the bums out. All of which lays the groundwork for yet another army intervention.

At first blush, the army appears to have little in common with feudal Pakistani politicians. Relatively few of its officers come from feudal or moneyed backgrounds, although some marry into them. They are predominantly the sons of the urban middle class, for whom the army offers a pathway to higher status and material well-being. Pervez Musharraf was the son of a midranking civil servant, as was Zia ul-Haq. Many officers are themselves the sons of officers, such as Ashfaq Kayani, who succeeded Musharraf as army chief. The enlisted ranks, or *jawans*, as they are called, come predominantly from rural backgrounds. Many of them hail from the so-called army triangle, consisting of Attock, Rawalpindi, and Jhelum districts in northern Punjab, which has been contributing soldiers to the army, first under British rule and now for Pakistan, for many generations. The army triangle used to furnish a disproportionate percentage of the officer corps as well, but in recent years the army has worked hard and with some success to broaden its recruitment base to better reflect the nation as a whole.

Unlike the feudal political class, which is narrowly focused on servicing its patronage networks, the army is ostensibly focused on the general welfare of the nation. It sees itself, and is seen by other Pakistanis, as the primary defender of national sovereignty and the ultimate guarantor of domestic stability. Its members take great pride in their supposed professionalism. The army views itself, and is viewed by most Pakistanis, as the only truly professional organization in the country. One former senior army officer tried to illustrate this professionalism to me by stressing that every coup attempted against the army leadership from within had failed, while every coup launched by the army leadership against civilian governments had succeeded. While this might strike a Western audience accustomed to civilian control over the military as damning the army with faint praise, in a third-world country where democracy has not yet become internalized, it actually carries some weight.

The army officer corps is an exclusive meritocracy and it is not easy to win admittance to the club. In a typical year only several hundred out of an applicant pool of fifteen thousand pass the rigorous examination process. Most of the senior army officers I knew were intelligent men who struck me as more sophisticated and worldly in their outlook than many of their feudal political counterparts. But they also seemed to harbor a single-minded mistrust of, and antipathy toward, India, a disposition that helps to define them as a class. The Indians unfairly took Kashmir, they insist. The Indians do not recognize the legitimacy of the Pakistani state. The Indians, if we let down our defenses, would be certain to try to do us harm. These attitudes have been drummed into generations of young army officers and have taken root in the institution as a whole.

Many Pakistanis, particularly in the press and among the liberal intelligentsia, believe that this anti-Indian mantra is purely self-interested, since it helps guarantee the army its privileged position in society. But I find this interpretation a bit too cynical. One of my best army contacts in Pakistan was a retired lieutenant general who headed a prominent Islamabad think tank. He was a soft-spoken, reflective, almost bookish man, who seemed remarkably mild-mannered for someone who had managed to reach the top of such a martial profession. We were talking about Kashmir and he told me he had reluctantly come to the conclusion that India would never relinquish it and that Pakistan would have to learn to live with this. But when I turned the subject to what would happen if another war were to erupt over Kashmir and Indian armor managed to break through Pakistani defenses, threatening to cut the country in half, I was taken aback by his answer. He looked at me gravely, his voice seeming to tremble with emotion. He said in that event Pakistan would have no choice but to use nuclear weapons.

The voices of Pakistani officers also sometimes tremble when talking about feudal politicians, for whom they feel disdain bordering on contempt. Army attitudes here, it would seem, have changed little since the time of Ayub. But this in no way distinguishes them from their Pakistani counterparts in academia, civil society, and the media, all of whom harbor similar attitudes. Nor would it be fair or accurate to describe Pakistan army officers as contemptuous of democracy and ready to launch a coup at the drop of a hat. In the fall of 1998, Jehangir Karamat, who preceded Pervez Musharraf as army chief, became embroiled in a dispute with Nawaz Sharif over a speech he delivered sharply criticizing the government and calling for establishment of a National Security Council, which would give the army a formal seat in the cabinet. At the time, Nawaz was becoming widely unpopular, not only for economic mismanagement but also for his increasingly dictatorial style. The air was full of coup talk, and I went to see my bookish lieutenant general, who happened to know Karamat well, to get his take on the situation. I half expected him to embrace the coup rumors, but his response, once again, surprised me. He said he was "one hundred percent certain" there would be no coup. When I asked how he could be so sure, he replied that the army chief believed in democracy. Karamat resigned the very next day.

The role of Islam in the Pakistan army is also sometimes misunderstood. Many officers are pious Muslims, some harbor fundamentalist views, and on occasion this has taken on a political cast. As we shall see in the following chapter, this occurred most notoriously during the regime of Zia ul-Haq. In 1995, a major general of radical Islamist sympathies named Abbasi tried to carry out a coup at army headquarters but failed miserably. This was one of the incidents the senior army officer I quoted earlier was referring to when he said that no coup against the army leadership had ever succeeded. Nonetheless, in response to this incident, the army started paying more attention to the religious beliefs of its officers and began diverting those suspected of harboring extremist views into unpromotable positions. In general, however, religion has not and does not play a major role in determining the priorities of the Pakistan army. Officers are and always have been evaluated by their peers based on professionalism and military competence, not on their religious beliefs. Exceptionally pious officers, identifiable by the fact that most of them have beards—indeed, they are called "beards" by their fellow officers—are a distinct minority within the upper reaches of the army.

During my tenure in Islamabad, there was an American officer attending the National War College—the elite army training school for newly minted flag rank officers—as an exchange student. I asked him to count "beards" among his Pakistani colleagues. In the prestigious War Wing, consisting of the fifty best and brightest Pakistani one-star generals, only four had beards. This does not mean such officers rarely reach the top. The two senior officers who launched the coup against Nawaz Sharif in October 1999, Mahmud Ahmed and Mohammed Aziz Khan, were reputed to be religious fundamentalists, although only Aziz sported a beard. The army chief on whose behalf they acted, Pervez Musharraf, was, by contrast, well-known in army circles as a man of distinctly moderate social and religious views, an Ayub rather than a Zia. In Pakistan, corporate army blood is thicker than fundamentalist Islamic water.

Of course, the Pakistan army is hardly unique among military organizations in having a strong corporate identity. What makes it distinctive, even exceptional, are the extraordinary lengths to which it goes in order to take care of its own. It oversees a vast industrial and agricultural empire whose main purpose is to ensure the welfare of retired army personnel. The army-owned Fauji Foundation and Army Welfare Trust are the two largest business conglomerates in the country. The Fauji Foundation oversees companies producing fertilizer, cement, and breakfast cereals; other Fauji enterprises drill for natural gas and manage oil terminals. The foundation is even into investment banking and stock brokering. The Army Welfare Trust is involved in many of the same kinds of enterprises under its own Askari label. It manages a sugar mill, hires out retired jawans as security guards, and leases helicopters and pilots for tourism and industry. Askari Leasing Limited is the largest leasing company in Pakistan. The army is also one of the largest landowners in the country, much of it agricultural. Although retired senior officers live far less ostentatiously than their feudal cousins, in my experience they live far better than their army pensions would seem to warrant.

This substantial involvement in industry and agriculture, designed specifically to protect the welfare of its members, bears many of the attributes of a patronage network, albeit a highly regimented one. This should come as no real surprise since the army is a product of the very same culture that gave rise to the feudal political system in Pakistan. This helps to explain why the army, when it does come to power, tends to govern in much the same way as its civilian counterparts. When Pervez Musharraf ousted Nawaz Sharif, there was a good deal of hope among Pakistanis fed up with the feudal way of doing business that the army would begin implementing the reforms that civilian politicians refused to make. At the beginning, Musharraf talked a good game, but he ended up doing very little. On the plus side, he generally respected freedom of the press and was considerably less confrontational than Sharif. But although he made a big show early on of criticizing the feudals for refusing to pay income taxes, he made no serious effort to follow through. He was quick to condemn the feudal political establishment for its self-absorption and rapaciousness but responded limply by introducing his own version of Ayub's threadbare Basic Democracies scheme.

The fact is that when push comes to shove, the army has a vested interest in maintaining the status quo. Not only does it seek to protect its agricultural and industrial holdings as any good feudal would, it also fears the potential chaos that would come with attempting to bring about fundamental change. In a country like Pakistan, in which feudal relationships are so firmly entrenched, it would be a mammoth and very probably bloody undertaking. The conservative ethos of the army, with its emphasis on order and discipline, is constitutionally at odds with such activity. Risking fundamental change would under-mine military preparedness and jeopardize the central mission of the army in protecting the nation against the presumed Indian threat. Even Zia, who in his efforts to Islamicize the country was by far the biggest exception to this rule, made no real attempt to dismantle the basic feudal culture of the country. Army governments are therefore essentially holding actions. Even when the army is in charge, its tendency is to focus on its own immediate corporate self-interest and kick serious problems down the road.

Like Ayub and Zia before him, Musharraf eventually felt the need to bring civilians back into government and began doing so even more quickly than his predecessors. Within a year of taking power, the army was trying to convince senior PML leaders, whose relations with Nawaz Sharif had been strained even before the coup due to his authoritarian style, to break with him and establish their own pro-army version of the party. As we have seen, this led to the formation of the PML-Q under Chaudhry Shujaat. Musharraf found himself obliged to move in this direction because of the one transcendent constraint under which any army operates. Although it enjoys a monopoly of physical force and can seize power any time it chooses, army rule lacks the legitimacy of democratically elected governments. This is one reason why every army chief who has seized power has felt the need to seek constitutional grounds, however specious, for doing so. This is not simply a point of political science. Army officers appear to have genuinely internalized the belief that democracy is preferable to dictatorship. A number of my senior army contacts told me they regarded the fact that Pakistan has failed to become a successful democracy as a black mark against their country, although they were less prepared to acknowledge their own considerable responsibility.

This represents something of a sea change in attitude since the time of Ayub and Zia and helps explain why exercising influence behind the scenes has become the default setting for army involvement in government. This was on clear display during the return to civilian rule after the death of Zia. The Eighth Amendment to the Pakistani constitution, promulgated in 1985 under the Zia presidency, gave the president rather than the prime minister the power to dissolve parliament. Zia's successors were relative figureheads, and during the decade between Zia and Musharraf, the army was able to conspire with them to remove three successive governments from power, two led by Benazir Bhutto and one by Nawaz Sharif. These actions were taken not on a whim but only after each government had blundered into economic and political crisis and lost most of its popular support. In each case, the results were not a return to army rule but the holding of new parliamentary elections, which were won all three times by the political opposition due to the widespread unpopularity of the deposed regime.

Thanks in large measure to these repeated interventions, there is a widely held belief, both in Pakistan and among Pakistan watchers elsewhere, that the army calls the shots regardless of whether it holds formal power. But if that were really the case, it seems unlikely the army would have felt the need to move against civilian governments as often as it did in the 1990s. The truth seems to be that it fully shared the frustration felt by the general public over the performance of these governments. Similarly, if the army was really in charge, it would not have been necessary for Jehangir Karamat to call for the creation of a National Security Council, and Nawaz Sharif would not have been in a position even to contemplate removing him from office.

This does not mean that the army has no influence over civilian governments. Far from it. Its influence on national security and defense is formidable and it does not shy away from expressing its displeasure when a civilian government does something it doesn't like. A good example is the Lahore Summit in early 1999, when Nawaz Sharif invited his Indian counterpart, Atal Vajpayee, to Pakistan in an effort to improve relations. The army was not happy with this and made its opposition known by boycotting the event. Then, several months later, it became enmeshed in a near war with India after provocatively occupying Indian border posts that had been abandoned for the winter at Kargil along the Line of Control in disputed Kashmir. It was widely believed at the time that the army had taken this action in order to torpedo the improvement in relations that Lahore had brought about. In the blame game that followed the subsequent Pakistani withdrawal from Kargil in the face of U.S. pressure and a massive Indian counterattack, both Pervez Musharraf, who was then still relatively new as army chief, and Nawaz Sharif used the press to criticize each other for what had proved to be a major military and public relations debacle. This formed the backdrop for the Musharraf coup that followed several months later.

Although the decade leading up to the coup featured a revolving door of incompetent civilian governments, the political system that emerged during this period was actually both resilient and fairly stable. The army used the Eighth Amendment as a kind of safety valve, permitting the political system to let off steam, while ensuring that each of the major parties was able to take its turn at the patronage feeding trough. When Nawaz Sharif disrupted this pattern by abolishing the Eighth Amendment in 1997, he removed this safety valve, leaving the army with little choice but to live with his incompetent, increasingly despotic rule or find some other way to move against him. The moment of truth came in October 1999, several months after Kargil, when Nawaz tried to fire Musharraf, whom he had come to regard as an intolerable threat. Confronted with the second premature dismissal of an army chief in the space of a year, the army decided it had to act or risk losing its institutional independence. Would the army have eventually moved against Nawaz in any event? My guess is that it probably would have, not because it coveted power but because Nawaz, like Zulfiqar Ali Bhutto before him, seemed determined to bring all major centers of power in Pakistan under his personal sway, something the army would not tolerate.

With no army to look over his shoulder, Musharraf managed to last considerably longer than his civilian predecessors. He was eventually brought down by accumulating unhappiness with his rule, much of it flowing from the alliance he forged with the United States in the aftermath of 9/11 and the subsequent terrorist blowback inside Pakistan. The immediate cause of his downfall, however, was a domestic political dispute, specifically, his firing of the Supreme Court chief justice, Iftikhar Chaudhry, whom he feared would find him ineligible to run for a second term as president. This effort at preemption triggered a revolt inside the legal community, whose rallies and street demonstrations attracted widespread media coverage and public support. The two main opposition political parties at the time, the PPP and PML-N, effectively piggybacked on what came to be known as the Lawyers' Movement, and with army popularity nosediving alongside that of Musharraf, his military colleagues finally persuaded him he had to go.

The Lawyers' Movement represented the first real stirrings of civil society in Pakistan. Its emergence raised hopes among liberals that the stranglehold on power exercised by the feudals and the army might someday be broken. But the protesting lawyers owed much of their success to the fact that Musharraf had already been seriously weakened. The outcome would almost certainly have been different had the drama played out several years earlier when Musharraf was popular. Once Musharraf passed from the scene, moreover, the protesting lawyers quickly faded back into the political woodwork. His departure paved the way for a full return to civilian feudal rule, with the army retreating to a respectful, if watchful, distance. The PPP and the PML-N emerged from their long sojourn in the political wilderness as the two most popular parties in the country, almost as if Musharraf had never happened. As before, their focus remained firmly fixed on servicing their patronage networks while studiously avoiding dealing with the serious problems that plague their country. The result has been government that is as predictable as it is ineffective. Political parties, and even leaders, may come and go, the army may come and go, but governance in Pakistan remains the same.

Yet despite the fact that the feudal political system delivers chronically bad government, no one seems concerned enough to seek genuinely fundamental change. Even the Lawyers' Movement was aimed primarily at protecting its own turf rather than transforming society as a whole. Unlike other nations in which secular political forces have risen up to challenge oligarchic rule, there is no real sign of this in Pakistan today. There are no Lenins or Fidels or Maos to be found. Ordinary Pakistanis grumble a lot, but they do not form revolutionary conspiracies or plot to take over the government. As election day dawns, they continue to wend their way to the polling stations to cast their ballots for one or another of the mainstream feudal parties. They still allow themselves to get their hopes up when the army takes over or a new civilian administration comes into power. And they still just shrug their shoulders when both of them eventually fail. They do all this—and continue to forbear—because in Pakistan the political system is simply a manifestation at the political level of underlying feudal patterns to which they have been acculturated for centuries.

Left strictly to its own devices, it is possible this dysfunctional system could muddle on indefinitely. But Pakistan does not have this luxury. A threat to the system has emerged and it is a serious one. Unlike Bolshevism and Maoism, which sprang up in opposition to the ruling elites in Russia and China, the threat in this case was nurtured from infancy by the same Pakistani political establishment whose leadership it now seeks to overthrow. It is the threat from radical Islam. Pakistan finds itself under armed attack in its tribal northwest by an indigenous enemy, the Pakistani Taliban, whose cause it once supported and whose Afghan counterparts it continues to support. This enemy, allied with Al Qaeda and aided and abetted by a growing Craigslist of Punjabi jihadist and sectarian groups, each of them once supported or tolerated by the state, has been able to commandeer large swaths of northwest Pakistan, while pursuing an effective terrorism campaign in the urban heartland.

To add insult to injury, the one jihadist group nurtured by the state that still pretends to remain loyal—the Lashkar-e-Taiba—has pursued a private vendetta against India that more than once has brought Pakistan to the brink of an unwanted war. The continuing proliferation of radical mosques and madrassas, which serve as feeder institutions for many of these groups, testifies to growing religious radicalization in areas such as the Seraiki belt of southern Punjab, where sectarian animosities have long held sway. Ruled by an uneasy coalition of feudal politicians and army officers, each with their own obsessions and disposed to turn a blind eye to the serious problems that plague their country, Pakistan seems ill equipped to deal with this rapidly metastasizing radical Islamic threat. How did the people responsible for governing manage to get themselves into such a parlous state? Since the radicalism they face is firmly rooted in religious belief, it is time to take a closer look at the role that religion plays in Pakistani society and politics.

3. Religion, Zia, and the Anti-Soviet Jihad in Afghanistan

Judged solely by the headlines, with their steady offering of religious violence, suicide bombings, gruesome beheadings, and terrorist extravaganzas such as the Mumbai massacre, carried out by the Lashkar-e-Taiba, headquarted near Lahore, it might seem that Pakistan is a nation of religious fanatics.

Nothing could be farther from the truth. Pakistani religion, much like Pakistani politics, is deeply rooted in the underlying feudal culture. Most Pakistanis, including most members of the political class, practice a form of Islam derived from Sufism and unique to South Asia, revolving around the veneration of holy men known as *pirs*. The most prominent pirs down through the centuries have come to be revered as saints. Their shrines, which can be found scattered throughout Pakistan, are not only sites of pilgrimage and worship but also play host to annual celebrations, known as *urs*, which commemorate the anniversaries of their deaths and rebirth into eternal life. These celebrations are renowned for their vibrant carnival atmosphere and colorful attractions, which frequently include not only the Pakistani version of amusement park rides, but freak shows and performances by transvestite dancers. This is definitely not the Islam of Osama bin Laden or the Taliban leader Mullah Omar. It is a picturesque religion and, for the most part, a tolerant and nonthreatening one.

Pakistani pirs share many of the same trappings as feudal land-owners. Many are landowners in their own right and some have even entered politics. Their function in feudal Pakistani culture can be viewed as a religious counterpart to the patron-client relations that bind together secular Pakistani society. Sharecroppers look to their landlords for basic staples and assistance in times of need, while politicians rely on their patronage networks to get them elected to office. But both patron and client look to their pirs to intercede on their behalf in their relationship with the Almighty. This intermediary role is what most distinguishes this South Asian version of Sufism from other varieties of Islam, where the relationship between believer and God is conceived of as direct.

It is not surprising that this form of Sufi Islam would take root in a culture based on ties of reciprocal obligation. Religious believers give love and support to their pirs in much the same way that sharecroppers grow crops for the landowners whose fields they work. They do so in the expectation of receiving help and support in return, the one in the religious realm, the other in the secular. In the feudal countryside, the religious believer and the sharecropper are frequently one and the same. The difference is that it is not just sharecroppers who look to their pirs to intercede with Allah on their behalf but also the landowners for whom they work. Much the same can be said for all inhabitants of rural society. As in the case of feudal politics, however, this form of Sufi Islam has long since ceased to be an exclusive phenomenon of the rural countryside. As Pakistanis have moved off the land and into the cities and towns, they have taken their religion with them. A pir maintained a home in central Islamabad not far from where I lived. It was crowded with well-wishers when he was in residence and lit up at night with strings of white lights that covered much of the house.

Pakistanis who practice this form of Islam are generally known as Barelvis. The name comes from the city of Bareilly in northern India, where a school was established around 1880 to defend and promote the traditional rural religion of the region. The particular brand of Sufi Islam practiced in South Asia is especially noteworthy for including significant borrowings from Hinduism, and is heir to a rich musical tradition, including a devotional form of singing known as *qawwali*, not seen elsewhere in Islam. These borrowings reflected the pragmatism of the first Sufi missionaries to visit the region, who assimilated

Hindu rituals into their own teachings in order to make Islam more attractive to potential converts. Given the distinctive, unorthodox nature of this form of Islam, it is not surprising it eventually provoked a backlash. This came in the form of the Deobandi sect, which took its name from the north Indian town of Deoband where its first school was established. Although the Deobandis continued to honor Sufi saints, they sought to purge South Asian Sufi Islam of its exotic practices and return it firmly to its roots in the classical texts of Islam, the Quran and the Hadith. The result was an austere back-to-the-basics brand of Islam that was highly critical not only of South Asian Sufi Islam but of other Islamic sects as well, directing special opprobrium at Shia Islam, which it regarded as heretical. Its missionaries carried the new faith throughout British India, finding particular resonance among the Pashtuns of the NWFP, whose own demanding tribal code of Pashtunwali proved fertile ground for its fundamentalist message. Even there, however, it failed to supplant the dominant Sufi tradition.

Today, the Deobandis remain most deeply entrenched among the Pashtuns, but they have attracted followers throughout Pakistan, particularly among the urban lower middle classes in Punjab and through the establishment of numerous mosques and madrassas, most notably in the Seraiki belt of south Punjab. Although most Deobandis are no more prone to violence than their Christian fundamentalist counterparts in the West, every jihadist group based in Pakistan save one is Deobandi, as are the Afghan Taliban. Whereas Barelvis tend to have a live-and-let-live approach toward other religious groups, the Deobandis are active proselytizers. Members of their Tablighi Jamaat travel throughout the world spreading their fundamentalist Deobandi message among local Muslim populations. Deobandis are also highly active in promoting their particular brand of Islamic education. More than half of all Pakistani madrassas are run by the Deobandi sect. It is a religion on the make.

The only other Sunni denomination of any size in Pakistan is the much smaller Ahle Hadith. Like the Deobandi sect, it espouses a fundamentalist form of Islam, which bears similarities to that practiced by the Wahhabis of Saudi Arabia, the sect from which Osama bin Laden and the Saudi royal family both spring. The differences between the Ahle Hadith and the Deobandi forms of Islamic fundamentalism rest largely on their differing views on interpreting the Quran and the Hadith, which in the case of the Ahle Hadith is even more literalist. The main claim to fame of the Ahle Hadith is that it is the parent sect of the one jihadist group in Pakistan that is not Deobandi, the Lashkar-e-Taiba.

These three Sunni sects live together in uneasy rivalry. The competition between the Barelvis and the Deobandis is more than a hundred years old. Although the Deoband school was formed in reaction to the distinctive brand of Sufi Islam practiced by most South Asian Muslims, it actually predated the Barelvi school by more than a decade. This is because the Barelvis established their own school in large part to defend the traditional religion of the subcontinent against the depredations of the Deobandi upstarts. The main sectarian divide in Pakistan, however, is not between Barelvis and Deobandis, but between Sunnis and Shiites, reflecting the major fault line within Islam as a whole. No one knows for certain what percentage of the Pakistani population is Shiite, since census takers are not permitted to ask that question. Rough estimates range from 15 to 25 percent. Much like the Barelvis, Pakistani Shiites are firmly rooted in the land and have their own Sufi traditions. They are well represented within the landed feudal aristocracy and have made their way comfortably into the corridors of power. Both Mohammed Ali Jinnah and Zulfiqar Ali Bhutto were Shiites. This helps explain why Jinnah conceived of Pakistan as a homeland for South Asian Muslims rather than an ideologically Islamic state. Even today there are many Shiite politicians in the PPP and both varieties of the PML. This speaks well of the religious tolerance of their Barelvi colleagues, whose politics may be combative but whose religion, by and large, is not.

There are two major religious political parties in Pakistan. The Jamiat Ulema-e-Islam, known almost exclusively as the JUI, is a regional party based in the NWFP and northern Baluchistan. It membership is Deobandi in religious orientation and ethnically Pashtun. It was formed just prior to partition after its founder broke with its Indian parent organization over the question of supporting a separate Pakistani state. Its main faction has long been headed by Fazlur Rehman, known popularly as Maulana Diesel due to some shady petroleum dealings he was involved in while a member of the second Benazir Bhutto government. In the NWFP, it is the religious alterative to the Awami National Party (ANP), which is the dominant Pashtun secular party.

The largest and most influential religious party in Pakistan, however, is the Jamaat-e-Islami. It was founded by Maulana Abul Ala Maududi, a journalist by profession who reinvented himself as a religious reformer and moved to Pakistan after partition. The Jamaat sees itself as the vanguard of a peaceful Islamic revolution that would establish sharia rule in the country, replacing secular authority with a moral and legal code based on the precedents set out in the Quran or derived from the life of the Prophet—what he said and did—as passed down in the Hadith. This call for the imposition of sharia is a cornerstone of political Islam that is shared by militant groups such as Al Qaeda and the Taliban as well as those prepared to work within the system, like the Jamaat. Although an exclusively South Asian phenomenon, the Jamaat is part of a broader movement of Islamic political parties. As Qazi Hussain Ahmed, its longtime leader, explained to me, it is closest in spirit to the Muslim Brotherhood of Egypt, as well as the Refah party of Turkey, which, although banned in 1998, was the forerunner of the current ruling party in Ankara. Unusually for a fundamentalist Islamic organization, it is nonsectarian in character. Its membership is drawn from all three major Sunni sects, although a senior official admitted to me that approximately two-thirds came from Deobandi backgrounds. It is also a vanguard party, which means it keeps its core membership deliberately low. Although it can count on the support of more than a million sympathizers, only a small cadre of twelve thousand enjoys full membership. It is a party not of the poor and disadvantaged but of the relatively well-to-do. Most of its support comes from the ranks of pious but well-educated middle-class professionals. In this sense, the Jamaat can be viewed as something of a middle-class reaction to a feudal political establishment that it regards as venal and hopelessly corrupt.

The Jamaat originally opposed the creation of Pakistan, which it feared would divide rather than unite South Asian Muslims, but it has since become strongly nationalistic. Maududi did not like Hindus, and the Jamaat, consequently, is virulently anti-Hindu—and therefore anti-Indian—in its basic orientation, a disposition that has not infrequently brought it into alliance with more secular Pakistani nationalists, including the army. It is also passionately committed to wresting Kashmir from Indian control.

Although the Jamaat-e-Islami and the JUI appeal to markedly different constituencies, they have long viewed themselves as rivals. But neither has ever done very well at the polls. Their electoral high-water mark came in the first-ever national elections in 1970, when they captured 10 percent of the vote. The JUI also did well in the 2002 provincial elections in the NWFP, when it was swept into power in the backlash generated by the U.S. invasion of Afghanistan. Aside from these atypical showings, the Jamaat and the JUI usually manage to win only a few seats here and there at the national and provincial levels. But this has sometimes been sufficient to gain them membership in coalition governments headed by the mainstream secular parties, where small numbers can pay big dividends. Their lack of success at the ballot box is not difficult to understand. Since they stand outside the feudal system, they are not tied into the fabric of patronage networks that define the political mainstream. As the Pakistani political scientist Mohammad Waseem told me, the religious parties do not know how to play at feudal politics, where constituents vote for candidates who succeed in convincing them they will do a better job of helping them pay an overdue electricity bill.

What the religious parties do have, reputedly, is street power: the inclination and ability to take to the streets in large enough numbers to cause serious disruptions to daily life and the implied threat of violence if they do not get their way. Although the reputation is real, the reality is somewhat different. The Jamaat did take an active role in demonstrations in 1953 that sought to outlaw the small but influential Ahmadi sect, which regards its founder as a successor to Mohammed, a heretical view even among moderate Muslims. It was also highly prominent in the street agitation that helped bring down Zulfiqar Ali Bhutto. Its student wing has long served as a force of intimidation and harassment at colleges and universities. But it is difficult to find recent instances where the religious parties have actually taken to the streets and done serious damage. A senior figure in the PPP made this point to me in describing a Jamaat-led march on the national assembly in Islamabad during the first Benazir Bhutto administration. The police had been given orders to stop the procession. Although the marchers managed to withstand two baton charges, they finally broke and ran when the police began firing live ammunition into the air. Our conversation took place shortly after the previously mentioned Lahore Summit, which Nawaz Sharif hosted for his Indian counterpart in early

1999. The PPP official noted with considerable satisfaction that the Jamaat had also vowed to disrupt that event but had been "routed by the Lahore police." The Musharraf government also successfully faced down demonstrations organized by the Jamaat in the wake of U.S. military operations in Afghanistan following 9/11. Nonetheless, in a country where those who rule are eager to avoid disruption, the threat of violence can often be as effective as the reality. Since the time of Zia ul-Haq, the religious parties have managed to trade on this weakness to bring pressure to bear on their more easily intimidated secular counterparts.

Zia was a senior officer in the Pakistan army who came from a pious Deobandi background. His rise to power was unexpected, one of those accidents of history that frequently determine the fate of nations. He emerged as army chief when Zulfiqar Ali Bhutto raised him up over several more senior generals because of his obsequious behavior in his dealings with the prime minister. If anything, his patent religiosity actually recommended him to Bhutto, who was advised that a pious general was less likely to challenge civilian authority. Obsequious or not, Zia nonetheless managed to summon up the will to move against his benefactor in the wake of the nationwide disturbances that broke out in reaction to the too-good-to-be-true results of the 1977 national assembly elections. Not content simply to remove Bhutto from office, he then conspired to have him convicted on murder charges and stood firm in the face of entreaties from world leaders that he spare his life. Zia feared that as long as Bhutto was alive, his hold on power—and his life—would be at risk.

With Bhutto permanently out of the way, Zia found himself facing the same question of legitimacy that confronts all Pakistani military rulers. His trump card was religion. As we have seen, Jinnah had conceived of Pakistan as a homeland for South Asian Muslims, not an ideologically Islamic state. The Jamaat-e-Islami had challenged this conception, but its views found only limited resonance in a state dominated by tolerant Barelvi Muslims prepared to leave the affairs of state to the feudal political establishment. In Zia ul-Haq, however, it finally had its man. He admired the Jamaat and decided to move the country firmly in its direction, implementing a series of measures specifically aimed at Islamizing the state along fundamentalist Sunni lines. Sharia was back in business.

At the top, he instituted a Federal Shariat Court, which had the ability to strike down laws found repugnant to Islam. He replaced portions of the Pakistani criminal code with a series of what were called Hudood ordinances. These retrograde statutes imposed punishments set out in the Quran and Hadith, including stoning, flogging, and amputation, for certain categories of crimes, such as rape, adultery, blasphemy, and theft, whose prosecution is regarded under traditional Islamic law as being the responsibility of the state. Perhaps fortunately, the equally draconian rules of evidence required for conviction, including testimony from two or more witnesses, meant that the most severe punishments were seldom imposed and in practice never carried out. The most notorious of the Hudood ordinances was the one covering rape. A woman charging rape had to produce four male witnesses to the crime, a virtually impossible undertaking. Failure to convict the accused rapist, however, could result in the woman being prosecuted for adultery since the charge of rape carries with it the implicit admission of having had sexual intercourse. The ordinance on blasphemy, meanwhile, was subsequently used by local authorities to harass members of Christian and other religious minorities.

Zia also began to roil sectarian waters by making the Muslim charitable contribution known as Zakat a mandatory tax. While acceptable to Sunnis, this was anathema to Shiites, who began to demonstrate against it. This and other moves at odds with Shiite jurisprudence were particularly incendiary because they occurred in the immediate afterglow of the Islamic revolution in Iran, which had substantially raised Shiite religious consciousness in Pakistan. The Shiite group Tehrik-e-Nifaz-e-Fiqh-e-Jafaria Pakistan (TNFJ) had already been established to protect and promote Shiite interests in the country and it took the lead in opposing the Zakat ordinance and other measures. Although Zia saw his mistake and exempted the Shiite community from compulsory Zakat, the first seeds of sectarian conflict between Sunni and Shia had been sown. Zia even managed to upset the Barelvi community, which was angered by government efforts to regulate mosques and shrines, which they believed favored the Deobandis. This increased tension between the two sects and led to a major confrontation at Badshahi mosque in Lahore in 1984. Zia's policies demonstrated the folly of trying to Islamize a society composed of divergent sectarian groups, each with a different take on what constitutes appropriate Islamic behavior. A major problem had been created where only minor ones existed before.

Like those who preceded him, and those who were to follow, Zia made no effort to improve public-funded education. But, uniquely, he cut spending for public schools and promoted the establishment of madrassas, even using Zakat funds to pay for them. These schools, operated by religious sects, the majority of them Deobandi, provided their students with a very narrow, almost exclusively religious, education. Since many of these institutions provided free room and board, they proved highly popular with poor families who had too many mouths to feed. The education provided did not furnish graduates with the credentials needed to make their way in the secular world. The more capable or ambitious would go on to become Islamic clerics known as mullahs, some of them eventually to open their own mosques. This created a snowball effect that gave rise to ever increasing numbers of madrassas, a phenomenon that continues.

The Islamization program launched by Zia created Islamic fundamentalist facts on the ground that his more secular successors have found difficult to roll back. The religious parties have been dogged in their efforts to protect the gains made under Zia by threatening to use street power against any attempt to reverse them. This was the fate of proposed changes to the blasphemy laws during the Musharraf era, although Musharraf did succeed in removing rape from the Hudood statutes. But the lingering effects of the Islamization campaign go beyond mere threats of street action. Prior to Zia there was no real consensus over whether Pakistan should be an ideologically Islamic state in addition to being a homeland for South Asian Muslims. The country emerged from the Zia era having internalized the belief that Pakistan should in some sense have an Islamic cast to it, although no one could define precisely what this meant. The need to uphold this injunction has become a Pakistani version of political correctness, with politicians afraid to criticize Zia-era reforms for fear of being labeled anti-Islamic. Even in an army that is still largely secular and nationalist in orientation, soldiers who die in combat are described in army press releases as having "embraced martyrdom."

Although Zia had begun his Islamization campaign shortly after seizing power in 1977, as of December 24, 1979, there were still no jihadist or violent sectarian groups in Pakistan. That was the day the

Soviet Union invaded Afghanistan. The ensuing decade of conflict would change Pakistan forever. Relations between Pakistan and Afghanistan on the eve of the Soviet invasion already had a long and unhappy history. The primary bone of contention concerned the fate of the Pashtuns, who lived on both sides of their common border. The problem extended well back into British times. British efforts to maintain a presence in Afghanistan as a hedge against Russian penetration of the subcontinent had foundered in 1842 when its entire garrison was massacred by Pashtun tribesmen in a horrific retreat from Kabul. Even then most Pashtuns did not live in Afghanistan but in the far western extremity of the Sikh Empire, whose capital lay far to the east at Lahore. When the British conquered the Sikhs in 1849, they found themselves ruling over a Pashtun population, centered on the Vale of Peshawar, that was already separated politically from its Afghan branch. This was not much of a hardship at the time since the borderlands were neither well-defined nor policed, and did not need to be.

Within thirty years, however, the situation had changed. The Russians had reached the northern borders of Afghanistan, and the British concluded it would be prudent to formalize their own border with Afghanistan as a hedge against further Russian penetration. In 1893, they sent the Indian foreign secretary, Sir Henry Mortimer Durand, to Kabul to negotiate the issue with the Afghan king. The border that was eventually agreed to, memorialized ever after as the Durand Line, left the British in possession of what came to be known as the NWFP and the tribal areas, both of which were subsequently broken off administratively from the Punjab, and then from each other, as buffer zones, formally separating what were to become the Pakistani Pashtuns from their Afghan brethren.

The Afghan king willingly signed off on the deal and even feted Durand once the agreement had been inked. But Afghan Pashtuns, who constituted the largest ethnic group in Afghanistan and dominated the government, were never happy with this political separation of the Pashtun people. Nonetheless, this is where matters stood for more than half a century, until the departure of the British and the creation of the new state of Pakistan gave them an opportunity to revisit the issue. By this time, the Pashtun population on the Pakistan side of the Durand Line had grown to twice the size of its Afghan counterpart. Despite this fact, Afghanistan not only voted against admitting Pakistan to the United Nations, Afghan representatives argued that the Durand Line had no standing since it had been negotiated with the British Empire, not with Pakistan. The Afghans called instead for the incorporation of the Pashtun areas of the British Raj into a greater Afghanistan, extending its borders to the banks of the Indus. In a referendum held by the British prior to partition, however, the Pashtuns of the NWFP voted overwhelmingly in favor of joining Pakistan. Needless to say, these developments did not get relations between the two countries off to a very good start.

The primary proponent of this Afghan irredentist policy was Mohammad Daoud, cousin to the Afghan king Zahir Shah and, needless to say, an ethnic Pashtun. He became foreign minister in 1953 and continued to assert Afghan claims on Pakistani territory, even sending troops into the tribal areas in 1960 in an abortive effort to make good on his claims through the use of force. In carrying out this adventure, however, Daoud had crossed more than the Durand Line, and he was eventually removed by the king. Nonetheless, he managed to resurrect his fortunes in the years that followed and was finally able to launch a successful coup against his royal cousin in 1973. With the support of local communists, he began moving the country closer to the Soviet Union, which became Afghanistan's largest benefactor. This resurfacing of its Afghan bête noire, and his growing alliance with the Soviet superpower, set off alarm bells inside Pakistan. In response, the Zulfiqar Ali Bhutto government began searching for ways to make life uncomfortable for the new regime. Its instrument of choice turned out to be a group of Afghan exiles who had set up shop in the NWFP capital of Peshawar after being forced out of Afghanistan by Daoud. They were members of the Jamiat-e-Islami, the similarly named Afghan cousin to the Pakistani Jamaat-e-Islami. The army would have another chance to employ the guerrilla strategy that had gone so badly awry during the 1965 war with India.

The choice of the Jamiat, which was headed by an ethnic Tajik theology professor named Burhanuddin Rabbani, was not an ideological one. The Afghan version of the Pakistani Jamaat was both conveniently located, due to its headquartering in Peshawar, and willing to aid the Pakistanis in attempting to undermine the Daoud government. Political infighting along ethnic lines would soon split the Jamiat-e Islami into two factions, one dominated by ethnic Tajiks under Rabbani and his chief lieutenant, Ahmed Shah Masood, the other by eth-

nic Pashtuns, headed by Gulbuddin Hekmatyar, who named his group
the Hezb-e Islami. But neither of these factions was able to make any
serious headway inside Afghanistan during these early days, even with
Pakistani support. Their most notable effort, a 1975 uprising led primarily by Masood forces in the Panjshir valley, was easily and ignominiously crushed.

Events, however, were evolving inside the Daoud regime itself.
Daoud was growing nervous about the Communists in his midst and
began purging them from his ranks. He reduced his reliance on Soviet
support and began reaching out to the shah of Iran and to India. He
even showed a willingness to negotiate with the Pakistanis. This policy
reversal alarmed both the Soviets and his erstwhile Afghan Communist colleagues. Pro-communist forces within the Afghan army finally
moved against Daoud in 1978, killing him and installing a Communist
regime, which quickly returned to the Soviet camp. The Soviets were
happy to see Afghanistan fall back into their laps, but their pleasure
turned to consternation the following year when an independent-
minded Communist, Hafizullah Amin, emerged on top after a power
struggle between competing factions. Unable to intimidate Amin into
line and unwilling to see Afghanistan escape from their clutches yet
again, they decided to invade the country, murdering Amin and installing a trusted rival in his place.

On the day the Soviets marched into Afghanistan, relations between the United States and Pakistan were in the deepest of deep
freezes. Barely a month before, a mob led by the student wing of the
Jamaat-e-Islami had attacked the U.S. embassy in Islamabad and
burned it to the ground. They were responding to rumors that the
United States was behind the seizure of the Grand Mosque in Mecca,
the holiest shrine in Islam, by a group of radical Islamists whose identity and motives were initially unclear. Two Americans and two local
Pakistani employees were killed in the embassy attack. A photo album
of the charred ruins of the old embassy is still kept in the ambassador's
office of the new chancery building. It is eerie and disquieting to flip
through page after page of familiar-looking but heavily gutted offices
and corridors, since the new embassy was built to the exact specifica-
tions of the old. The main difference is that the easily surmounted
chain-link fence that had surrounded the embassy compound was replaced by a thick redbrick wall twelve feet high, topped out with razor

wire. To this day Embassy Islamabad looks more like a maximum-security prison than a diplomatic establishment.

The students who led the assault on the embassy were following in the footsteps of the Iranian students who had overrun the U.S. embassy in Tehran ten months earlier, and may have been trying to emulate them. In retrospect, 1979 looms as a pivotal year in the emergence of radical Islam, with the Iranian revolution and the seizure of the Grand Mosque serving as opening salvos in a rejection of Western influence that has yet to run its course. Its intellectual roots lay somewhat further back in time, in the writings of Syed Qutb, an Egyptian theologian and member of the Muslim Brotherhood. Although Qutb was executed by the secular Gamal Abdul Nasser in 1966, his condemnation of Western values, contempt for secular Muslim rulers, and support for violent jihad inspired successive generations of radical Islamists. The dramatic events of 1979 can be viewed as a symbolic passing of the torch from the secular, frequently left-wing, nationalist movements, such as the PLO, that had previously dominated Islamic opposition to the West to those motivated by fundamentalist religious beliefs and infused with the spirit of jihad.

Such thoughts were no doubt far from the minds of the beleaguered American employees of the embassy in Islamabad who escaped from their attackers by locking themselves in the steel-reinforced chancery vault. There they waited as hours passed and the floor beneath them grew hotter from the fire that was raging below. They could hear gunfire pouring down from the roof above. Although army headquarters was only half an hour away, Pakistani security personnel were nowhere to be seen and finally appeared only late in the day. Well before that happened, the frightened Americans sweltering inside the vault finally convinced themselves they would rather be shot than fry and proceeded to make their way out. Luckily for them, the embassy compound had been reduced to charred ruins by this time and the satiated mob had gradually drifted away. As these dramatic events were playing themselves out, Zia ul-Haq was engaged in a leisurely bicycle tour of the neighboring city of Rawalpindi intended to demonstrate the benefits of a healthy life. He may well have felt he had good reason to leave the United States in the lurch. In April, seven months before the burning of the embassy, the Carter administration had suspended all economic and military aid to Pakistan under the Symington

Amendment. The intent was to signal U.S. displeasure with Pakistani efforts to develop a nuclear weapon, as well as unhappiness with the continuing Zia dictatorship, which two years after his coup showed every indication of becoming permanent.

The events culminating in the attack on Embassy Islamabad were merely the most recent in a long, mostly downhill slide in U.S.-Pakistani relations. Pakistan had been a close U.S. ally in its early years, joining two different U.S. defense alliances during the first decade of its existence. The first dark clouds had appeared on the horizon in 1962, when the United States supported Pakistan's enemy, India, in its losing war against the Communist Chinese. Then, as we saw in chapter 1, during the 1965 conflict over Kashmir, the United States had pulled the rug out from under the Ayub regime by refusing to provide Pakistan with the military spare parts it needed to continue the war. These events thoroughly disaffected Zulfiqar Ali Bhutto, then the foreign minister, whose policy preferences migrated toward friendship with China and membership in the Non-Aligned Movement. Even though the United States subsequently provided diplomatic support to Pakistan during its conflict with India over Bangladesh, the Pakistanis considered it too little too late. This would all change, however, on the day the Soviet Union marched into Afghanistan.

The United States saw the Soviet invasion of Afghanistan exclusively through the prism of the Cold War. Although the Soviets had sponsored proxy wars in various parts of the globe, this was the first time since the end of World War II that the Soviets had invaded a country that was not a member of the Warsaw Pact. The United States feared the Soviets might have designs not only on Afghanistan but also on Pakistan itself, aimed at securing a warm-water port on the Arabian Sea and projecting Soviet power into the Middle East. The Pakistanis had no time for such geostrategic ponderings. They were simply alarmed at the sudden appearance of a hostile superpower on their western flank, supporting a Communist government no more wedded to the Durand Line than its Daoud predecessor had been. The partnership between the United States and Pakistan that subsequently ensued was a marriage of convenience. Even though the ashes of its burned-out embassy had not yet been completely cleared away, the United States now had more important things on its mind. It extended an olive branch to the Zia government and offered its support.

The deal that gradually emerged divided up responsibilities. The Pakistanis would organize, train, and equip insurgent forces to infiltrate into Afghanistan to undertake guerrilla operations against the Soviets. The United States would pay for it. Zia had already identified the resources he would use in the effort. On seizing power, he had picked up where Bhutto left off by continuing to provide financial support to the Hekmatyar and Rabbani forces in their Peshawar exile. Given their strong ties to Zia's ally, the Pakistani Jamaat-e-Islami, his interest in using them was not merely pragmatic but also ideological. And now he had the prospect of real money to make it happen. Zia rejected the initial Carter administration offer of $400 million, but the incoming Reagan administration was considerably more generous, upping the offer to $3.2 billion. The Saudis, who feared Soviet penetration into the region every bit as much as the United States, agreed to match the U.S. financial contribution dollar for dollar. The Chinese and Egyptians also promised to help out.

Zia looked to his military spy service, the Inter-Services Intelligence Directorate, universally known as ISI, to manage the Afghan insurgency. ISI was staffed largely by seconded army officers and had been in existence since 1948, the year following independence. But its role in running the anti-Soviet insurgency in Afghanistan brought it to a frontline prominence in Pakistani affairs of state that it would never completely relinquish. Later it would serve as the primary instrument through which Pakistani governments did business with radical Islamic groups and through which the army, working behind the scenes, attempted to influence domestic politics. A myth has arisen over the years that ISI is a rogue organization that pursues its own foreign and domestic policy agendas. It is not completely clear where and how this stereotype emerged. The most likely explanation is that the high visibility of the organization, whose operatives are suspected by some to lurk behind every tree, played a substantial role. The army itself may also share responsibility, disseminating such rumors as a way of distancing itself from some of ISI's more controversial acts.

I have discussed this issue with a number of former senior army officers over the years, and they categorically reject this stereotype. They all insist, and emphatically so, that ISI acts only under policy guidelines laid out by the army leadership or in response to direct orders emanating from army headquarters. In defense of their position, they point out that most ISI officers are seconded from the army and dependent on it for further promotion. They note that the head of ISI more often than not enjoys close personal and professional ties to the army chief. The current chief, Ashfaq Kayani, was actually head of ISI under Musharraf. My officer contacts also insist, as noted earlier, that the Pakistan army is a professional organization whose officers are not inclined to insubordination. Some would even be willing to admit that, even though ISI technically falls under civilian control when feudal politicians are in power, its primary allegiance always remains to its parent institution.

As the ISI-directed insurgency gathered steam, the Pakistanis began referring to the insurgents as mujahideen and to the insurgency itself as a jihad. This supported the fiction that the insurgent forces were inspired by religious zeal and acting on their own rather than under the direction of Pakistani authorities. It also portrayed them in a positive light to their domestic audience by wrapping them in an Islamic flag. This was the very same tactic that had been used by the Ayub government during the 1965 war with India when the irregular forces that were infiltrated into Kashmir were also referred to as mujahideen. It was even more important in the Afghan context because the Pakistanis wished to avoid giving the Soviets a pretext to attack them by publicly admitting they were supporting the mujahideen forces. The primary difference between the 1965 precedent and the Afghan example is that in the Afghan case the most important insurgent groups actually did have a religious pedigree. But there was also an important similarity between the two insurgencies. Like their predecessors in 1965, the Afghan mujahideen harbored nationalistic goals. They wanted to drive the Soviets out of their homeland and wrest control of the state from their indigenous Communist puppets. This was jihad with a patriotic touch.

Preeminent among the groups fighting the Soviets were the Hezb-e Islami of Gulbuddin Hekmatyar and the Jamiat-e Islami forces commanded by Ahmed Shah Masood. They recruited fighters inside Afghanistan, many of whom flocked to their banners in patriotic opposition to the Soviet occupation. Given their Jamaat origins, their forces were not exclusively Deobandi. Many recruits were followers of Sufi Islam, which even today commands the allegiance of most Pashtun Afghans, despite the inroads made by the Deobandis. Even Shiites were welcomed into the mujahideen ranks. Taking advantage of local knowledge, these forces attacked Soviet convoys and launched devastating raids against Soviet garrisons and outposts inside Afghan cities and towns. As the fighting escalated, up to three million Afghans eventually fled across the border seeking safe haven in refugee camps set up in the NWFP and tribal areas. These served as additional recruiting grounds for the mujahideen forces.

More extreme in both his religion and methods than Masood, Hekmatyar gradually emerged as the ISI favorite. He was not only an effective commander but also an Afghan Pashtun prepared to cooperate with Pakistan, a highly desirable characteristic in the eyes of Pakistanis long troubled by hostile Afghan designs on their Pashtun lands. He was also the mujahideen leader with the closest ties to the Jamaat-e-Islami in Pakistan. This was just the kind of Afghan leadership ISI hoped would emerge from the conflict when and if the Soviets departed. Masood and his political master, Burhanuddin Rabbani, on the other hand, were ethnic Tajiks, more oriented toward Central Asia and with no special ties to Pakistan. Never close to begin with, relations between Hekmatyar and Masood became further strained over time.

Although these Afghan groups dominated the anti-Soviet struggle throughout its course, it did not take long for outsiders harboring a more globalist Islamic agenda to enter the fray. Prominent among them was a Saudi-based Palestinian theologian named Abdullah Yusuf Azzam, who had been deeply influenced by the writings of Syed Qutb. Shortly after the Soviet invasion, he had written a tract on "Defense of the Muslim Lands" in which he implored Muslims to undertake jihad to liberate Palestine and Afghanistan from infidel rule. There was nothing nationalist in this sort of appeal. It outlined a strictly jihadist agenda aimed at rescuing Muslim populations from the depredations of Western influence. Azzam subsequently moved to Peshawar, capital of the NWFP, where he attracted like-minded young recruits, including his former pupil Osama bin Laden, whose father was a wealthy Saudi construction magnate with strong ties to the Saudi royal family. Another recruit, a radical Egyptian physician named Ayman al-Zawahiri, who had been imprisoned for his activities following the 1981 assassination of Egyptian president Anwar Sadat, arrived in Peshawar to serve at a local charity hospital and decided to stay.

Unlike Qutb and Azzam, bin Laden and al-Zawahiri were neither theologians nor mullahs. They were well-educated members of the secular establishment, who were inspired by the writings of Qutb and Azzam and suffused with feelings of Muslim victimization at the hands of the West. In many ways, they can be viewed as radical Islamic counterparts to the secular upper-middle-class activists of the New Left who gravitated to groups like the Weather Underground and the Baader-Meinhof gang in the late 1960s. Personally well-off, but surrounded by what they regarded as multiple injustices, they demonized those in authority whom they considered responsible and were prepared to act with great brutality against them in pursuit of their romanticized revolutionary goals. Thanks to funds provided by bin Laden and a number of Saudi-based charity organizations, young radical Islamists from the Middle East and in some cases even farther afield flocked to Pakistan to join their ranks. Unable or unwilling to peer far enough into the future, the United States was itself inclined to look favorably on the recruitment of these foreign jihadists into the mujahideen. Although these outsiders made up only a small percentage of the mujahideen forces deployed, they constituted the first significant coming together of revolutionary jihadists from across the Islamic world, a phenomenon that would in time give birth to Al Qaeda.

Although most of these foreign recruits were Wahhabist, Deobandis also felt the call of jihad. Within Pakistan, the first jihadists emerged not from the educated upper middle class but from Deobandi madrassas. The first Pakistani jihadist organization was formed in 1980 by students from the most prominent Deobandi madrassa, the Jamia Uloom al-Islamia in Karachi. They had been inspired by the ongoing insurrection against the Soviet Communists and decided to do something about it. Traveling to Peshawar in the hope of joining the mujahideen, they made contact with similarly minded local Pashtuns and together with them established the Harakat ul-Jihad-e-Islami (HUJI). Most of their recruits came from the dozens, perhaps hundreds, of madrassas that the JUI had begun to establish in the NWFP with encouragement from the Zia government. These madrassas took advantage of resources made available through Zakat but were also beneficiaries of Saudi money that flowed into the coffers of the JUI following the Soviet invasion even though it was not a Wahhabist organization. In these dramatic circumstances, the Saudis were not disposed to let simple differences over Islamic jurisprudence stand in the way.

Although not itself a jihadist organization—then or now—the JUI was eager to become a major player in Afghanistan. It wanted to match— if possible, surpass—the exploits of its Jamaat-e-Islami rival, whose Afghan sister organizations were shouldering the great burden of the fighting. Its embarrassment at standing on the sidelines stemmed in large part from the fact that it, like the majority of the mujahideen forces, was Pashtun in composition. To redress the imbalance, it became particularly active in recruiting Afghan refugees into its madrassas, from whose ranks many of the Taliban would later emerge. But it was also happy to see its Pakistani students join the newly established HUJI or move directly into the ranks of the Afghan mujahideen. Approximately 4,000 HUJI recruits out of a total mujahideen force of 150,000 ended up fighting with the mujahideen during the Soviet occupation, a modest but not insignificant contribution. They were there still, a jihadist force in waiting, when the last Soviet soldier departed Afghanistan in February 1989.

But the anti-Soviet struggle had a more significant effect on Pakistan than the production of four thousand indigenous jihadists. The radical Islamist ferment that drove JUI madrassa students into the HUJI was accompanied by the weaponization of the NWFP and tribal areas as small arms siphoned off from the Afghan fighting flooded into the region, producing what came to be known as the Kalashnikov culture. I asked one of the largest landowners in the NWFP what this meant, and he replied that when he was a young man his father and his fellow landowners owned all the guns, but now the mullahs had them too. This easy access to arms, which gradually expanded outward from the NWFP, proved to be an important enabler contributing to the rise of violent sectarianism in the country. But that spark was to come not in the NWFP, whose Pashtun population was overwhelmingly Sunni in composition, but in the adjacent Seraiki belt of south Punjab, an area that although primarily Sunni had long been dominated by wealthy Shiite landowners.

It was in the Seraiki belt that a mullah by the name of Haq Nawaz Jhangvi founded the Sipah-e-Sahaba Pakistan (SSP) in 1985. This was a militant Deobandi pressure group that developed the trappings of both a terrorist organization and a political party. Very much a child of its time, it arose in reaction to the increased politicization of the Pakistani Shiite community brought about by the Iranian revolution and

Zia's parallel efforts to Islamize Pakistan along Sunni lines. On one level, it sought to provide a Sunni counterweight to the Shiite pressure group, the TNFJ, which continued to champion Shiite interests following its success in getting the Shiite community exempted from mandatory Zakat. But the ultimate goal of the organization was not simply to promote Sunni interests. It sought to demonize the Shiite community by having it designated a non-Muslim minority, the same fate that had been visited on the Ahmadi minority a decade earlier. The SSP was able to gain traction in the Seraiki belt primarily due to the strong hostility felt by the majority Sunni population toward the wealthy Shiite feudal landowners who dominated the politics and economy of the region. Much of its original support came from members of the urban middle class, many of them local businessmen. During this period there was also a substantial increase in Deobandi mosques and madrassas in the Seraiki belt, fostered by the same anti-Shiite hostility. The madrassas, many of which enjoyed links to JUI counterpart institutions in the NWFP, drew many of their students from the families of local Sunni sharecroppers who toiled for Shiite masters.

It is perhaps not surprising that with jihad raging in Afghanistan and the region overrun with arms, the animosity between the SSP and TNFJ would erupt into violence. In 1988, Arif Husayn al-Husayni, who had succeeded to the leadership of the TNFJ and driven it in an increasingly confrontational direction, was assassinated, presumably by SSP gunmen. Two years later, the Shiites managed to exact their revenge by gunning down the Sipah-e-Sahaba founder, Haq Nawaz Jhangvi. The spate of reprisal killings that followed the Jhangvi assassination, which included the murder of an Iranian diplomat in Lahore, led to the formation of the Sipah-e Mohammed, a small and more militant offshoot of the TNFJ, in 1991. Many of its founding members were veterans of the anti-Soviet jihad, having been welcomed into the ranks of the overwhelmingly Sunni mujahideen despite their Shiite orientation. That was forgotten now as they embraced the cause of sectarian violence. Their TNFJ parent organization, meanwhile, moved in the opposite direction, changing its name and adopting less confrontational tactics.

Although the Sipah-e-Sahaba did little to tone down its own rhetoric, it did begin to demonstrate an interest in mainstream politics, running for seats in the national assembly as early as 1988. Haq Nawaz

Jhangvi failed in his own election bid that year, but after his assassination in 1990, the new deputy leader of the group, Maulana Isar al-Qasimi, was successful, demonstrating just how strong anti-Shiite sentiment had become in the Seraiki belt by this time. By 1994, the Sipah-e-Sahaba had spun off its own version of the Sipah-e Mohammed. The Lashkar-e-Jhangvi, as it was called in honor of the SSP founder, was similar in size and ambition to its Shiite counterpart and, like the Sipah-e Mohammed, was composed largely of mujahideen veterans. The two groups would engage in tit-for-tat killings over the course of the next several years, with the radical Deobandi group getting the better of them. By the time I arrived in Pakistan in 1998, the Lashkar-e-Jhangvi was deeply enmeshed in sectarian violence and already emerging as the first radical Islamic group to turn decisively against the state.

Although many of these developments still lay in the future when the Soviets left Afghanistan in 1989, the groundwork for the violent sectarianism that divides Pakistan to this day had been laid. This impulse within the Deobandi community would gradually merge with the jihadist impulse represented by the HUJI, represented in the founding of the Jaish-e-Mohammed at the turn of the millennium. But this possibility was far from the minds of Pakistani authorities on that February day. Not only were the Soviets departing, but the United States was also pulling the plug, ending its financial assistance, dramatically reducing its diplomatic involvement, and leaving the Pakistanis alone to deal with the unwelcome detritus of the anti-Soviet jihad. The Afghan Communist government left behind by the Soviets did not collapse as everyone expected but continued to hold out against the mujahideen. There was no victorious march into Kabul. There was no end to the fighting. What was to become known as the Afghan civil war was about to begin.

The United States, reveling in the withdrawal of Soviet forces and the collapse of the Soviet empire in Eastern Europe, moved on to other issues, including nuclear proliferation. In October 1990, little more than a year and a half later, the United States leveled punishing sanctions against its erstwhile ally. This was done under terms of the Pressler Amendment, a legislative effort that, like its Symington predecessor, sought to pressure Pakistan into terminating its nuclear program. There was never any prospect that the Pakistanis would do this since they regarded, and continue to regard, the possession of nuclear weapons as the foundation stone of their national security, given the fact that India was also a nuclear power. The Pressler sanctions served to remind the Pakistanis of the inconstancy and unreliability of American support. The great majority of Pakistanis, both civilian and military, considered the imposition of Pressler as a slap in the face and an act of betrayal from which U.S.-Pakistani relations have never fully recovered.

But at the same time, the Pakistanis had reason to feel satisfied with their accomplishments in Afghanistan. They had not done it alone, it was true. U.S. and Saudi financial support had made a decisive difference. Stinger antiaircraft missiles, in particular, which were provided to the mujahideen beginning in 1986, gave them the final advantage they needed to persuade the Soviets to withdraw. But ISI believed it had learned an important lesson nonetheless. It had seen how a relatively small group of highly motivated insurgents, acting under their guidance and driven by Islamic religious zeal, could force even a superpower to its knees. This was a lesson it was not inclined to forget. But Pakistan had also changed. The first jihadist and violent sectarian groups had been formed. The madrassas that fed their ranks were continuing to proliferate, not just in the Pashtun lands in the northwest but also in the Seraiki belt of south Punjab. Although radical Islamists constituted only a minuscule percentage of Pakistani society as a whole, their eagerness to pursue jihad made them a potentially invaluable weapon, provided their extremism could be harnessed to a Pakistani cause. Encouraged by their success in Afghanistan, ISI was inclined to see them as an opportunity rather than a threat. All that was needed was a cause.

4. Kashmir, India, and the Institutionalization of Jihad

It is 1986 in a Muslim village in Indian Kashmir. Crowds have gathered around two shops in the village center to listen to radio commentary of the final stage of an important international cricket match between Pakistan and India. The Pakistanis have trailed throughout the contest and their cause seems hopeless. They are down to their very last ball and still trail by several runs. The only way they can win is with the cricket equivalent of a home run, an event much more rare in cricket than in American baseball. Somehow, their batsman, Javed Miandad, manages to do just that, swinging mightily and driving the ball into the stands, snatching dramatic victory from the jaws of what seemed to be certain defeat. The villagers listening to the match can scarcely believe what they are hearing. They explode with joy at this sudden, miraculous turn of events. The irony, of course, is that they are citizens of India and they have been rooting for Pakistan to defeat their own national team. This vivid childhood memory, related by the Indian journalist Basharat Peer in his book, *Curfewed Night*, testifies as much as a single event can to the alienation felt by Muslims in Kashmir toward the country in which they live. Whatever else they may wish for in life, they do not want to be part of India. A great deal has happened in the twenty-five years since Miandad's moment of cricket glory, but time—and the deaths of more than twenty thousand people in an insurrection against Indian rule—have not changed this basic fact. The Kashmiri Muslims are a captive people.

They had failed to rise up in 1965 when Ayub sent army-led irregulars into the Vale of Kashmir in the hope of fomenting an uprising. But they would finally do so a quarter century later, just three years after the cricket match, in what the Kashmiris refer to as their intifada. The events of the years in between the two events help to explain why. As we saw in chapter 1, six years after Ayub launched his abortive effort in Kashmir, Pakistan had blundered into a war with India once again, this one resulting in the loss of Bangladesh. This cataclysmic event had a profound impact not only on Pakistan but also on the still imprisoned Kashmiri leader, Sheikh Abdullah. The Indians had released him once again in 1968, when almost the entire population of Srinagar turned out to greet him, but he remained as defiant as ever and was returned to prison, just as in 1965. But three years later, in the aftermath of the massive Pakistani defeat of 1971, he had finally come to the bitter conclusion that his hopes for an independent Kashmir were never going to be realized. After four more years of soul-searching, an aging man nearing the end of his life, he was finally ready to collaborate, entering into negotiations with New Delhi and agreeing to drop his demands for self-determination. In exchange for this he was returned to power in Srinagar as chief minister in February 1975.

The agreement with New Delhi remained in force for the better part of a decade. Sheikh Abdullah finally died in 1982 and was replaced by his son Farooq, who had earned something of a reputation as a playboy. The politically naive Farooq made an early miscalculation, agreeing to take part in an electoral coalition against the ruling Congress party in the run-up to the 1984 Indian parliamentary elections. Congress regarded this as a violation of its 1975 understanding with his father and maneuvered behind the scenes to have him removed by his own party in an almost exact replay of the putsch that had deposed Sheikh Abdullah in 1953. This provoked widespread demonstrations throughout Kashmir, which the Indian government managed to suppress through a liberal use of curfews and the introduction of paramilitary police. Two years later, the Indian government decided to impose direct rule from New Delhi in response to attacks by Kashmiri Muslims on members of the minority Hindu community. At the end of 1986, Farooq Abdullah, impatient to return to power, finally decided to do his own deal with the Indians. Like his father before him, he agreed to toe the New Delhi line in exchange for being returned to office.

Unlike his legendary father, however, Farooq was unable to carry his fellow Kashmiris with him. They reacted to his capitulation not with resigned acceptance but with contempt. This time they were determined to resist. A broad-based coalition of opposition parties was hastily put together to contest local Kashmiri elections scheduled for the coming spring. The coalition performed well, but to little avail; the election ended up being rigged by Abdullah with support from his new masters in New Delhi. In one case, the routed Abdullah candidate was called back to the vote-counting center to be informed that he had actually won the contest, while the winning candidate was carted off to jail. Such blatant attempts at vote rigging only served to further inflame Kashmiri public opinion. Abdullah had won the election but lost the Kashmiri people. More important, a fuse had been lit that has not been fully extinguished to this day.

Over the course of the next two years, just as the last Soviet forces were pulling out of Afghanistan, a growing wave of civil disobedience and violence began sweeping over the valley. Periodic strikes became interspersed with large-scale demonstrations. Government installations were bombed. In late 1989, the first assassinations of government officials and suspected informants took place. By January of the following year, the increasing anarchy prompted New Delhi to bring the valley under direct rule once again. During three days of protest that same month, more than three hundred unarmed Kashmiri demonstrators were killed by paramilitary forces sent in to put down the protests. A signal feature of the early days of the intifada was the sudden disappearance of young Kashmiri males from their homes. Most were aspiring members of the Jammu Kashmir Liberation Front (JKLF), a separatist group that had been formed in 1977 to carry on the struggle for independence abandoned by Sheikh Abdullah two years before. But contrary to expectations, they had not been arrested by the Indian authorities. They had instead made their way by various means and circuitous routes to the Line of Control separating Indian Kashmir from Azad Kashmir. From there they had crossed over into Pakistani-held territory.

Waiting on the other side was the Pakistan army. Despite their preoccupation with Afghanistan during the Soviet occupation, the Pakistanis had never fully taken their eyes off Kashmir. They had established contact with the JKLF as early as 1984 in the hope of conspiring against the Indians but were as surprised as New Delhi by the speed and intensity with which the intifada arose and gathered strength. Already gearing down from Afghanistan, they perceived an opportunity to do to the Indians in Kashmir what they had just done to the Russians in Afghanistan, employing much the same resources and techniques. Here was another opportunity to use the guerrilla warfare doctrine that had worked so well in Afghanistan. They began to train and equip the young JKLF recruits who were streaming across the Line of Control and then helped them infiltrate back into the valley, where they would attack the Indian army and paramilitary forces that were pouring into Kashmir in an effort to put the rebellion down. There was one big problem with the JKLF, however. It was a secular organization and fought well and with great determination, which was fine with the Pakistanis. The problem was that it was separatist. Its leaders had no interest in throwing off Indian rule only to become part of an impoverished Pakistani state prone to military dictatorship. Their goal, which had once been the goal of Sheikh Abdullah, was an independent Kashmiri state.

The Pakistanis had been happy to support the JKLF during the opening phases of the insurrection. But this was primarily a tactical move designed to increase the pressure on an Indian government already struggling with the intifada. They had no interest in seeing their efforts repaid by the establishment of an independent country. They began looking around for a more palatable alternative to the JKLF, one that would support their political goals in Kashmir. It did not particularly matter to them whether its motivations were religious or secular, nationalist or jihadist, so long as it was prepared to take up the struggle to make Kashmir part of Pakistan. Their search did not take long. Within the first two years of the intifada, three possibilities would emerge and the Pakistanis would take advantage of each.

The first was the Hizbul Mujahideen, formed in 1989 as the armed wing of the Kashmir branch of the Jamaat-e-Islami. The Kashmiri Jamaat occupied a niche in the disputed territory similar to the one the Jamiat-e Islami and Hezb-e Islami had occupied in Afghanistan during the anti-Soviet jihad. The primary difference was that it was even more closely tied to its Pakistani parent organization. It was well established in the valley and had been an active if not very successful player in local Kashmiri politics, having contested the 1987 elections as a member of the opposition coalition. When the intifada began to emerge, therefore, it is hardly surprising that some of its members would also begin making their way across the Line of Control to be welcomed with open arms by ISI. One of them, Yusuf Shah, had been the opposition candidate stripped of his victory and thrown into jail in the case cited earlier in the chapter. He would soon adopt the nom de guerre of Salahuddin and assume the leadership of the Hizbul Mujahideen.

Over the course of the next two years, the Pakistanis would steadily shift resources away from the JKLF and toward the Hizbul Mujahideen until young men coming across the LOC for training had little choice but to join the latter whether or not they were Jamaat-e-Islami supporters. After suffering debilitating casualties during the initial stages of the intifada, and bereft of Pakistani support, the JKLF would eventually abandon the armed struggle, while the Hizbul Mujahideen would become the dominant insurgent group in Kashmir. Although the Hizbul Mujahideen leaders shared the religious pedigree of their Afghan counterparts, their motivations were never purely jihadist either. The group was overwhelmingly Kashmiri in its makeup and its primary goal was to drive the Indians from its homeland. This was a goal it shared with the JKLF, but it parted company with its secular counterparts over the future status of the disputed territory. The Hizbul Mujahideen loyally followed the lead of its Pakistani parent organization in favoring the incorporation of Kashmir into Pakistan and was more than happy to cooperate with ISI and the Pakistan army to this end. I asked the Jamaat-e-Islami leader Qazi Hussain Ahmed how the Hizbul Mujahideen, which he professed to control, could take orders from both his leadership and from ISI. He pondered for a moment and then a slight smile crept across his face. "This is Pakistan," he replied.

The Hizbul Mujahideen was soon joined in Kashmir by two other groups, both of which harbored more straightforward jihadist motivations. As we saw, the HUJI had emerged during the anti-Soviet jihad as the first indigenous Pakistani jihadist group. Although most of its members were Pashtun, they, like the Arab mujahideen, had been radicalized by their Afghan experience and were eager for new opportunities to pursue the jihadist cause. As luck would have it, the Kashmiri intifada began to gather strength just as the last Soviets left Afghanistan. It required little imagination on the part of the HUJI leadership to see in it a potential jihadist cause. With the Soviets beaten, they decided to shift their attention to the northeast and help their Muslim brothers in Kashmir drive the infidel Hindus out of the valley. It is not certain when the first HUJI volunteers arrived in Kashmir or in what strength. There is some indication that ISI may have been reluctant to help them at first, out of fear of Indian retaliation over the introduction of Pakistani nationals. Frictions within the HUJI leadership precipitated a split around this time, and it was not until 1993 that it reunited under a new name, the Harakat-ul-Ansar (HUA). By this time, ISI appears to have overcome any previous reluctance to using Pakistani nationals in Kashmir, and HUA foot soldiers began making their way across the Line of Control. Back in Pakistan, meanwhile, the HUA was at work broadening its membership into the Deobandi-rich Seraiki belt. Prominent among the new recruits was the soon to become notorious Maulana Masood Azhar from Bahawalpur, who quickly rose to become a senior HUA ideologue.

At about the same time, a new group, calling itself the Lashkar-e-Taiba, also appeared on the scene. It was established as the jihadist wing of the Da'wa wal Irshad, an Ahle Hadith missionary organization that had been formed several years earlier to promote the growth of this, the smallest of the three main Sunni sects in Pakistan. The Da'wa wal Irshad had been founded by Hafiz Saeed, a professor of religious studies at a Lahore engineering university. He had been encouraged by none other than Abdullah Azzam, the Wahhabist cleric who, as we saw earlier, had recruited Osama bin Laden into the Afghan mujahideen and whose "Defense of the Muslim Lands" had become the international jihadist manifesto. The subsequent creation of the Lashkar-e-Taiba, which means "Army of the Pure," coincided with the beginning of the Kashmir intifada, suggesting that it was specifically established for the purpose of pursuing jihad in Kashmir. Hafiz Saeed has certainly never been shy about proclaiming the primary objective of the group, which is to liberate Kashmir as a first step toward freeing the entire Muslim population of India.

It is unclear whether ISI encouraged the formation of the Lashkar-e-Taiba or merely took advantage of it. According to the South Asia Terrorism Portal, an Indian website that tracks jihadist groups in Kashmir, its presence in the valley was first reported in 1993. While this timing is consistent with an ISI role in its formation, no smoking gun has ever been found. What does seem clear is that during the early stages of the intifada, ISI established relations with both the Lashkar and the HUA and did so with the intention of using them in the same way it had used Arab jihadists and Pakistani volunteers during the anti-Soviet jihad. This does not mean it shared their religious beliefs or subscribed to their ultimate objectives any more than the United States shared the views of Arab jihadists such as Osama bin Laden when it agreed to welcome them into the ranks of the mujahideen. Rather, the Pakistanis perceived these groups as instruments of foreign policy that could be used to contest Indian supremacy in Kashmir. The fact that the Lashkar and HUA were Pakistani groups was no doubt regarded as a point in their favor, since they were fellow countrymen rather than outsiders and might be presumed to harbor some residual loyalty to the state. It is also quite clear to me, from numerous discussions I had with retired senior army officers close to the situation at the time, that they thought they could control them.

The evidence seems to indicate that ISI came to rely increasingly on the Lashkar and HUA as the decade drew on. Part of the reason for this had to do with events inside Kashmir itself. Kashmir increasingly took on the appearance of an armed camp, as India flooded ever larger numbers of troops into the region, by some accounts as many as half a million men. This represented a significant portion of the Indian army, a level of commitment approaching that of the United States during the height of the Vietnam War. Basharat Peer titles one of his chapters "Bunkeristan" in order to convey the overwhelming Indian security presence in the valley at the time, manifested by thousands of bunkers and military encampments, which scarred urban landscapes and rural countryside alike. The Indians would respond to attacks on their convoys and installations by rousting nearby villages and neighborhoods. The men and teenage boys would be herded together for interrogation, with local informers on hand to finger possible jihadist collaborators, who would be carted away to special interrogation facilities where many were tortured. This practice steadily gnawed away at the strength and morale of the Hizbul Mujahideen. Although it continued to be the largest insurgent group in Kashmir, fewer and fewer potential recruits made their way across the Line of Control into Azad (free) Kashmir for training. To compensate, ISI turned increasingly to the Pakistani jihadists.

By the time I arrived in Islamabad in 1998, the insurrection in Kashmir had degenerated into an interminable slugging match. Pakistan and India were locked in a relentless artillery duel across the Line of Control. Pakistan army units would lay down artillery barrages as covering fire for incipient infiltrators and the Indians would answer back in kind. The innocent civilians who continued to inhabit both sides of the border frequently got caught in the crossfire and paid for it with their lives. The Hizbul Mujahideen, the Lashkar-e-Taiba, and the HUA remained the primary insurgent groups active in the valley. By this time, however, the HUA had run afoul of the United States, which had officially designated it as a terrorist organization. The United States had taken this step in the wake of the 1995 kidnapping of five young Western tourists hiking in the valley by an HUA-affiliated group. One of the hikers was later found beheaded, another managed to escape, while three others were never located. This one event attracted almost as much Western media attention as the entire Kashmir intifada and helped poison Western attitudes toward Pakistani efforts in Kashmir. It also helped discredit the Kashmiri insurrection itself, which became tainted by association. In response to these events, the HUA changed its name to the Harakat ul-Mujahideen (HUM), presumably in the hope that no one would notice.

The Lashkar-e-Taiba, meanwhile, had managed to build up an increasingly large profile inside Pakistan itself, with two thousand offices scattered around the country, many of them designed to perform charitable works. It had constructed a vast religious headquarters complex at Muridke just to the north of Lahore on the Grand Trunk Road, housing a large mosque, a madrassa, a hospital, a marketplace, and residential housing. According to Pakistani press accounts I read at the time, its annual conventions at Muridke were gigantic extravaganzas that attracted upward of a hundred thousand people. The Lashkar also established its own chain of religious schools, which provided a much more well-rounded education than that offered at the Deobandi madrassas. Many of its recruits were drawn from the ranks of lower-middle-class public school dropouts, but it also attracted a significant number of university graduates. These included physicians and other health workers who played an important role in its increasingly sought after charitable activities. Whereas the HUM drew its membership from the NWFP and the Seraiki belt of southern Punjab, the Lashkar mined a much broader geographical area, although primarily centered on Punjab. My impression at the time, which was shared by most Pakistani jihad watchers, was that the Lashkar-e-Taiba was the Kashmir-focused group most closely linked to, and favored by, ISI. It was an organization that seemed clearly on the way up.

By this time the Kashmiri insurgency was almost a decade old. But despite the insertion of three different jihadist groups into the fighting, the Indians showed no signs of leaving. The Pakistanis, however, had succeeded in getting their attention. In 1996, New Delhi had decided to launch what it billed, apparently without irony, as a good-neighbor policy, aimed at opening up a dialogue with Islamabad. The two sides met at just below the foreign minister level and put together the framework for what was called a "composite dialogue," in which they agreed to discuss all outstanding issues between them, including Kashmir. These were the first major bilateral negotiations between India and Pakistan in almost a quarter century. The two sides had last met at the Simla conference in 1972 in the immediate aftermath of the Bangladesh war. Simla had proved to be a seminal event in relations between the two countries, though not necessarily for the good. The two sides had managed to reach agreement on the geographical coordinates of the cease-fire line that ran through the disputed Kashmiri territory, which they renamed the Line of Control. Unfortunately, they neglected to give the precise coordinates for the LOC as it crossed through the remote Siachen Glacier region in the heart of the Karakorum Mountains in the extreme northern part of Kashmir. This became a bone of contention a decade later when Pakistan began issuing climbing permits to mountaineers. The Indians got wind of this and began moving troops onto the glacier, soon to be matched by the Pakistanis, leading to combat and eventual stalemate at twenty thousand feet, the highest war zone in the world, one in which most of the casualties resulted from frostbite and avalanches rather than firearms and artillery fire.

The most fateful decision to come out of the Simla conference, however, was an agreement that the two sides would settle their outstanding differences over Kashmir through bilateral negotiations. This is an obstacle the Indians have tried to hide behind ever since in discouraging any outside involvement. Their position is a bit disingenu-ous since the Simla agreement also permits efforts to settle differences by "any other peaceful means mutually agreed upon" by the two sides. Nonetheless, the Indians have stuck passionately to their position on bilateral negotiations despite the fact that they had previously accepted both the United States and Britain as mediators in six rounds of nego-tiations with Pakistan on Kashmir that took place in 1962 and 1963. During those negotiations, the two outside mediators had actually put specific ideas of their own on the table, concluding that both India and Pakistan should have "a substantial position in the Vale." The In-dians were not happy with the outsiders meddling with what they re-garded as their ownership of the Kashmir valley, and the talks went nowhere. India has subsequently used the Simla agreement to ensure that the episode is never repeated. By the time I got to Pakistan, the Kennedy-era talks had been long forgotten and the United States had come to regard the Indian refusal to permit outside mediation on Kashmir as the diplomatic equivalent of holy writ.

Although the Indians and Pakistanis had finally agreed to talk again in 1996, the composite dialogue made no immediate breakthroughs and was finally brought to a halt by the nuclear weapons tests con-ducted in May 1998, first by India and then—in direct and deliberate response—by Pakistan. While the Pakistani tests demonstrated that Pakistan had managed to develop its own nuclear capability, they forced the United States to reimpose Pressler Amendment sanctions, which Benazir Bhutto had managed to get lifted just two years earlier. In an effort to regain international favor, her successor as prime min-ister, Nawaz Sharif, who had ordered the nuclear tests, invited his Indian counterpart, Atal Vajpayee, to a summit meeting in Lahore eight months later, in early 1999. As we have seen, this was the event that Pervez Musharraf and the rest of the military brass had boycotted and where Jamaat-e-Islami protesters, of street power fame, had been routed by the Lahore police. The summit was made particularly mem-orable by the decision of the Indian prime minister to pay his respects at the Minar-e-Pakistan monument in Lahore, where Jinnah and the Muslim League had first gone on record in 1940 as favoring the cre-ation of a separate political entity for South Asian Muslims. The two leaders publicly agreed to restart the composite dialogue, but more important, they agreed behind the scenes to establish a secret negotiation aimed at making rapid progress on a settlement to the Kashmir dispute.

Unbeknownst to the rest of the world, the back-channel negotiators had already finished their first round of discussions in the spring of 1999 when media reports began to surface that mujahideen had occupied a number of Indian army outposts abandoned during the winter in the mountains above the town of Kargil along the Line of Control. Time would reveal that these were not mujahideen at all but rather Pakistan army forces dressed in khaki whose apparent intention was to cut the main supply route to Indian forces on the Siachen Glacier. The Pakistani claim that religiously motivated civilians were the culprits was yet another in a long line of attempts to secure plausible deniability for their actions extending back to the 1965 war. The Indians, who no doubt had their own suspicions early on, were determined to evict whoever was responsible, and they began pouring men and matériel into the Kargil salient, where fighting ensued at altitudes of well over ten thousand feet.

The United States also doubted that Kargil was a mujahideen operation and began pressuring the Pakistanis early on to withdraw the forces involved. Whatever the United States might have thought about the merits of the Kashmir dispute, it was not prepared to countenance efforts to resolve it through the overt use of military force, particularly when the two protagonists were nuclear armed. As India began streaming forces into the Kargil area to drive the Pakistanis from the heights, U.S. officials began to ratchet up the pressure on Islamabad, even sending General Anthony Zinni, the head of U.S. Central Command, to the capital to remonstrate with Nawaz and his army chief. Unnerved by the U.S. pressure, and spooked by the nearly universal condemnation of Pakistani actions, Nawaz Sharif began looking desperately for a way out. He persuaded the Clinton administration to let him fly to Washington on short notice for consultations that would allow him to back down gracefully. In an unprecedented July 4 meeting with President Clinton at Blair House, he pledged to work to restore the original cease-fire line in the Kargil area in return for Clinton's promise to help restart the Lahore process, which had come to an unceremonious halt as a result of the fighting.

I was surprised at the time how easily the Pakistanis had succumbed to U.S. pressure. After all, Pakistan had already been heavily sanctioned by the United States for its nuclear activities. What more could we do? Yet Nawaz Sharif had reacted as if he had been caught doing something wrong and expected to be punished for it. It began to dawn on me that Pakistanis seemed to believe, almost reflexively, that the United States had considerably more clout than it actually did. This attitude seemed linked to the view, which appeared to be widely held, that the United States was somehow manipulating events behind the scenes. This view was a commonplace in the Pakistani press and not infrequently encountered at dinner parties. It seemed to reflect a distinctive Pakistani fondness for conspiracy theories, their readiness to believe that the United States was behind the siege of Mecca in 1979 being a well-known example. I noted earlier that many Pakistanis seemed to believe there was an ISI operative lurking behind every tree. Well, many of these same people also seemed to think there was an American lurking behind every ISI operative, telling him what to do. As I have continued to follow events in Pakistan—many of which are chronicled later in this book—I have been struck by how much mileage the United States continues to be able to extract out of overblown Pakistani perceptions of American power. U.S. pressure seems to work even in the absence of U.S. threats, when there is little more behind it than vague imaginings. This isn't simply my view. A number of my best and most influential Pakistani contacts, both civilian and military, have conceded to me—somewhat ruefully, I might add—that the phenomenon is real.

Although the Pakistanis did withdraw from Kargil following the July 4 meeting in Washington, this was hardly the end of the matter. The incident generated further bad blood between Sharif and Pervez Musharraf, who used the media to publicly blame each other for the debacle. Nawaz claimed he had not been adequately informed about what was going on; Musharraf begged to differ. It now appears that the decision to occupy the Indian outposts at Kargil was made well before the Lahore summit, but it is much less clear to what end this was done. It is possible that the army saw it as a way to short-circuit an overture to India that was already on the horizon, or it may have been a badly misjudged effort to force concessions from India at the negotiating table. Whatever the motive, and whether or not Nawaz knew about it, the die had been cast. The prime minister, who was already wildly unpopular in Pakistan after two years of singularly bad governance, had no chance of winning the battle for public opinion. Coup talk filled the air. Increasingly beleaguered and convinced that Musharraf would move against him at some point, Nawaz decided to act. On October 12, just three months after his White House backdown, he attempted to fire Musharraf while the army chief was out of contact in a commercial jetliner returning from a conference in Sri Lanka. But the army was having none of it. Key Musharraf subordinates quickly sprang into action and Nawaz soon found himself out of a job, imprisoned in the army fort at Attock on the banks of the Indus, and before long, on a commercial jetliner on the way to exile in Saudi Arabia.

The composite dialogue and the second prime ministership of Nawaz Sharif were not the only casualties of the Kargil adventure. A much more sensitive negotiating process had also been brought to an end. Not long after Kargil, and against the backdrop of the Nawaz-Musharraf backbiting in the press, I had lunch with Niaz Naik, a retired high-ranking Pakistani diplomat. He surprised me by revealing that the Indian and Pakistani prime ministers had established a secret back-channel negotiation at Lahore. He knew this because he was the Pakistani representative. He proceeded to explain that he and his counterpart, an Indian businessman named R. K. Mishra, had been tasked to deliver a draft Kashmir agreement before the end of the year. During their first and only round of talks, in New Delhi, shortly before Kargil sabotaged the process, they had discussed the outlines of a possible territorial settlement. Naik said he had proposed that Indian-held Kashmir be divided along the line of the Chenab River. This would have given the heavily Muslim Kashmir valley, which lies to the north of the river, to Pakistan, with the largely Hindu area of Jammu to the south remaining in Indian hands. Although Mishra had been noncommittal—I suspect he may have been dumbfounded or was just being polite—Naik appeared to believe that the Indians might actually agree to this. This struck me as improbable in the extreme, since it would have required India to surrender most of the territory then under its control, including the biggest prize of all, the Vale of Kashmir. It is hard to see how this could be viewed as anything less than complete Indian capitulation to bottom-line Pakistani demands. Yet Naik seemed to think it was doable.

It is this glaring lack of perspective and inability to comprehend the art of the possible that lies at the heart of Western frustration with the Pakistani obsession over Kashmir. Although I have never taken a poll, my strong impression, based on numerous conversations over the years, is that most U.S. officials involved in South Asia and familiar with the origins of the dispute sympathize with the position that Kashmir should have gone to Pakistan, given the fact the population was overwhelmingly Muslim. The one wild card here is the position of Sheikh Abdullah, who was not only the most popular Muslim politician in Kashmir at the time but also a friend of Nehru's and sympathetic to the ruling Congress party. The plebiscite mandated by the UN after partition could have settled the matter once and for all, but the Indians were never really prepared to risk putting their hold on the valley to a vote. Once Sheikh Abdullah started falling out with them a few short years later, it became completely out the question.

But all this is irrelevant. The very fact that India refused to countenance a plebiscite at the time testifies to its reluctance to let the valley go. It has held on to it with the greatest tenacity ever since, prepared to act as ruthlessly as necessary to ensure that Kashmir remains in Indian hands, even to the point of deploying a significant percentage of the Indian army in the region. Nor is the reason for this dogged determination difficult to fathom. India is not now nor has it ever been a monolithic state. It is a patchwork of different ethnic, cultural, linguistic, and religious groups. The Kashmir intifada erupted at a time when India was already struggling with a Sikh insurgency in the state of Punjab. The Indians fear that giving in to bottom-line Pakistani demands in Kashmir—or Kashmiri demands for independence— could spark insurrections elsewhere in India. This they cannot and will not risk, no matter what price has to be paid.

Perceiving this, Western officials tend to be impatient with the Pakistanis. Their policy toward Kashmir seems pointless because it has no chance whatsoever of achieving success. How could anyone believe the Indians might actually be persuaded to abandon the Vale of Kashmir? Yet many Pakistanis did, and still do, believe it. Niaz Naik, who was otherwise the most moderate of men, presumably believed it. So does the army as an institution, although I encountered more than one retired senior officer willing to admit it was a lost cause. Many feudal politicians appear to be passionate on the subject, particularly those from the Punjab, which lies next door to Kashmir and enjoyed historically close ties to it until the Indians severed the link. By the time I got to Pakistan, however, support for the Kashmir cause had become such an item of political correctness inside the country that it was hard to tell what people actually believed. The two groups most vocal in advocating a hard-line position on Kashmir were strange bed-fellows. One consisted of secular nationalists, active in the media and reputedly close to the army, who were popularly known as Kashmir screamers. The other group, not surprisingly, consisted of those who harbored religious motivations. I vividly remember a conversation in which a senior Jamaat-e-Islami official insisted that the mujahideen would drive the Indians out of Kashmir just as they had driven the Soviets out of Afghanistan.

It was, in fact, Pakistan's use of jihadist groups in Kashmir that lost them all hope of a sympathetic ear in Washington. The United States, it is true, had supported using jihadists during the anti-Soviet jihad in Afghanistan, but this was before they had begun turning against the West. I first arrived in Pakistan four days before Al Qaeda bombed the U.S. embassies in Nairobi and Dar es Salaam. As I explore in greater detail later on, by this time Al Qaeda was operating openly in Afghanistan under the protection of the Taliban, who were Pakistani clients in the Afghan civil war that followed the Soviet departure. In response to the East Africa bombings, the United States launched cruise missiles against suspected Al Qaeda training camps in Khost province, not far from the Pakistani border. Most of the victims, however, turned out to be members of the HUM, one of several groups that were making use of the large camp complex at the time. It was clear that Al Qaeda and the HUM shared more than just training facilities. They also shared the same basic jihadist philosophy and antipathy toward the West, even though the HUM at the time was almost exclusively focused on Kashmir. As we saw earlier, this was the group the United States had desig-nated as a terrorist organization following the kidnapping and murder of the Western hikers in Kashmir in 1995. It is difficult to feel sympa-thy for a government prepared to employ groups that are virulently anti-American in pursuit of a hopeless cause.

The misgivings of the embassy community, and Washington more generally, were further exacerbated by an incident that occurred barely a month after Musharraf seized power. My ambassador, Bill Milam, and I were on our way to a meeting with Musharraf at his official resi-dence on a hill overlooking Islamabad. As we got out of our car, we heard what sounded like a loud bang down in the city below but gave it no further thought as we went inside. When we emerged an hour later and headed back to our car, we found our extremely agitated driver pointing excitedly at a phone lying off the hook on the backseat of our limousine. The deputy chief of mission was on the line explaining in an agitated voice that the embassy had just been the target of a rocket attack, which appeared to have failed. She encouraged us to wait until our security people could give the all clear, but we raced back to the embassy anyway and made our way quickly to our offices on the second floor. Looking out the large picture windows that lined one side of the building, we could see in the distance, across an empty field about a quarter of a mile away, the burning hulk of a large SUV. The perpetrators had apparently removed the backseat and remotely detonated a rocket they had mounted in its place. The embassy had escaped being hit because they had underestimated the force of the recoil, which made the vehicle jerk violently to one side, causing the projectile to literally miss by a mile. For all we knew at the time, this was HUM payback for their deaths at Khost.

If the Pakistanis understood the impact of such events on American sensibilities, they failed to take them into account. The only concession I encountered occurred in a meeting Musharraf had with the visiting assistant secretary for South Asia, Karl Inderfurth, not long after this event. In extolling the virtues of the Kashmiri insurgents, he avoided referring to them as jihadists or even as mujahideen, preferring instead to use the secular expression "freedom fighters." His audience was not amused. U.S. frustration reached its symbolic limit several months later, in March 2000, when Bill Clinton visited Pakistan amid the draconian security precautions described on the first page of this book. The centerpiece of his visit—his very reason for coming—was to deliver a live television address to the Pakistani people urging them to abandon their obsession with Kashmir, a fixation without hope of fulfillment that only served to open Pakistan up to the forces of religious extremism. He was telling them it was time to move on.

They did not listen. Even as the president was speaking, ISI was grooming a new jihadist group to take the field in Kashmir. Just a few months earlier, on Christmas Eve, HUM militants had hijacked an Indian Airlines plane shortly after taking off from Kathmandu airport in

Nepal. The hijackers originally asked to be flown to Lahore, but Pakistani officials refused to let the plane enter their airspace. Already low on fuel, it landed instead at Amritsar just across the border in India. When it appeared the Indian authorities were trying to block the runway to prevent the plane from leaving, the hijackers forced the pilot to take off. It headed for Lahore, where local officials once again refused it permission to land, even turning off the runway lights. It was only when the desperate pilot almost crashed the plane in an effort to land on a nearby road that they finally relented. The plane landed, was refueled, and took off again, landing first in Dubai, where most of the women and children were released, before heading for what turned out to be its final destination, the Taliban capital of Kandahar in southern Afghanistan.

Kandahar was a good choice, because the HUM had a presence there, as the casualty list from the U.S. cruise missile attack on Khost the previous year had demonstrated. In the negotiations that ensued, the hijackers agreed to release the plane and its passengers in return for the release of several jihadists being held in Indian custody. One was Omar Sheikh, a British-born jihadist who was later to play a central role in the kidnapping and murder of Daniel Pearl. But the big fish was Maulana Masood Azhar, the HUM leader from Bahawalpur in the Seraiki belt who had been captured in Kashmir in 1994. A man of some scholarly pretensions, he followed in the footsteps of the original founders of the HUM by studying at the Jamia Uloom al-Islamia madrassa in Karachi. After being delivered by the Indians to Kandahar, he had disappeared, only to resurface several months later in Pakistan, where he announced the formation of a new jihadist group, the Jaish-e-Mohammed, or Army of Mohammed. It remains unclear whether he had fallen out with the existing HUM leadership or had simply decided to go his own way. But he succeeded in carrying virtually the entire south Punjab membership of the HUM with him. The HUM was left with its Pashtun rump and quickly faded into relative obscurity.

Many analysts who follow such things believe ISI played a part if not in the actual hijacking, at least in the creation of the Jaish-e-Mohammed, which, given its south Punjab base, they may have believed they could more easily keep track of and control. They may also have wanted a group that was more narrowly focused on Kashmir than the HUM, which also had a foothold in Afghanistan. As is so often the case in such matters, documentary evidence is lacking and the principals involved have not seen fit to comment. What does seem clear is that Azhar intended the Jaish to be a somewhat different kind of organization. Within a few months of its creation, reports began to surface that some of its cadres had infiltrated Kashmir. But there were also reports that it was involved in sectarian operations against Shiites in Punjab, making it the first group to bridge the divide between home-grown sectarianism and foreign jihad. Some analysts have suggested that the Jaish made common cause with the more overtly sectarian Sipah-e-Sahaba and its even more militant Lashkar-e-Jhangvi offshoot. Be that as it may, it clearly recruited from the same Deobandi milieu as these other groups, and it would not be at all surprising if they were inclined to cooperate, as in later years would increasingly appear to be the case.

The introduction of the Jaish-e-Mohammed into the Kashmir fray coincided with a change in the character of the insurgency there. As we have seen, the massive Indian security presence had made it increasingly difficult for the Hizbul Mujahideen to operate. By 1996, the Kashmiri population was suffering from war weariness and the Indians felt confident enough to hold the first elections in the valley since the intifada had begun. Even though the opposition boycotted the elections, the steam was going out of the insurrection. Never able to match the Hizbul Mujahideen in numbers, the Lashkar-e-Taiba eventually decided to adopt tactics more suited to its circumstances. It shifted its focus away from large-scale assaults, which were not only increasingly harder to mount but also likely to result in significant attrition of its forces, to much smaller-scale, virtually suicidal attacks by very small groups—frequently just two-man teams—against well-defended but high-value Indian targets. The first such attack reportedly took place in July 1999 when two Lashkar militants burst into a camp manned by Indian paramilitary forces, lobbing grenades and with guns blazing. Fifty-five such attacks took place during the following three years, targeted primarily against police, paramilitary, and army camps. This included attacks mounted by the Jaish-e-Mohammed, which adopted similar tactics when its operatives moved into Kashmir in 2000. The Lashkar-e-Taiba called such attacks *fidayeen*, or life daring, and they represented a change not just in tactics but also in the nature of the attacks, since they carried with them the prospect of almost certain death.

It is highly likely that ISI knew and approved of this change in tactics. There were too many of these attacks over too long a period of time for this not to have been the case. No senior army officer retired or otherwise would admit to this, but more than one of my acquaintances did acknowledge a grudging admiration for the courage displayed by the jihadists, even though they conceded they were fanatics. The extent of ISI and Pakistan army involvement becomes harder to assess as these fidayeen attacks moved up the escalatory ladder to encompass more spectacular and incendiary attacks, some inside the Indian heartland itself. A fidayeen team attacked the Red Fort in New Delhi in December 2000. A month later, another team stormed into the terminal at Srinagar airport. The legislative assembly in Srinagar was attacked in October 2001. Two months later, on December 13, five men attacked the parliament building in the heart of New Delhi. Although they failed in their main goal of assassinating as many high-ranking Indians as possible, the audacity of this event, which brought the Kashmir conflict to the very seat of Indian political power, inflamed Indian public opinion. New Delhi deployed forces to the international frontier, a move reciprocated by the Pakistanis, which brought the two countries to what seemed to be the brink of war.

U.S. crisis diplomacy, aided by Pakistan's decision to publicly ban the Lashkar-e-Taiba and Jaish-e-Mohammed in January 2002, helped calm the waters, but in May another fidayeen team attacked a residential compound in Jammu housing the families of Indian army soldiers serving in Kashmir. Thirty-three people were killed, many of them women and children. This attack proved to have an even more incendiary impact, accompanied this time by nuclear saber rattling on both sides. The United States was sufficiently alarmed by the prospect of war that it evacuated families and nonessential personnel from its embassy and consulates in India, a decision that had a bracing effect on Indian decision makers. At the end of the day, a pledge by Pervez Musharraf to permanently cut off infiltration into Kashmir gave the two sides the cover they needed to back down from the brink. In the meantime, nothing much really changed for the jihadists. Hafiz Saeed and Masood Azhar were detained for several months, but little occurred that could reasonably be described as a crackdown on their organizations. The Lashkar-e-Taiba and Jaish-e-Mohammed lay low for a while, changed their names, and were soon back in business. The Pakistanis had no intention of seriously going after them. In Pakistan, the names are sometimes changed, not to protect the innocent but to enable jihadist collaborators to survive.

Opinions differ on how close India and Pakistan came to war on these occasions. My own sense is that they did not come very close at all. The great dilemma facing India in contemplating war with Pakistan, whatever the provocation might be, is that any success it enjoyed on the battlefield would put it at greater risk of coming under nuclear attack. What would the Pakistanis do, after all, if Lahore was under siege and about to fall, or if an Indian armored breakthrough farther to the south threatened to cut Pakistan in two? The retired lieutenant general whose emotional reaction I described in chapter 2 seemed to harbor few doubts that the Pakistanis would feel obliged to resort to nuclear weapons. The Indians are undoubtedly well aware that such attitudes exist within the Pakistan army officer corps and cannot be sure they are founded on bluff. A good part of the Indian frustration in being victimized by spectacular fidayeen attacks is that they genuinely feel the deterrent effect of the Pakistani nuclear arsenal, which is capable of destroying most, if not all, of India's large cities.

This raises the question of whether ISI approved or knew of the New Delhi and Jammu attacks in advance. No smoking gun has ever been found, so the matter must remain in the realm of speculation. It is relatively easy to understand how fidayeen attacks against police and military targets in Kashmir would advance Pakistani political objectives by keeping up the pressure on Indian security forces in the valley. But it becomes significantly more difficult to make a convincing case that it would serve Pakistani interests to physically attack the seat of Indian government or massacre defenseless women and children. Such incidents, as the Mumbai attack would demonstrate once again seven years later, only harden world opinion against the Pakistani cause. Kargil should have been fresh enough in the memory to convince even Pervez Musharraf of this fact. Nor could the Pakistanis be certain that such incidents, given their incendiary nature, would not lead to war, with potentially catastrophic results.

It is important to keep in mind here that Pakistani jihadist groups such as the Lashkar-e-Taiba and Jaish-e-Mohammed, whatever their relationship with ISI, are not and never have been simply instruments of Pakistani foreign policy. These groups have their own worldview and their own political goals, which sometimes overlap with those of their Pakistani benefactors but are distinctly and even radically different. Although both sides seek to drive the Indians out of Kashmir, the Pakistani political establishment, civilian and military, does not seek restoration of a universal Islamic caliphate or the imposition of sharia rule in Pakistan, or anywhere else. Groups such as the Lashkar and Jaish care not a whit about world public opinion and may see opportunity in the chaos that would surely flow from war between India and Pakistan. They are also well aware that the Pakistani authorities have regarded them as a critical weapon in their struggle with India over Kashmir. They probably see in this dependency all the license they need to pursue their own jihadist agenda.

Regardless of who bore ultimate responsibility for them, these events proved a bitter pill for the Indians to swallow. What, after all, did they have to show for their more than fifty years of suzerainty in Kashmir? A hostile and permanently disaffected Muslim population in the valley. Up to half a million troops permanently tied down. The implacable hostility of their closest neighbor. The prospect of further terrorist spectaculars in the heart of their country, any retribution for which could easily lead to war and the possible nuclear destruction of their largest cities. The knowledge that if they were actually to decide to cut their losses in Kashmir and run, the precedent could well inspire others, causing India to begin to unravel along ethnic, linguistic, and religious lines. Would the founders of the Indian nation have gone to the aid of Hari Singh had they been able to peer through the fog of time and see what would come of their decision? They had alternatives then. It is not so clear what their alternatives are now.

As for the Pakistanis, they thought they were being clever when they decided to take the lessons they had learned in Afghanistan and impose them on Kashmir. It was an inexpensive way to put pressure on the Indians and to tie down a sizable portion of their army. They no doubt harbored high hopes of forcing them to the negotiating table and, perhaps in time, even out of the valley. But they failed to appreciate that the groups they had chosen for the task had a significantly different agenda. What, after all, were the ultimate goals of the Lashkar-e-

Taiba and Jaish-e-Mohammed? Did anyone really believe that after driving the Indians from Kashmir they would lay down their arms and return to their homes in Pakistan to live in peace and harmony under the beneficent rule of a secular Pakistani establishment dominated by feudal politicians and the army?

I suspect that no one gave it very much thought at all. Those who did think about it almost certainly regarded it as a problem for tomorrow, a distant threat that could safely be left until later. The firm belief within ISI, supported by the leadership of the army and the civilians who ruled Pakistan for much of this period, was that they could control the jihadists. And why not? This had been their experience in running the mujahideen in Afghanistan. But they failed to fully understand whom and what they were dealing with. They were beginning to learn that they could control or influence radical Islamists only up to the point where their interests began to diverge. Beyond that point lay the steps of the Indian parliament building in New Delhi and the dead bodies of the wives and children of Indian soldiers in Jammu. But Kashmir was not the only place where the Pakistanis were beginning to learn this difficult lesson. Afghanistan, to their surprise and great dismay, had also come back to haunt them.

5. *The Taliban, bin Laden, and the Road to 9/11*

It was not supposed to be that way. Everyone thought that when the Soviet Union pulled out of Afghanistan, the puppet Communist government it left behind, headed by Mohammed Najibullah, would quickly give way to the Afghan mujahideen. But the Soviets kept their pocketbooks open and the regime did not fall. Not in 1989, nor in the next year, nor in the year after that. ISI had continued to channel most of its funding to Gulbuddin Hekmatyar, who was its clear-cut choice to seize power in Kabul once the Communists had been overthrown. But neither he nor his main rival, Ahmed Shah Masood, was able to force his way into Kabul. It was only at the beginning of 1992, with the final collapse of the Soviet Union, that the ground underneath Najibullah finally began to give way. The new Russian republic took him off the payroll, sharply reducing the incentive his military commanders had to continue supporting him. The decisive move came in February, when the commander of his ethnic Uzbek forces, General Dostam, decided to defect to the mujahideen. This was a setback not only for Najibullah but for the Pakistanis as well, since Dostam joined the contest on the side of Masood rather than of Hekmatyar.

Under the combined weight of Masood and Dostam, Kabul finally fell. The ousted Najibullah sought refuge in the UN compound, where he would remain until his brutal death several years later. ISI and

Hekmatyar found themselves on the outside looking in. The latter had only himself to blame. Before moving into the city, Masood had offered him an opportunity to share in its taking, but Hekmatyar had instead tried to beat him to the punch. He failed at this but succeeded in alienating his former mujahideen rival once and for all, laying the groundwork for yet another phase of the seemingly endless Afghan civil war, as the two warlords, soon to be joined by other contenders, squared off against each other in a Sisyphean struggle for power. The Afghan people were condemned to continue their sufferings, none more so than the Pashtuns of the Kandahar region in the south. Here, the situation bordered on anarchy, with no single commander able to dominate the political landscape. The region was tormented instead by a collection of local warlords who, in the manner of provincial despots since time immemorial, proceeded to rape, pillage, and burn.

Among those dismayed and angered by this turn of events was a group of local former madrassa students. Some were old enough to have fought with the mujahideen during the anti-Soviet jihad, while others had fled with their families into the various refugee camps set up by the Pakistanis in the NWFP. Almost all had managed to find their way into the numerous madrassas the JUI had established in the region in its effort to make itself a player in the mujahideen struggle in Afghanistan. There they received a strict Deobandi education, learning to recite the Quran and the basics of Deobandi jurisprudence, which they filtered through the prism of their own Pashtun tribal customs. Those too young to have fought with the mujahideen would no doubt have listened attentively to the stories told by more senior students of the heroic struggle against the godless Soviets, which had finally obliged them to leave. But as these madrassa students began returning to the Pashtun lands of southern Afghanistan following the completion of their studies, they had received a severe shock. The defeat of the Soviets had not ushered in an Islamic millennium. The lands of their birth had instead fallen into anarchy and ruin. Not only was there no central authority, but the grab bag of local warlords who competed for power in the region were lawless and corrupt. At first the former madrassa students did little more than complain among themselves about the evil and injustice in their midst. But they eventually decided to do something about it.

As told by the Pakistani journalist Ahmed Rashid, their first resort to arms came in the spring of 1994 in response to the kidnapping and rape of two teenage girls by the military commander of a local warlord. A young mullah by the name of Omar gathered together thirty of his companions and attacked the outpost where the girls were being held, freeing them and hanging the commander from the barrel of one of his own tanks. Unlike most of his colleagues, Mullah Omar had studied at a local Afghan madrassa rather than in Pakistan. He was a rural, backwater Pashtun who, like his Pakistani madrassa colleagues, filtered his fundamentalist Deobandi views through the austere lens of the demanding ancient Pashtun tribal code of Pashtunwali, with its emphasis on honor, revenge, and rough frontier justice. According to this ethnoreligious amalgam, a good Muslim was obliged not only to rescue the innocent from the clutches of local despots but also to hang the perpetrators from the barrel of a tank. The Taliban had been born.

Uplifted by this event, which won them substantial local renown, Omar and his compatriots achieved one success after another in the Kandahar area. Omar became a Robin Hood figure, moving from place to place, helping the poor against their warlord oppressors. As luck would have it, these events were transpiring just as ISI was growing impatient with its own man in Afghanistan, Gulbuddin Hekmatyar, who had a talent for making enemies. Some of his difficulties stemmed from the fact that his recruitment base was demographically limited. Consistent with his origins in the Jamaat-e-Islami movement, he drew most of his support from educated urban Pashtuns, a relatively small percentage of the overwhelmingly rural and illiterate Afghan population. The Taliban suffered from no such difficulty, drawing their strength not simply from Pakistani madrassas but also from the uneducated rural Pashtun countryside—men much like Mullah Omar himself.

Quite by chance, the Taliban had an ally in the Pakistani government. Benazir Bhutto had won a narrow victory in national assembly elections held in 1993 but needed support from some of the smaller parties to form a government. The JUI had managed to win only four seats, but its leader, Fazlur Rehman, suddenly found himself being courted by the PPP. In return for his support, Benazir agreed to make him chairman of the national assembly foreign affairs committee. When the Taliban, most of whom had emerged from his madrassas, suddenly burst into the spotlight in the spring and summer of 1994, he was there to plead their case to the defense minister, Naseerullah

Babar, a retired army general and longtime Bhutto supporter, who just happened to be an ethnic Pashtun. The JUI leader argued that the strong madrassa ties the Taliban had to Pakistan would make them a more reliable ally than the prickly Hekmatyar, and that with proper support they could succeed where Hekmatyar had failed. Babar was persuaded by the argument and took the matter to Bhutto, who was inclined to agree. She was attracted by the possibility the Taliban might be able to bring sufficient stability to their home base in the Kandahar area to enable Pakistan to open up trade routes to Central Asia through southern Afghanistan. ISI, however, proved to be an obstacle. It conceded that Hekmatyar was a disappointment but noted that his forces were at least keeping Masood pinned down in Kabul. This was important because Masood and his political master, Burhanuddin Rabbani, had turned firmly against Pakistan due to its support for Hekmatyar. ISI feared that if the pressure Hekmatyar was exerting was removed and Masood and Rabbani managed to consolidate their control over the country, they would inevitably gravitate toward India.

In this case, however, it was the civilians who prevailed. ISI agreed to provide the Taliban with support in what amounted to a trial run. The payoff was immediate. The Taliban first managed to successfully escort a Pakistani convoy through warlord-held territory. But by November they had succeeded in capturing Kandahar itself. This news electrified the ranks of young Afghan and Pakistani students enrolled at the JUI madrassas in the NWFP. With encouragement from their mullahs, more than ten thousand left their modest lodgings and rallied to the Taliban banner in southern Afghanistan. Mullah Omar and his lieutenants proceeded to institute their unique blend of Pashtun tribal customs and fundamentalist sharia rule on the inhabitants of Kandahar and its environs, shutting down schools for girls, banishing women from public view, requiring men to grow beards, outlawing television and movies, lopping off hands and feet for petty crimes, and hanging more defeated adversaries from the barrels of their growing arsenal of tanks.

Although the Taliban would suffer more than one setback during the next two years, thanks to growing ISI support and their own increasing prowess on the battlefield, they proved to be an inexorable tide. Within a year they had seized all of southern Afghanistan. In September 1995 they captured Herat, the largest city in the western part of the country. Exactly one year later—a mere two and a half years after Mullah Omar had rescued the two young girls—the Taliban swept into Kabul, driving the Masood forces out of the city and bringing the Afghan capital under their draconian rule. The luckless Hekmatyar, who had finally made peace with Masood the previous spring and subsequently become prime minister in the Kabul government, found himself out of a job and soon afterward in Iranian exile. The Taliban, meanwhile, in their first political act after taking control of Kabul, hauled the former Communist ruler Najibullah out of the UN compound where he had spent the previous four years, castrated him, dragged him on the ground from the back of a jeep, and finally hanged him with steel wire, not from a tank barrel but from a traffic control post in the center of town.

By the time I got to Islamabad in early August 1998, the Taliban were poised to overrun the northwestern stronghold of Mazar-e-Sharif. This had been the site of their biggest ever military setback the year before, when three thousand Taliban soldiers had been massacred by local forces. They were about to take their revenge and with it bring 80 percent of the country under their control. Their primary adversary, the Northern Alliance, the name by which the forces of Masood and his on-again, off-again ally General Dostam were known by this time, were hunkered down in a narrow swath of the country north of Kabul centered on the Panjshir Valley, where Masood was based.

The day I landed in Pakistan, relations between the United States and the Taliban were neither good nor bad. The United States had closed its embassy in Kabul in 1989 due to the widespread breakdown of law and order at the beginning of the Afghan civil war. Afghanistan was covered instead by the U.S. embassy in Islamabad, and most meetings with the Taliban took place in the Pakistani capital, where the Taliban maintained an embassy they had commandeered from the Northern Alliance representatives. It was located in a quiet, leafy residential neighborhood that just happened to be across the street and a few houses down from where I lived. At the time, the United States was officially neutral in the Afghan civil war. The U.S. view was that the issue should be settled not on the battlefield but through UN-led negotiations aimed at producing a broad-based coalition government. Needless to say, this policy was unlikely to find favor in Kandahar, given the dominant Taliban position in the country. What the Taliban wanted from the United States more than anything else was recognition of that dominance. But they were far from hostile. They began virtually every meeting with U.S. officials by thanking the United States for its support for the mujahideen in their struggle against the Soviet occupation.

There was a rather large fly in the ointment, however: Osama bin Laden. He had returned to Saudi Arabia following the Soviet withdrawal from Afghanistan but soon fell out with the Saudi government over its decision to permit the United States to use Saudi territory as its primary base of operations during the 1991 Gulf War. He considered the stationing of what he called "Crusader" forces in the "Land of the Two Holy Places" to be sacrilege and began to speak out openly and brazenly against it. This did not endear him to the Saudi royal family, and bin Laden was eventually pressured into leaving the kingdom, seeking refuge in Sudan where, during the next several years, he set about cobbling together what would become known to the world as Al Qaeda. His anti-U.S. rantings and repeated threats to begin attacking U.S. interests, however, attracted growing attention and concern in Washington, which began pressuring the Sudanese authorities to evict him. This they eventually agreed to do, and bin Laden, with limited options, decided to return to the one place where he thought he would feel welcome. He arrived back in Afghanistan in May 1996, four months before the Taliban moved into Kabul.

Bin Laden settled first in his old haunts of Jalalabad in the eastern part of Afghanistan not far from the Pakistani border in an area that was then outside of Taliban control. It was from here that he issued the first of his two anti-U.S. fatwas. Early in 1997, he managed to insinuate himself into the good graces of the Taliban and moved to their home base in Kandahar. He also managed to buy his way into a large training complex that had been established at Khost to the south of Jalalabad. This complex already served as a training facility for the Pakistani jihadist group the HUM, which, thanks in part to funding provided by ISI, used it to prepare its foot soldiers for service in Kashmir. Bin Laden converted a portion of the complex for use by his own Al Qaeda forces. There he was joined by Ayman al-Zawahiri, who had amalgamated his own Egyptian Islamic Jihad into Al Qaeda. Bin Laden authored, and both men signed, yet another fatwa against the United States in February 1998. This one called on Muslims to kill Americans and destroy their property wherever they could be found. This call to arms raised further alarms in Washington, which took advantage of a scheduled trip to Kabul by Bill Richardson, the U.S. ambassador to the UN, to raise the issue with the Taliban. Their reaction was primarily one of puzzlement. Bin Laden was not a mullah and so could not legitimately promulgate such a decree.

Four days after I arrived in Pakistan, bin Laden tried to make good on his fatwa by bombing the U.S. embassies in Nairobi and Dar es Salaam. It was August 7, 1998. More than two hundred people were killed, twelve of them Americans. There were going to be repercussions. Two weeks later the United States evacuated its diplomatic facilities in Pakistan as a precautionary move. All family members and nonessential personnel were flown out of the country. Two days after their departure, cruise missiles from U.S. ships stationed off the Pakistani coast slammed into the Khost training complex, where bin Laden was believed to be present. Mostly they just pounded sand. A number of camp residents were killed, but none of them were members of Al Qaeda. As noted earlier, the majority of the victims were unsuspecting members of the HUM. Bin Laden had apparently left the area several hours before the attack. The United States also bombed a chemical factory in Sudan that was believed to have links to bin Laden.

The East African bombings, and the failed retaliation at Khost, inaugurated three years of unsuccessful U.S. efforts to bring bin Laden to justice leading up to the attacks on the World Trade Center and the Pentagon on 9/11. The United States was not prepared to go to war with the Taliban over the East Africa attacks. The precise relationship between bin Laden and the Taliban leadership was unknown, and the provocation was not considered sufficient justification. There was no clamor inside Washington or within the country as a whole for that kind of drastic action. Instead, the United States made use of clandestine sources on the ground in Afghanistan in an effort to try to locate bin Laden, while maintaining ships in the Arabian Sea prepared to launch cruise missiles if his whereabouts could be pinpointed. Reported sightings did occur, but although some in Washington were prepared to take the risk, the intelligence was never deemed reliable enough, nor the risk of killing innocent bystanders small enough, to justify an attack, particularly in the aftermath of the Khost failure. Nor was the United States prepared to join forces with the Northern Alliance against the Taliban in what seemed a hopeless cause. The Masood forces were having difficulty just holding on and did not have the necessary manpower to turn the situation around even if the United States had dropped its neutrality and decided to throw material support its way.

The most Washington was prepared to do was give the Taliban stern warnings that if Al Qaeda carried out any further attacks, the Taliban would be held personally responsible. This became an almost ritualistic incantation in meetings with Taliban officials during the three years I was in Islamabad. It is not clear what they thought of this vague threat, but it did not appear to have them shaking in their sandals. Their stated reasons for refusing to move against bin Laden varied over time. The one most commonly cited was that he was a guest and therefore could not be turned over due to the Pashtun tribal custom of Pashtunwali. It was difficult to dismiss this out of hand since the obligation to extend protection to guests is an important tenet of the Pashtunwali code. At other times the Taliban expressed at least a superficial willingness to take steps against bin Laden. They asked to see evidence implicating him in the East Africa bombings and raised the possibility of setting up a commission of religious scholars to examine it. In the immediate aftermath of the bombings, they declared they had placed restrictions on bin Laden himself and his activities. The following February they claimed he had absconded to parts unknown. The most far-fetched excuse they managed to trot out was that the Afghan people would rise against them if they tried to throw bin Laden out. During this period, as they offered one dubious excuse after another, it became increasingly clear that they were intended primarily as off-putters and time wasters, designed to keep stringing the United States along.

The one thing the Taliban most wanted from the United States was recognition. Despite the fact that they controlled more than 80 percent of Afghan territory, the only countries that recognized them as the legitimate government of Afghanistan were Pakistan, the UAE, and Saudi Arabia. The Saudis had been early backers of the Taliban and had been extremely unhappy at the support they subsequently extended to bin Laden, but they were never quite willing to pull the plug on them. Against this backdrop, U.S. recognition of the Taliban would have presented an enormous coup, providing them with the international respectability they craved, matching the success they had achieved on the battlefield. But the United States was never willing to offer diplomatic recognition in return for bin Laden, nor did the Taliban ever attempt to explicitly link the two. Although the United States wanted bin Laden badly, it was not prepared to recognize a regime that made a virtue out of seventh-century brutality. To do so would have been regarded as cynical in the extreme. There was also strong domestic opposition to recognizing a regime that harbored retrograde attitudes toward women, having forced females out of schools and required women to wear the burqa in public and submit to purdah in private.

But there is good reason to believe the Taliban would never have accepted such a tradeoff in any event. When I arrived in Pakistan, the nature of the relationship between bin Laden and Mullah Omar was still unclear. At first the Pashtunwali argument seemed to make some sense. But during my first year at the embassy, we began to pick up press reports from Taliban media outlets that condemned the presence of U.S. forces on Saudi territory. Not only had these and similar pronouncements not been heard from the Taliban before, they echoed positions long associated with Al Qaeda and appeared to be taken directly from the Al Qaeda press kit. They were not the sorts of posturings you would have expected from the provincial backwater Pashtuns who led the Taliban movement if left to their own devices. Why, after all, should Mullah Omar care about who the Saudis let into their own country? It was evidence not only that the Taliban were buying into the Al Qaeda message but also that bin Laden had succeeded in becoming a political mentor to Mullah Omar rather than simply an honored guest. At about the same time, reports started surfacing in the Pakistani press that bin Laden had married one of his sons to a daughter of Mullah Omar, or perhaps it was the other way around; it was never made precisely clear. Although it might seem unlikely that a wealthy, well-educated Saudi would consent to have one of his children married to the son or daughter of an illiterate rural Pashtun, such rumors were widely believed at the time.

Time, of course, would demonstrate that Mullah Omar was prepared to stick with bin Laden to the bitter end. But few believed this until it became a reality, and so the United States continued seeking ways to try to pry the two men apart. Not surprisingly, this included direct pressure on not only the Taliban themselves but also their primary benefactors, the Pakistanis. The East Africa bombings had put the Pakistanis in a difficult position. They had made the decision to back the Taliban in the Afghan civil war and it seemed to have paid off handsomely for them. Thanks in large measure to substantial Pakistani support, the Taliban had managed to bring almost the entire country under their control. There was good reason to believe that Masood would eventually fall and that Pakistan would emerge from the conflict with a friendly power on its western flank, providing the Pakistanis with what they liked to refer to as strategic depth in the event of war with India. But the presence of Osama bin Laden on Afghan soil was a serious complicating factor. They gained nothing from his presence but potentially stood to lose a great deal.

After the East Africa bombings, the United States began ratcheting up the pressure on Pakistan to use its influence in Kandahar to bring bin Laden to justice. In practice, however, this amounted to little more than hectoring. As we have seen, the United States had already reimposed Pressler Amendment sanctions on Pakistan in response to its May 1998 nuclear tests and had relatively few usable arrows left in its quiver. The Pakistanis were not only well aware of this fact, they were resentful that the United States had found yet another issue to beat them over the head with. The fact that Washington had recently forced them to back down over Kargil, while castigating them for supporting jihadist groups in Kashmir, did not help their disposition either. In my discussions with Pakistani officials during this period, Afghanistan was the one issue that was most likely to set them off. I vividly remember a conversation I had with Ehsan ul-Haq, at the time the director general for army military intelligence and later the head of ISI. It was something of a coup to get an appointment with him, since senior military officers were reluctant to meet with U.S. officials outside the normal chain of command. He received me at his Rawalpindi residence, and we had a very pleasant conversation until I touched on the subject of bin Laden. His demeanor changed rapidly to one of frustrated irritation. "I cannot understand why you Americans are so concerned about Afghanistan," he replied. On another occasion, my best army contact in Pakistan, a retired general with close ties to Musharraf who always spoke frankly to me about the army and its aims, told me he simply could not grasp U.S. concern with just one man.

It was more than just irritation. These officers found it difficult to understand why the United States took bin Laden so seriously. Although Al Qaeda, it was true, had succeeded in bombing two U.S. embassies, it was still a relatively small organization that posed no conceivable strategic threat to the United States. This perception was combined with resentment, widely felt within Pakistani ruling circles, that the United States was seeking to undermine something they regarded as critically important to the defense of their country and that they had worked very hard to achieve. As they saw it, they had borne the brunt of the struggle against the Soviet occupation of Afghanistan and had earned the right to have a friendly government in Kabul. Yet here was the all-powerful United States, quick to criticize them at every turn—for their nuclear weapons program, for their Kargil adventure, for training jihadist groups and helping them infiltrate into Kashmir—now giving them a hard time over this.

It is unclear how hard the Pakistanis pushed the Taliban on the bin Laden matter. There were a considerable number of ISI officers working with the Taliban in Afghanistan, and had they wanted to they could have found a way to gain physical access to the Al Qaeda leader. In the wake of the Kargil crisis, Nawaz Sharif reportedly agreed to put together a commando unit to go after bin Laden, but he was toppled in the Musharraf coup before his sincerity could be tested. Despite this agreement, it is, frankly, doubtful that the Pakistanis would actually have gone after bin Laden, since this could have severely damaged their relationship with the Taliban. Whatever else bin Laden may have been, he was their honored guest. They would not have taken kindly to the Pakistanis assassinating him on their home turf or snatching him unceremoniously from under their noses. Although the Taliban might have gotten over it—after all, they had nowhere else to look for support—this would have required the Pakistanis to assume far more risk than they were willing to under the circumstances.

The Pakistanis did, however, make two well-publicized trips to Kandahar to press Mullah Omar on bin Laden: one when Nawaz Sharif was prime minister, the other after the Musharraf coup. The first was by the ISI chief, Ziauddin, the second by his born-again Islamic fundamentalist successor, Mahmud Ahmed. Both generals had agreed to make the pitch after visiting Washington and being taken to the woodshed by Under Secretary of State Thomas Pickering. In both cases, they were turned away empty-handed, recipients of the same kind of off-putting replies for which Mullah Omar was becoming justly renowned. But the Pakistanis refused to press the matter. They were unwilling to risk their relationship with the Taliban over the Al Qaeda presence in Afghanistan. It was clear to me at the time that their policy on bin Laden was driven primarily by hope. The Pakistanis hoped that Al Qaeda would not succeed in attacking the United States again or, if it did succeed, that the United States would not retaliate in a way that would undermine Taliban ascendency in Afghanistan.

The Pakistanis did manage to dodge some bullets. In the run-up to the millennium celebrations at the end of 1999, Al Qaeda tried to carry out a number of terrorist spectaculars. A bin Laden operative with an automobile full of explosives was picked up on a car ferry entering Washington State from Canada. He had planned to detonate his car bomb at Los Angeles International Airport. Jordanian intelligence short-circuited a plot to bomb the Radisson hotel in Amman, where a large group of American and Israeli tourists were planning to hold a millennium party. Early in January 2000, Al Qaeda attempted to bomb a U.S. destroyer, *The Sullivans*, in the Yemeni port of Aden. Luckily, the launch containing the explosives sank due to its heavy weight before it could reach its target. The fact that there had even been such an attempt remained unknown for several years. In October 2000, bin Laden operatives finally managed to get it right when they carried out a similar attack against the USS *Cole*, blowing a gaping hole in its side and killing seventeen U.S. sailors in the process. Here, too, the Pakistanis were lucky, because U.S. intelligence was not able to trace the operation with certainty back to an Al Qaeda source. On 9/11, however, their luck ran out.

Although the Taliban remained on their side of the Durand Line during the three years I served in Pakistan, a phenomenon known as Talibanization did make an appearance. This referred not to something done by the Taliban but to efforts by radical Islamists in Pakistan to impose their fundamentalist views on the community around them. The phenomenon was typically associated with raids on video shops or movie theaters and other symbols of Western cultural influence. Such activities tended to occur in areas where radical mosques or madrassas were actively engaged in proselytizing or were otherwise throwing their weight around. During my time in Pakistan, the phenomenon was almost exclusively restricted to the NWFP, where reports of such activities would surface from time to time in the local press. But I remember at least one report involving the Seraiki belt. This came from a south Punjabi politician who complained to me that Talibanization was taking root in his district. When I pressed him on the matter, he admitted the activities involved could be traced back to students from local madrassas. His concern was that their actions seemed to be finding resonance among at least a portion of the local population.

The emergence of Talibanization coincided with the rapid proliferation of radical Deobandi mosques and madrassas, which continued unchecked even after the Soviet departure from Afghanistan. Although most of these institutions were located in the NWFP and the Seraiki belt, they could be found just about anywhere. I vividly remember a trip I took to Gilgit, a bustling frontier town in the far north of Pakistan in the heart of the Karakorum Mountains. I was walking over the main bridge across the Indus in the center of town with my local guide when he pointed to a large building at the far end of the bridge. "That," he said, "is our radical mosque." I later learned that Gilgit was home to a majority Shiite population and had a history of sectarian violence, making it an obvious stopping-off point for sectarian-minded Deobandis looking for trouble. No one knows for sure how many such mosques existed in Pakistan, then or now, since no comprehensive survey has been undertaken. But if radical mosques can be found in Gilgit they can probably be found in just about any city or town of any size in Pakistan.

The situation is similar with respect to madrassas. In 2003, the Pakistani government estimated there were just over ten thousand madrassas in the country, the majority of them Deobandi. In 2005, the Musharraf government finally set about trying to register them. By 2007, it claimed to have registered more than fourteen thousand. No one believes that the government succeeded in registering them all, and estimates that they number around twenty thousand are common, with some estimates considerably higher. But the fact is that no one really knows for certain. Nor is it clear what percentage of madrassas can be considered radical—those institutions that preach jihad and sectarian hatred and actively encourage their students to join jihadist and sectarian groups, with whom many of them have ties. Ten to fifteen percent is a commonly cited statistic, but this is at best an educated guess. It was this radical subset of Deobandi madrassas that served as feeder institutions for the Taliban during their rise to power in Afghanistan, as well as for the jihadist and sectarian groups that were active in Pakistan during my tenure there. It was mullahs and students from these very same institutions whose strong-arm tactics in parts of the NWFP and the Seraiki belt also gave rise to the use of the term *Talibanization*.

Talibanization was not something the people who ran Pakistan sought, but it was an inevitable consequence of their policies. The number of madrassas continued to grow over time because the authorities did nothing to stop it. Any mullah or Deobandi group that wanted to open a radical mosque or establish a radical madrassa was able to do so free from any hindrance by the state. The authorities were disinclined to move against them or even to regulate them in any meaningful way because the Taliban and the jihadist groups into whom they fed recruits served what were perceived to be vital Pakistani state interests. This was not just a Deobandi dispensation. The Lashkar-e-Taiba, which searched the bazaars of Punjab and Sindh trolling for public school dropouts, was also left severely alone. Any effort to bring these groups to book would have risked causing severe damage to Pakistani foreign policy.

But there was a problem. The same radical mosques and madrassas that provided recruits for jihadist groups serving Pakistani interests in Kashmir and Afghanistan also preached sectarian hatred at home. They included on their enemies list not simply those who they believed had oppressed Muslims, such as Christians, Hindus, and Jews, but also those who professed to be Muslims but who in their judgment were not, such as Shiites and Ahmadis. Although many students from radical Deobandi madrassas went off to fight jihad abroad, others stayed home to join the sectarian Sipah-e-Sahaba and its even more violent Lashkar-e-Jhangvi offspring. At first the Pakistani authorities were inclined to see Deobandi sectarianism as a counterweight to the growth in Shiite assertiveness following the Iranian revolution. It posed no problem so long as its targets were confined to militants associated with their radical Shiite counterparts, such as the Sipah-e-Mohammed. But this forbearance gave way to dismay when the Lashkar-e-Jhangvi began to target and assassinate prominent members of the Shiite community and to target Shiite religious processions and celebrations. This spread alarm throughout the entire Shiite community, many of whom, as noted, held prominent positions in the feudal political establishment.

As a purely practical matter, it was difficult to attack the problem at its source. The Pakistanis were unwilling to crack down on the mosques and madrassas that fed the sectarian groups because of their links to the jihadist groups at work in Afghanistan and Kashmir. The waters became further muddied when the Sipah-e-Sahaba started sending recruits off to fight alongside the Taliban in Afghanistan and even more so when the Jaish-e-Mohammed was formed with the specific intent of pursuing both jihadist and sectarian ambitions. As we saw in chapter 3, the Sipah-e-Sahaba had begun to show an interest in electoral politics almost from the beginning. The Pakistani authorities tried to counter its more violent tendencies by actively supporting these moves toward the political mainstream. The SSP was encouraged to field candidates for seats in the Punjab provincial assembly, and one successful candidate actually secured a ministerial post in the Punjab provincial government, which at the time was in the hands of the PPP. But at the same time, the authorities took a hard line against the Lashkar-e-Jhangvi, which flatly refused to end its own campaign of violence against the Shiite community.

The government crackdown on the Lashkar was in full swing when I arrived in Pakistan. The press carried periodic reports of Lashkar militants being shot while attempting to escape from police custody. These events were sufficiently common that they came to be known in the media vernacular as false encounters. The portrait that emerged of the Lashkar-e-Jhangvi was of a very small but ruthless organization led by a fanatical former SSP assassin, Riaz Basra. In what would become a familiar phenomenon in later years, the Lashkar reacted to government efforts to curtail its activities by turning against the state. It threatened to kill police officers involved in hunting them down and in some instances made good on the threats. Nor did the Lashkar shy away from attacking the very highest levels of government. In January 1999, the Lashkar narrowly failed in an effort to assassinate Prime Minister Nawaz Sharif. Riaz Basra fled to Afghanistan and managed to hide out there for a time, but he returned to Pakistan and was finally tracked down and killed in yet another false encounter with police in May 2002.

The crackdown against the Lashkar-e-Jhangvi appeared to be an effort by the Pakistanis to draw a line between good and bad radical Islamic groups. The good ones were those that served the country's foreign policy interests, such as the Lashkar-e-Taiba and the Jaish-e-Mohammed. Even though the Jaish occasionally carried out sectarian attacks against Shiite targets inside Pakistan itself, the authorities were prepared to look the other way because of its participation in the Kashmir jihad. ISI no doubt had a word with Masood Azhar from time to time and hoped that that would suffice. The bad groups, on the other hand, were those whose activities failed to serve Pakistani foreign policy objectives or were otherwise deemed harmful to the state. The Lashkar-e-Jhangvi was the first such group, but it was destined not to be the last. The one constant would be the reluctance of the authorities to go after the radical mosques and madrassas that fed both good and bad radical Islamic groups. As we shall see in chapter 7, the one major exception to this, the crackdown against the Lal Masjid mosque and madrassa complex in the center of Islamabad in the summer of 2007, resulted in a bloodbath and public relations disaster. The Pakistanis have never repeated it, not simply because to do so would invite further violence, potentially on a massive scale if multiple targets were hit, but also because it would jeopardize their supply of good jihadists. The Pakistanis have learned the hard way that you have to take the bad with the good.

The reports of Talibanization that surfaced from time to time during my years in Pakistan reflected spontaneous efforts by radical Deobandi madrassa students to rid nearby communities of Western cultural influences. But they were not part of any broader organized effort to impose the Deobandi vision of sharia rule on Pakistan, because at the time there was none. The one exception was in the Swat Valley of the NWFP. Here, in 1989, an apostate member of the Jamaat-e-Islami by the name of Sufi Mohammed founded an organization called the Tehrik-e-Nafaz-e-Shariat-e-Mohammadi (TNSM). Sufi Mohammed had lost patience with the Jamaat's willingness to pursue fundamentalist change working from within the system. He was prepared to use the TNSM to bring sharia rule back to the Swat Valley by force, if necessary. This was easier said than done; Swat at the time was not just another valley. Covered by pristine forests and surrounded by beautiful mountains of Alpine character, it was the most popular outdoor vacation spot in Pakistan, particularly among the feudal elite.

Prior to its full incorporation into the NWFP in 1970, the judicial system in what had been the Provincially Administered Tribal Area of Swat had actually been governed by sharia law. In 1994, Sufi Mohammed issued a proclamation demanding that it be reimposed not only there but in all of Malakand division, of which Swat is a relatively small part. When the Pakistani authorities ignored this, he took matters into his own hands, ordering his followers to seize government buildings in the valley. The surprised authorities sent in forces to regain control but had no stomach for a prolonged fight. Instead they attempted to buy off Sufi Mohammed by agreeing to his bottom-line demand to restore sharia rule to the region. This would turn out to be the first of many such deals that the Pakistani authorities would negotiate with radical Islamists in the years to come, in which they would cave in to fundamentalist demands and, by so doing, gradually abandon the writ of the state in the area concerned in order to avoid having to put up a fight.

When I was serving in Pakistan, the authorities appeared to regard the TNSM as an annoyance, but nothing more. In the aftermath of the sharia deal, ISI had been tasked to watch over Sufi Mohammed and temper his more extreme ambitions. At one point during this period, he announced plans to march on Islamabad. I asked one of my most knowledgeable former senior army contacts how the authorities planned to prevent this. He said that ISI would have a word with Sufi Mohammed behind the scenes and convince him it was not in his interest to proceed with the march. Various threats would be deployed or hinted at. I asked what would happen if these threats failed to move the TNSM leader and he decided to carry out the march nonetheless. The general smiled and replied that the whole point was to prevent the march from ever taking place. This was how ISI worked. If the march did take place, that would mean the army had lost control.

Presumably, ISI succeeded, because the march did not take place. Swat remained a sideshow until just after 9/11. That was when Sufi Mohammed sent seven thousand followers into Afghanistan to fight alongside the Taliban against the gathering American assault. Most ended up being killed or captured in the fighting that followed. Sufi Mohammed survived, but the Pakistani authorities decided to arrest him on his return to Pakistan and subsequently reasserted their control over Swat and the rest of Malakand division. In seeking to impose sharia rule in Swat, Sufi Mohammed, like the Lashkar-e-Jhangvi, had turned against the state. By sending forces into Afghanistan, he had given the Pakistanis a pretext to move against him. In so doing, they were able to rid themselves of a nuisance while providing the United States with some early evidence that they were serious about cooperating in the war on terror. This was not to be the end of the story, however. Sufi Mohammed was in prison, but his son-in-law, Mullah Fazlullah, would rebuild the TNSM in his absence and one day join forces with the Pakistani Taliban.

Although ISI had managed to dissuade Sufi Mohammed from marching on Islamabad, it was becoming increasingly clear that it could not simply bend radical Islamists to its will anytime it wanted. The example of the Taliban and Al Qaeda was already near at hand. Pakistani efforts to persuade Mullah Omar to turn over bin Laden had clearly failed. Within Pakistan itself, the Pakistanis had actively encouraged the growth of the Lashkar-e-Taiba and Jaish-e-Mohammed, but evidence would soon mount that they exercised far from complete control over them as well. The only goal these jihadist groups seemed to share with the people who ran Pakistan was the desire to liberate Kashmir from Indian rule. The Lashkar-e-Taiba, in particular, appeared to be growing rapidly in size and strength; I wondered what would happen if it ever decided to turn against the state. Then there were the sectarian groups that continued to spread their messages of hatred, which they exercised at the point of a gun. How could they remain at peace indefinitely with a Pakistan dominated by followers of a tolerant, nonthreatening form of Sufi Islam? And what would the future be like a decade or two or three down the road if the radical mosques and madrassas that provided the cannon fodder for most of these groups continued to multiply unchecked and unregulated by the state?

Living in Islamabad as a U.S. diplomat, I felt a palpable sense of vulnerability. On one occasion, following a large reception at my house, a reporter who had left the party drunk returned to his office to file a story about it, in which he not only divulged my address but called attention to the fact that my father-in-law, Thomas Pickering, was currently the third ranking official in the State Department. My wife and I were seriously alarmed by this disclosure, which not only shouted out where we lived but also gave Al Qaeda or the HUM or some other group additional motivation to target us. Our alarm was shared by the security people at the embassy, who quickly rushed to our neighborhood to look for signs of possible surveillance. They did not expect to find anything right away, but to their dismay they immediately noticed several men who appeared to be watching our house. My family and I were quickly moved into a small apartment on the embassy compound, while our security people tried to determine who the watchers were. It took them five weeks to get their answer. The Pakistanis finally revealed that the culprits were security men from the Taliban embassy, who had no interest in us at all but were watching the street for signs that their own embassy was being surveilled. It was then that it began to dawn on me that I probably lived on one of the safest streets in Islamabad, a place where everyone seemed to be watching everyone else.

It was against this backdrop that I sat down to research what was probably one of the longest cable messages ever sent to Washington by a Foreign Service officer serving in the field, describing the growth of radical Islam in Pakistan and assessing the threat it posed to the state. I saw it then pretty much the same way I see it now. The Pakistani political establishment, civilian and military alike, had allowed militant Islamic fundamentalism to take root for reasons of state. They saw the use of radical Islamists as a relatively low-cost and seemingly highly effective way to pursue important foreign policy interests, particularly against India. They thought they could control them, even though the first signs to the contrary had already appeared. Although these forces did share certain goals with the people who ran Pakistan, the alliance between them was a tenuous one, permanently in danger of breaking down, as it already had with the Lashkar-e-Jhangvi. The longer these forces were allowed to flourish unchecked by the state, the more difficult they would be to contain. I saw no reasonable prospect that the woeful civilian security forces, in particular the police, would be able to handle such a threat. At the end of the day, it would come down to the army, the only truly professional organization in Pakistan, which believed, in its hubris, that it could control all these forces but was unable to see past the expediency of the moment to the dangers that lurked beyond.

In retrospect, the most interesting fact about my cable was that it was written before a single Taliban militant or Al Qaeda operative had been driven onto Pakistani soil. That future was not and could not be foreseen. My analysis had been based on the assumption that the Taliban and Al Qaeda would remain an Afghan phenomenon. The threat that I perceived had nothing to do with them. Its focus was squarely on forces that were indigenous to Pakistan, already active on Pakistani soil. As I returned home in July 2001, sad to leave such a fascinating place but happy nonetheless to have survived, I had no idea the situation was about to get worse. A whole lot worse.

6. The Tribal Areas, 9/11, and the Rise of the Pakistani Taliban

Places change. When I served in Pakistan, the tribal areas were a political dead zone. Nothing much was happening there, at least nothing worth reporting back to Washington. During my three years in Islamabad, my political section produced exactly one telegram reporting on events in the area. This covered sectarian tensions in Kurram agency, where a substantial Shiite community lived in the midst of a Sunni majority, many of them sectarian Deobandis. As noted earlier, the British had created the tribal areas originally to serve as a final buffer between the Raj and Afghanistan. The British exercised influence through the presence of a political agent, but the local Pashtuns were given wide latitude to manage their own affairs through their tribal councils. It was a way of life they had practiced for centuries. When Pakistan came into being, the Pakistani authorities merely continued the British practice. By agreement with the tribes, the regular Pakistan army stayed out. Territorial defense was provided instead by a poorly trained, locally recruited paramilitary force known as the Frontier Corps. Its officers, however, were seconded from the regular army, within whose ranks assignment to the corps was regarded as a career death sentence.

I visited the tribal areas twice, both times on trips through the rugged and historic Khyber Pass. On my first trip through, in early 1999, we drove to Michni Point, a small Frontier Corps outpost located on a promontory overlooking the Afghan border crossing at Torkham, which commanded a panoramic view of the rugged, mountainous Afghan countryside beyond. It was a sleepy place. The Taliban were running things on the far side of the border, and Pakistan was their closest ally. The only incident of note occurred as we were driving back to Peshawar. As we descended the pass on a switchback road, I saw what looked remarkably like a line of ants moving across the far horizon. As we got closer, I was finally able to make out that they were men, hundreds of them, stretching single file into the distance as far as the eye could see, making their way along a path through the hills that eventually converged with our road.

Besides their sheer numbers, what made their presence noteworthy was what they were carrying, most of it strapped to their backs. It was a department store in motion. There was brand-new stereo equipment, a number of good-sized television sets, an assortment of video recorders, and even a flotilla of small European-sized refrigerators. We passed by several bicyclists, each with three or four additional bikes ingeniously strapped to their sides, so that their wheels ran along the ground beside them. These were smugglers, on their way to the bazaars that had cropped up in the Afghan refugee camps that lined the road between Peshawar and Khyber tribal agency. I never tried to get to the bottom of where all these goods had come from, although someone in Afghanistan, presumably the Taliban, must have been making a profit off of it. This seemed obvious from the fact that the Pakistani authorities—the one party clearly not making money—were doing nothing to try to stop it.

The tribal areas had been a much different place during the Soviet occupation of Afghanistan. During that era, the men moving through the harsh terrain had been carrying rifles rather than refrigerators and were moving in the opposite direction. Despite the presence of Soviet forces on the other side of the Durand Line, the mujahideen had no trouble making their way into Afghanistan, since the border between the two countries was as porous as a sieve. In addition to two major checkpoints, one at Torkham, the other at Chaman in Baluchistan on the main road from Quetta to Kandahar, there are twenty crossing points manned by customs and police officials. These are the official crossing points, but there are 111 more known but unmanned crossings in the northern part of the border region, encompassing the northern tribal areas and the NWFP, and a further 229 crossings in the southern tribal areas and Baluchistan. There are also literally hundreds of footpaths and goat tracks that crisscross the border, used predominantly by the local Pashtuns, for whom the Durand Line is merely an abstraction. In the months immediately following 9/11, armed men in substantial numbers would once again take to these paths and byways. But they would be desperate men fleeing for their lives.

As with the Kennedy assassination, most Americans remember what they were doing when the World Trade Center was struck. I was in a conference room at the State Department waiting for a staff meeting to begin. I had returned to Washington to head up the NATO office at State and was sitting patiently with my fellow European Bureau office directors waiting for our assistant secretary to appear. She arrived several minutes late and apologized, saying she had been delayed by the news that a plane had just crashed into the World Trade Center. I asked if it was terrorism, but she said she didn't know. We carried on with the meeting and were just finishing up when a bureau secretary rushed in to say another plane had struck the Trade Center and that the Pentagon had also been hit. Almost as if on cue, the loudspeaker came to life, ordering us to evacuate the building immediately.

By an amazing coincidence, General Mahmud, the head of ISI, was in Washington for consultations that fateful day. That morning he was up on Capitol Hill for meetings with members of the Senate Intelligence Committee. He too had been startled by the evacuation alarms that were sounding throughout official Washington that morning and had fled in confusion with the rest of the federal government. He was summoned to the State Department the very next day for a meeting with Deputy Secretary Richard Armitage. Although some accounts of this meeting suggest that Armitage told Mahmud that Pakistan would have to decide whether it was with the United States or against it, or that he threatened to bomb Pakistan back to the Stone Age, a Pakistani source with direct knowledge of the event told me that the mood had been somber and that Armitage had said simply that the United States would look to its friends for help. Secretary Colin Powell called Musharraf the same day to convey a similar message.

Whatever was said during these conversations, the Pakistanis wasted no time in deciding to cooperate. The attack on the World Trade Center was the most dramatic terrorist act in history. Musharraf sensed immediately that the U.S. reaction was likely to be swift and punishing. It was clear to him that the Pakistani position in Afghanistan, based as it was on support for the Taliban, was in mortal jeopardy. Unless the Taliban quickly agreed to turn bin Laden over, there was a good chance the United States would go to war. The prospect that the seven-year-long Pakistani investment in the Taliban might come to naught was bad enough. But the prospect of becoming an enemy of the United States was arguably worse. Musharraf confesses in his memoirs that he believed the United States might actually attack Pakistan. But even if the United States did not attempt to bomb Pakistan back to the Stone Age, it had a variety of other weapons, both diplomatic and economic, at its disposal. Pakistan had no interest in being labeled a terrorist state or seeing its access to international financial institutions blocked. There was also the Indian dimension to consider. New Delhi had wasted little time in offering to let the United States use Indian military bases for staging attacks into Afghanistan. The possibility that the United States might seek to make common cause with India against them undoubtedly weighed heavily on the Pakistanis. Far better to go along with the United States and try to make the best out of a very bad situation.

The list of demands presented to Pakistan on September 13 confirmed that the United States meant business. The Pakistanis were asked to grant the United States blanket rights to overfly Pakistani territory. The United States requested access to Pakistani seaports, air bases, and strategic border crossings. Pakistan was told it had to break off relations with the Taliban and to prevent madrassa students from crossing into Afghanistan to swell the Taliban ranks. The United States demanded that Pakistan close its borders to Al Qaeda and end all logistical support for the organization. This last requirement, which implied that Pakistan had been actively supporting Al Qaeda all along, demonstrated just how suspicious the United States was of Pakistani motives and behavior at the time. As I argued in the previous chapter, this suspicion was almost certainly unfounded. The Pakistanis had every reason to keep their distance from bin Laden before 9/11 since Al Qaeda designs against the United States were hardly a secret, and if they ever came to fruition would be certain to undermine Pakistani interests in Afghanistan.

The Pakistanis were taken aback by the sweeping nature of some

U.S. demands, in particular for blanket overflight and landing rights. They came back with counteroffers of more limited, but still generous, access, which the United States readily accepted. Not surprisingly, there was one point on which Musharraf insisted: the United States must hold its fire until the Pakistanis had one last opportunity to persuade Mullah Omar to turn over bin Laden. This was granted and, on his return to Pakistan, General Mahmud was once again dispatched to Kandahar. As in the past, he got nowhere. This time around Mullah Omar wanted to see evidence that Al Qaeda had been involved in the attacks, yet another time waster. A second and final attempt at the end of September also failed. The Pakistani journalist Ahmed Rashid suggests that Mahmud—who was a born-again Islamic fundamentalist—actually encouraged Omar to stand fast, but this seems unlikely, even for Mahmud, since Pakistan had everything to gain from having the Taliban part ways with Al Qaeda and a good deal to lose if they did not. Whatever actually transpired, Mullah Omar decided to stick with bin Laden to the bitter end, paving the way for the U.S. assault on the Taliban regime, which began on October 7, less than a month after 9/11.

As Operation Enduring Freedom unfolded, the concept of operations that emerged saw the United States acting as the air wing of the Northern Alliance, launching devastating aerial attacks against the Taliban front lines, which crumbled in their wake. Keep in mind that the Taliban at the time were a field army and not the insurgent guerrilla force the mujahideen had been before them or that they themselves were soon to become. By November 9, the strategic northwestern bastion of Mazar-e-Sharif had fallen. Kabul fell three days later. On December 7, Kandahar surrendered, and the following month Mullah Omar himself narrowly avoided capture by fleeing from his hideout in the mountains of Helmand province on a motorbike. Meanwhile, the man who had cost him his regime was fleeing for his own life. Osama bin Laden was in the eastern Afghan city of Jalalabad as Northern Alliance forces began to close in. He and some of his men, along with their Taliban protectors, retreated south to an extensive mountain cave system known as Tora Bora. This was soon besieged by Northern Alliance forces and subjected to withering aerial bombardment by U.S. military aircraft. At one point an enormous fifteen-thousand-pound bomb was rolled out the back of a C-130 cargo plane. Bin Laden was surely a goner. But when the smoke finally cleared after two weeks of pounding and the besiegers pored through the caves, bin Laden was nowhere to be found.

Some retreating Taliban managed to find refuge in the remote mountain fastnesses of southern Afghanistan. But most Taliban and Al Qaeda fighters fled south and east toward the Durand Line. What is not completely clear is what was waiting for them on the other side. There is some evidence that the Pakistanis sent forces into the tribal areas during this period, ostensibly to guard the border, although estimates of the number deployed vary wildly. Whatever their number, they do not appear to have had much success. Ahmed Rashid claims that while some Al Qaeda foot soldiers were detained, escaping Taliban forces were allowed to pass through unmolested. U.S. officers in Afghanistan told him sometime later that they believed the Pakistanis deliberately left much of the border unguarded. Nonetheless, the U.S. Central Command saw fit to praise Pakistani efforts at the time, and a Centcom liaison officer in Islamabad produced a highly flattering account of the Pakistani contribution, titled "Pakistan—An Enduring Friend," in the *Marine Corps Gazette*. Given the hundreds of crossing points between Afghanistan and Pakistan, it would have been a Herculean task for the Pakistanis to have guarded them all. But despite the early U.S. hyperbole about Pakistani cooperation, there is no concrete evidence the Pakistanis made even the slightest effort to emulate the labors of Hercules.

Evidence suggests that Osama bin Laden made his escape from Tora Bora into Kurram tribal agency, across the Durand Line just a few miles to the south. By some accounts he briefly reentered Afghanistan before making his way into North Waziristan, where his trail finally ran completely cold. Other senior Al Qaeda operatives also made their way across the Durand Line, but they appear not to have stopped for long in the tribal areas. Instead, they made their way into Pakistan proper and were eventually brought to justice. Abu Zubaydah, a member of the Al Qaeda inner circle, was the first to be apprehended. He was severely wounded in a shoot-out in the Punjab city of Faisalabad in March 2002. Khalid al-Attash, a key suspect in the USS *Cole* bombing, was captured in Karachi the following month. Another Al Qaeda leader, Ramzi bin al-Shibh, was arrested in Karachi in September. The biggest fish of all, Khalid Sheikh Mohammed, number three in Al Qaeda and the mastermind of 9/11, was run to ground in Rawalpindi, just down the road from Islamabad, the following March, when he was unceremoniously rousted from his bed. The Pakistanis subsequently turned these and the dozens of less senior Al Qaeda militants who were arrested with them over to U.S. authorities.

These arrests appear to have been carried out with the full cooperation of the Pakistani authorities. This was probably the very least they could do and still convince the Americans they were cooperating with them in the global war on terrorism. The one common thread that links them is that they took place well inside Pakistan itself, in Karachi and some of the larger cities of Punjab. These senior Al Qaeda operatives had gravitated to these sprawling urban jungles presumably because they afforded more ready access to the outside world and because they believed, mistakenly as it turned out, that they were safer places in which to hide. There also appears to have been a support network available to help them there. During my three years in Pakistan, there was an assumption that Al Qaeda operatives could more or less come and go as they pleased. It was concern that Al Qaeda might retaliate against the U.S. diplomatic community in Pakistan following the August 1998 cruise missile attacks that prompted Washington to evacuate its embassy and consulates shortly before the attack. It was concern that Al Qaeda might try to bring down Air Force One that led the Secret Service to implement its elaborate multiple airplanes ruse during President Clinton's visit to Islamabad in March 2000. Whether or not a formal network existed, Al Qaeda took advantage of relationships it had established with Pakistani jihadists in places like the Khost camp complex in the years leading up to 9/11. The close association between Al Qaeda and the Taliban, whose ranks included many Pakistanis, also provided Al Qaeda with potential access to an extensive network of radical Deobandi mosques and madrassas inside Pakistan itself.

The Al Qaeda operatives who fled into urban Pakistan following 9/11 did not simply hunker down. They began plotting attacks against Western targets in the country. Their first and most notorious victim was the American journalist Daniel Pearl, who was kidnapped in Karachi in February 2002. No less a person than Khalid Sheikh Mohammed was directly involved in the plot and several years later boasted to a U.S. military tribunal that he himself had beheaded Pearl with his "blessed right hand." But this was not just an Al Qaeda operation.

Pakistanis with ties to local jihadist and sectarian groups participated in this and subsequent attacks. The British-born Omar Sheikh, who was close to the Jaish-e-Mohammed founder, Masood Azhar, was a key figure in the kidnapping, as was Amjad Farooqi, who was also a Jaish member.

In the months following the Pearl kidnapping there were additional attacks against Western targets. A grenade attack inside a Protestant church not far from the U.S. embassy in March killed five people. Two of the dead, a mother and her teenage daughter, were members of a U.S. embassy family; the father and young son were wounded in the attack. This event sent shock waves through the U.S. diplomatic community. The State Department had evacuated family members in the immediate aftermath of 9/11 but had rashly allowed them to return not long afterward. They would be pulled out once again after the church attack, and this time they would not return. The department decided to designate all its diplomatic facilities in Pakistan as unaccompanied posts—meaning no dependents were allowed—and that is what they remain to this day. But U.S. diplomatic personnel were not the only victims of the Al Qaeda–orchestrated campaign. Two months after the attack on the church, eleven French naval workers were killed in a car bombing in Karachi. The following month, a bomb exploded outside the U.S. consulate in Karachi, killing twelve Pakistani bystanders. In August, six Pakistani employees were killed at a missionary school attended by foreign students in the former British hill station of Murree, not far from Islamabad.

The fact that Pakistanis participated in these attacks embarrassed the authorities. Even more embarrassing, many of them belonged to groups such as the Jaish-e-Mohammed that were serving Pakistani interests in Kashmir. In order to deflect attention from its allies, the government blamed most of the attacks on the Lashkar-e-Jhangvi, with which it had long been at war and had formally banned even before 9/11. While it is true that Musharraf had also banned the Jaish-e-Mohammed, as well as the Lashkar-e-Taiba, in January 2002, this had nothing to do with the Al Qaeda attacks against Western targets, which had not yet even begun—the Pearl kidnapping took place the following month—but was in response to the fidayeen attack on the Indian parliament in New Delhi the previous month. As we saw in chapter 4, banning these groups was a purely cosmetic gesture aimed at placating Musharraf's new Washington allies. He wanted to demonstrate that he was tough against Islamic extremism while continuing to support favored Islamic extremists, including the Jaish. This is why Sipah-e-Sahaba was also banned at this time. Although its leader, Azam Tariq, was placed under house arrest, he was released several months later and allowed to run for a seat in the national assembly, which he won.

Nonetheless, there was a price to be paid for siding with the United States. The Musharraf government had to face down a steady drumbeat of protest demonstrations organized by the Jamaat-e-Islami and JUI. It also had to deal with Al Qaeda. The Pakistani role in the apprehension of several of Al Qaeda's most senior operatives did not escape its attention, and the arrest of Khalid Sheikh Mohammed in March 2003 appears to have been the final straw. Al Qaeda and its Pakistani allies proceeded to shift their target from Westerners to high-ranking Pakistani officials. In December 2003, there were two separate assassination attempts against Pervez Musharraf. The first was carried out by militants affiliated with Jaish-e-Mohammed. The second was masterminded by Abu Faraj Al-Libbi, who had succeeded Khalid Sheikh Mohammed as the number three in Al Qaeda. His chief collaborator was Amjad Farooqi, the Jaish member who had played a prominent role in the Pearl kidnapping. In June 2004, there was an attack on the Karachi corps commander, Lieutenant General Ahsan Hayat, by a small group with ties to Al Qaeda that called itself Jundullah. A month later, a suicide bomber with links to the Jaish tried to assassinate Pakistani prime minister Shaukat Aziz.

Although several of the Pakistanis involved in these attacks were members of Jaish-e-Mohammed, there was not then, nor has there ever been, any crackdown on the group as a whole. Like Azam Tariq of the Sipah-e-Sahaba, the Jaish leader Masood Azhar was placed under house arrest when Musharraf instituted his cosmetic ban on radical Islamic groups in January 2002. But the restrictions on Azhar were removed later the same year and he was never personally implicated in the assassination attempts against Musharraf and the others. His organization remains active in Kashmir today. What appears to have happened is that some Jaish-e-Mohammed members—Amjad Farooqi is a classic example—shifted their loyalties from their parent organization to Al Qaeda. The reason for this is not difficult to fathom. Pakistani jihadists had considerably more in common philosophically with Al Qaeda than they did with the people who ruled Pakistan. To the extent that they cooperated with the government, they did so because they shared the Pakistani goal of liberating Kashmir from Indian rule. But for some members of Jaish-e-Mohammed and similar groups, the Pakistani decision to support the U.S. war on terror, and subsequent efforts to apprehend senior Al Qaeda operatives, proved to be a bridge too far. Unhappy at the continuing cooperation between their parent organizations and ISI, they shifted their allegiances and turned against the state.

Although the Pakistanis were all smiles when it came to helping the United States track down Al Qaeda leaders in urban areas, this was not matched by similar efforts in the tribal regions. This was where the vast majority of Al Qaeda militants had ended up, but they were intermingled with the Taliban forces that had also taken refuge there. Going into the tribal areas in search of Al Qaeda risked coming to blows with their former allies, and this the Pakistanis had no desire to do. They conceived their role in the war on terror to be one of helping the United States apprehend Al Qaeda leaders. And this they were doing—in urban Pakistan. Armed confrontation with the Taliban was not part of the deal. Nor was this simply their interpretation. The United States had not asked Pakistan to make war on the Taliban. It had demanded only that the Pakistanis break off relations with them and terminate their material support. As we have seen, Centcom was full of praise for Pakistani cooperation in the early phases of Operation Enduring Freedom. It even expressed understanding at the difficulties the Pakistanis faced in trying to prevent fleeing Taliban and Al Qaeda forces from entering Pakistan. The laid-back U.S. attitude toward the Taliban was driven in large part by the belief that they were a beaten force. The overwhelming U.S. preoccupation was with Al Qaeda. So long as Pakistan continued to produce results, there was little pressure to do more.

The Pakistanis had what they considered to be very good reasons for not wanting to make enemies of the Taliban. For starters, the Taliban were not simply an Afghan force. Numerous Pakistani volunteers had swelled their ranks over the years—most of them Pashtuns—and they had fled back onto their home turf during the opening stages of

Operation Enduring Freedom. Taking up arms against fellow country-men was likely to prove strongly unpopular, both within the ranks of the army, which would have to do the fighting, and among the popula-tion as a whole. The Afghan Taliban also remained highly popular among ordinary Pakistanis long accustomed to viewing them as trusted allies. Going after Al Qaeda was one thing; taking on the Taliban was quite another. The Taliban enjoyed their greatest popularity among their fellow Pashtuns, so much so that their defeat at the hands of the Americans and their Northern Alliance allies triggered a backlash in the NWFP provincial elections held in October 2002. The JUI, from whose madrassas so many of the Taliban had sprung, swept to a land-slide victory, totally routing the traditionally dominant political party in the province, the secular nationalist ANP. Needless to say, the new JUI provincial government had even less interest in taking on the Tali-ban than the Musharraf government did.

But the primary Pakistani motivator was concern over the future of Afghanistan. However unreliable the Taliban had proved to be, they had at least been allies. The same could not be said for the leaders of the Northern Alliance, who now walked the corridors of power in Ka-bul. They had gravitated inexorably toward India during the Afghan civil war in reaction to Pakistani support for their adversaries, Hek-matyar in the first instance and the Taliban after him. The Pakistanis watched with increasing concern as the Indians began carving out a substantial presence in Afghanistan. They not only opened an em-bassy in Kabul but also established consulates in the four major pro-vincial centers outside the capital (Jalalabad, Kandahar, Herat, and Mazar-e-Sharif). The only other country where they had this many diplomatic posts was the United States. The Pakistanis believed the Indians were using their diplomatic presence in Kandahar to support rebellious tribesmen in Baluchistan engaged in a long-running dispute with Islamabad over the control of natural resources. Along with the substantial Indian diplomatic presence in Afghanistan came offers of assistance, eventually amounting to well over a billion dollars. In the year after 9/11, India donated one million tons of wheat to Afghani-stan, the largest pledge in the history of the World Food Programme. Over the next several years, it would go on to build roads, power plants, satellite transmitters, and even the new parliament building in Kabul. As far as the Pakistanis were concerned, the only possible motive for this Indian generosity was an anti-Pakistani one. They were jockeying for influence in Afghanistan and their embassy and consulates were nests of spies.

Nor did the emergence of Hamid Karzai as president of Afghanistan provide them with any grounds for optimism. Karzai was an ethnic Pashtun, it was true, and leader of one of the largest Pashtun tribes in the country. A native of Kandahar, he had been an early supporter of the Taliban but had turned against them, reportedly due to the growing influence of Al Qaeda within their ranks. Obliged to leave Afghanistan, he had settled into an uneasy exile in Pakistan. There, in the Baluchistan capital of Quetta in 1999, Taliban operatives had gunned down his father, possibly with ISI assistance, or so Karzai believed. Although he avoided assassination himself and managed to hold on in Quetta for two more years, he had been visited by ISI officials not long before 9/11 and told he would have to leave the country. There was, therefore, no love lost between Karzai and the Pakistani authorities. Against the backdrop of this and the other factors, it is not surprising the Pakistanis would want to hedge their Taliban bets. Someday the United States would leave Afghanistan. Helping the United States track down the senior leaders of Al Qaeda would serve to hasten that day. Although the Taliban had proved themselves to be difficult allies, they remained far preferable to the alternative that was taking shape on the far side of the Durand Line. Better just to leave them be and wait for better days.

The United States, meanwhile, had already begun to take its eye off the ball. I got an early preview of this in October 2001 just as the first U.S. bombs were raining down on the Taliban. As the new director of the NATO office at the State Department, I was taking my first trip out to alliance headquarters in Brussels. Making the rounds of senior U.S. officials there, I eventually found myself in the office of Evan Galbraith, the U.S. defense advisor. A political appointee, he had been ambassador to France during the Reagan administration. Toward the end of an otherwise unremarkable conversation, he mentioned he had been in Washington shortly after 9/11 and had attended a meeting chaired by Richard Perle, one of the most influential foreign policy thinkers in the Republican party. Although Galbraith did not say so, it was probably a meeting of the Defense Policy Board, which Perle chaired at the time. Galbraith said Perle had argued that the United

States should use the opening provided by 9/11 to invade Iraq and overthrow Saddam Hussain. He wanted to know what I thought of the idea. I was shocked more than anything else. I had no idea that Iraq had become such an obsession in Republican foreign-policy circles. Not wanting to seem impolite, I simply told him I thought we needed to take care of Afghanistan and Al Qaeda before thinking about invading anyplace else.

So it did not come as a total shock to me when the Bush administration began driving the nation toward war in Iraq. When the war began in March 2003, it did so with shock and awe and what turned out to be misplaced confidence in the ability of the United States to rapidly liberate the country and depart. In removing the Baathist regime from power, the United States also destroyed virtually every instrument of governance in the country. The result was something very close to anarchy, rendered more threatening still by the emergence of a dangerous insurgency that soon developed a nasty Al Qaeda edge to it. The United States found itself forced to assume the running of the country and to pour in ever increasing numbers of troops just to keep events from spinning further out of control. Within a year there would be more than 130,000 U.S. troops on the ground in Iraq, twice the number that had carried out the original invasion. This contrasted dramatically with the situation in Afghanistan, where the United States was maintaining a skeleton crew of fifteen thousand soldiers. With Iraq firmly on center stage, Afghanistan had become a military and foreign policy backwater.

Eager to close the books on Operation Enduring Freedom, Defense Secretary Donald Rumsfeld had stopped in Kabul the same month that Baghdad fell to announce the end of major combat operations in Afghanistan. The irony is that he spoke just as the Taliban were beginning to reestablish themselves there. Last seen fleeing Helmand province on a motorbike, Mullah Omar had turned up in Baluchistan province next door in Pakistan, where he set up shop somewhere in the environs of Quetta. Many of his surviving lieutenants had also taken refuge there, or in the tribal areas to the north, where they proceeded to reconstitute their forces. They were now returning to Afghanistan, not as rulers but as insurgents, following in the footsteps of their mujahideen predecessors, who, they remembered, had driven out the Soviets a generation earlier. Other Taliban forces began emerging from their mountain hideouts inside Afghanistan to join them. In the south, several Taliban commanders, led by the mullahs Baradar and Dadullah, spearheaded the Taliban resurgence. In the east, Taliban efforts centered on what came to be known as the Haqqani network. Home-based in Miranshah in the North Waziristan tribal area, it was led by Jalaluddin Haqqani and his son Sirajuddin. During the anti-Soviet jihad, the elder Haqqani had been a prominent mujahid who enjoyed personal ties to Osama bin Laden. As a senior member of an important Hezb-e Islami faction, he had also been close to ISI. During the Afghan civil war, he had eventually switched sides, joining the Taliban in 1995 when they were already at the gates of Kabul. Gulbuddin Hekmatyar was also returning to the fray. Released from exile in Iran, he made his way back to Pakistan, where he was persuaded to cooperate with his former Taliban adversaries. The Taliban appear to have had little difficulty attracting new recruits to compensate for those lost in the earlier fighting. A distinct element of Pashtun nationalism appears to have been at work here, since the new Karzai government, and the newly minted Afghan army, were heavily dominated by ethnic Tajiks and Uzbeks from the victorious National Alliance. As these various Taliban forces began moving back across the Durand Line, there is no evidence that the Pakistanis did anything to stop them.

Despite the reemergence of the Taliban, U.S. focus was still very much on Al Qaeda. Washington had been grateful to Pakistan for its help against Al Qaeda, but with the apprehension of Khalid Sheikh Mohammed, the supply of senior Al Qaeda operatives available for arrest in urban Pakistan had just about dried up. The biggest catch, Osama bin Laden, remained embarrassingly at large, presumably holed up somewhere in the tribal areas. No one knew for sure. What the United States did know for certain was that there was a substantial Al Qaeda presence there. This consisted not only of its Arab core but other foreign jihadists who had also gone to Afghanistan to fight with them alongside the Taliban prior to 9/11. This included Uzbeks associated with the radical Islamic Movement of Uzbekistan (IMU), as well as assorted Chechen militants and even a small handful of Uighurs from Xinxiang province in China. The Pakistanis soon began referring to them collectively as foreign fighters. Unlike the senior Al Qaeda officials who had been run to ground in urban Pakistan, these militants had fled into the tribal areas and stayed there. Although their presence was hardly a secret, the Pakistanis had never done anything about it. Not one high-profile Al Qaeda operative had ever been arrested in the tribal areas. This fact eventually began to gnaw away at Washington. Frustrated by its failure to capture bin Laden and chagrined at the unmolested Al Qaeda presence on Pakistani soil, the United States began to ratchet up the pressure on Islamabad to take action.

The Pakistanis were extremely reluctant to do so. But they were also reluctant to risk their relationship with the United States. This had already paid off handsomely in debt forgiveness and the promise of $3 billion in economic and military aid. Islamabad may also have feared the United States would decide to act on its own. Ahmed Rashid suggests that Colin Powell actually threatened this, but a former senior Pakistani official who had considerable experience dealing with the United States denied this, telling me it was not the U.S. style to threaten. This was certainly my own experience. The United States would make more or less clear what it wanted the Pakistanis to do and continue to hammer home the point. It was left to the Pakistani imagination to determine what might happen if they failed to comply. In this instance, the Pakistanis were afraid that unilateral U.S. action in the tribal areas would outrage public opinion and jeopardize support for the Musharraf government. This was hardly a stretch. Ever since the loss of Kashmir at the founding of the state, the Pakistani people had been conditioned to believe that India harbored designs on their territory, and this had made them particularly sensitive to potential violations of their sovereignty. These fears would prove to be well founded later when U.S. Predator missile attacks in the tribal areas produced just such a reaction. But Musharraf also had his own reasons for finally deciding to move against Al Qaeda in the tribal areas: it had just tried to kill him.

In March 2004, the Pakistanis finally made their move. Local Frontier Corps troops surrounded and attacked a suspected Taliban stronghold at Kalosha in South Waziristan that was believed to harbor Al Qaeda militants and other foreign fighters. The attack was not a bolt from the blue. Pakistani authorities had told local tribal leaders the month before that they intended to begin "search-and-cordon" operations against Al Qaeda forces in the area. Unfortunately, the poorly trained Frontier Corps forces used in the Kalosha operation walked into something approaching a trap and ended up suffering extensive casualties. Reinforcements were called in and an initial force of seven hundred quickly swelled to seven thousand. Although the Pakistanis finally succeeded in overrunning the stronghold, the engagement triggered attacks against Pakistani military convoys and outposts in the area. A number of Frontier Corps troops reportedly deserted, reluctant to fight against fellow Pashtuns.

Having gotten a good deal more than they bargained for, and afraid the situation might spiral out of control, the Pakistanis offered to deal. Their primary interlocutor, as it turned out, was himself a Pakistani. His name was Nek Mohammed and he was the leader of the local Taliban forces in the area. It was his compound that the Frontier Corps had attacked at Kalosha. His exploits during the fighting, when he drove the IMU leader Tahir Yuldashev through the Pakistani lines to safety, had already made him something of a celebrity. The agreement he subsequently reached with the Pakistani authorities in the nearby village of Shakai only cemented his reputation. The army agreed to abandon its efforts to root out Al Qaeda militants and to confine its troops to their barracks. Nek Mohammed, in return, pledged to halt his hit-and-run attacks on government forces and ensure that the foreign fighters under his protection registered with the local authorities.

The Shakai agreement represented a significant climb down by the Pakistanis and was perceived as a victory for Nek Mohammed. The fact that the army had agreed to conduct the negotiations at the Deobandi mosque where the Taliban leader worshipped was widely regarded as a significant concession. The mountain had come to Mohammed. Flush with success, he made no effort to deliver up his foreign associates for registration, prompting an embarrassed army to renew its aggressive search-and-cordon activities, which only served to trigger further clashes. This was to be the first of many such deals to break down. Nek Mohammed ended up being killed just a few months later in what was later revealed as the very first U.S. Predator missile attack in Pakistan. At the time, the Pakistanis had claimed that one of their aircraft had done the deed. The most likely explanation is that the Americans offered to target Mohammed if the Pakistanis could locate him. The Pakistanis agreed to this but insisted that the United States not publicize or admit its involvement in the affair. Encouraged at the Pakistani decision to begin hunting down Al Qaeda militants in the tribal areas, and pleased by the willingness to permit Predators to operate on their territory, the United States was more than happy to oblige. Yet another precedent had been established. As for Nek Mohammed, he was dead, but his legacy would prove to be a lasting one. He had given birth to what would come to be known as the Pakistani Taliban.

The next significant Pakistani Taliban leader to emerge was Baitullah Mehsud. A member of the Mehsud tribe in the north of South Waziristan, he would go on to achieve even greater notoriety than his predecessor but end his life in the very same way. He appears to have begun more or less where Nek Mohammed left off, providing shelter to Al Qaeda militants and other foreign fighters, while periodically skirmishing with Pakistan army forces sent in to look for them. For the army it was déjà vu all over again. Reluctant to continue the clashes or send in more troops, it decided to resurrect its Shakai precedent and try to put together a deal with him. In this one, signed in February 2005, almost a year after Kalosha, the Pakistanis agreed to pull regular army forces out of South Waziristan and confine the Frontier Corps to its bases. Mehsud promised to end his own attacks against army convoys and outposts and to stop harboring foreign fighters. The Pakistanis were probably under no illusion that Mehsud would follow through on his Al Qaeda pledge and, in agreeing to confine their own troops to barracks, had deprived themselves of any mechanism for enforcing it. As in their earlier deal with Nek Mohammed, their goal seems to have been simply to end the fighting. In the event, it did them little good. With no army to oppose him, Mehsud was able to bring most of South Waziristan under his sway, disposing of any tribal leaders who tried to stop him and introducing rough Taliban justice along the way. In June 2005, he finally jettisoned his agreement with the army altogether, resuming his attacks against government forces.

His example, meanwhile, was being replicated in many other parts of the tribal areas, as well as in the Swat Valley of the NWFP. Hafiz Gul Bahadur established a Pakistani Taliban organization in North Waziristan, in the same area occupied by the Haqqani network. Maulvi Nazir, from the same tribe as Nek Mohammed, established a group in South Waziristan just to the south of the Mehsud forces. Fakir Mohammed followed suit in Bajaur tribal area, and Mullah Fazlullah, who had succeeded his imprisoned father-in-law, Sufi Mohammed, as leader of the TNSM in the Swat Valley, began reviving that organization along Pakistani Taliban lines. Although these were the most important Pakistani Taliban leaders to emerge during this period, they had counterparts who led smaller or less important groups in most of the other tribal areas. Most of these early organizations were autonomous groups with essentially local objectives. Fakir Mohammad was something of an exception. As a young man, he had been a follower of the TNSM leader Sufi Mohammed and had spent considerable time in Swat. In some cases, these new Pakistani Taliban had been spurred to action by the same circumstances that had motivated Nek Mohammed. The army had gone looking for Al Qaeda militants under their protection and they had resisted. Some were no doubt also inspired by the well-publicized successes achieved by Nek Mohammed and Baitullah Mehsud in South Waziristan and hoped to duplicate them on their own home turf.

These Pakistani Taliban were hardened fighters, veterans of the Afghan civil war, and with help from Al Qaeda militants and other foreign fighters in their midst, they possessed the means to wrest control of their home territories from the traditional tribal leaders. Tribal area madrassa students, who a few years earlier would have headed to Afghanistan to join the Taliban, flocked to their banners. So too did disaffected members of Punjab-based groups such as the Jaish-e-Mohammed, many of whom had already begun working with Al Qaeda in urban Pakistan in helping to carry out the attacks against Western targets and Pakistani government officials that took place in the years immediately following 9/11. It seems likely that Al Qaeda encouragement also played a significant role in the formation of these groups. Al Qaeda leaders not only had a personal stake in resisting Pakistani efforts to root them out but also viewed the tribal areas as their default home base until Afghanistan could be reclaimed. Their encouragement succeeded because, when forced to choose between the state and Al Qaeda, many Pakistani Taliban made precisely the same choice made previously by their Punjabi Deobandi brethren. They would side with Al Qaeda and make war against the state.

The common thread that united these various Taliban groups was their Pakistani nationality. The Pakistan army appears to have left Afghan Taliban forces inside Pakistan severely alone. This included not only Mullah Omar, home-based in Baluchistan with senior command-ers in what came to be known as the Quetta Shura, but also the Haqqani network, headquartered in Miranshah in North Waziristan. Gulbuddin Hekmatyar, who was also based in the tribal areas, was similarly left alone. This does not mean there were no Al Qaeda mili-tants in the areas under Afghan Taliban control. That presence was and remains significant, but there is no evidence the Pakistan army has ever conducted operations against the Haqqani network or Hek-matyar. The army even maintains a Frontier Corps outpost in Miran-shah, cheek by jowl with the Haqqanis. It was to this outpost that the *New York Times* correspondent David Rohde escaped in 2009 after fleeing a son of Jalaluddin Haqqani who was holding him hostage just down the road. The Pakistanis appear to have targeted Al Qaeda forces exclusively under the protection of Pakistani Taliban—beginning with the attack at Kalosha—not because the Taliban involved were Paki-stanis but because they were not Afghans. It is not difficult to fathom why. The Pakistanis left the Afghan Taliban alone not only because they saw a possible future role for them in Afghanistan but also be-cause they did not want to risk the consequences of their defeat. If the Afghan Taliban were to suddenly pass from the scene, the United States would almost certainly withdraw from Afghanistan, leaving In-dia as the dominant outside power in what they already regarded as a hostile Afghan state.

From the Pakistani perspective, coming to blows with the Pakistani Taliban was the best of an extremely bad bargain. By finally moving into the tribal areas to search for Al Qaeda, they had demonstrated to the United States that they meant business. They also stood to score points with the Americans for taking on the Taliban, in view of the increasing threat to U.S. forces in Afghanistan posed by the growing Taliban insurgency there. Although it was true that they were going after the Pakistani Taliban and leaving the Afghan variety alone, at this point in time there was no reason to believe the United States appreci-ated the distinction. Besides, even if the Pakistanis were targeting only the Pakistani Taliban, the fact that some Taliban forces were fighting against Pakistani troops in the tribal areas meant they were not fight-ing against U.S. forces in Afghanistan. And for that the United States should be grateful.

Although not directed against them, the fighting in the tribal areas still managed to complicate life for the Afghan Taliban. It drained away forces that would otherwise have been fighting in Afghanistan. They were no doubt unhappy with the Pakistanis for having gone into the tribal areas in the first place, but they were in no real position to resist, since Pakistani tolerance of their presence there and in Baluchistan was critical to what they were trying to do in Afghanistan. It is possible—indeed, likely—that ISI had already provided them with assurances that they had nothing to fear so long as they stayed out of the line of fire. They were well aware that their Pakistani Taliban counterparts had come to blows with the army for extending protection to Al Qaeda. But there is no evidence that they ever encouraged the Pakistani Taliban to turn against their Arab guests or the other foreign fighters in their midst. Indeed, they continued to extend protection to Al Qaeda themselves. Having lost control of Afghanistan because of them, they were unwilling to abandon them just to get it back.

Nonetheless, the Afghan Taliban had a powerful interest in seeing the fighting in the tribal areas come to an end. In June 2006, Sirajuddin Haqqani, who had replaced his father as day-to-day leader of the Haqqani network, became personally involved. He appears to have acted in response to clashes taking place in his own backyard between the army and forces loyal to Hafiz Gul Bahadur. He issued a proclamation stating that while jihad in Afghanistan should continue to "the last drop of blood," fighting against the Pakistan army "did not conform to Taliban policy." Baitullah Mehsud appears to have responded positively, renewing his own cease-fire with the army. Maulvi Nazir in South Waziristan and Gul Bahadur in North Waziristan also followed suit. The latter cease-fire paved the way for the North Waziristan peace agreement, which was finalized in September. As it had in previous accords, the army agreed to stop its aggressive patrolling and confine its forces to barracks. The Pakistani Taliban, in return, promised to stop attacking army forces and to refrain from carrying out cross-border operations into Afghanistan. Al Qaeda militants and other foreign fighters were required to leave North Waziristan. But there was an out clause: those who were unable to leave could stay so long as they remained peaceful and abided by the terms of the agreement.

It is easy to see what the Pakistani authorities liked about the agreement. It promised to end the fighting, which was deeply unpopular in the army as well as among ordinary Pakistanis. Going after Al

Qaeda militants was one thing, but the Taliban had been allies prior to 9/11. The Pakistani Taliban were also fellow Pakistanis, which made it that much worse. Worse still, the fighting was being done at the behest of the United States, which was responsible for having driven the Taliban and Al Qaeda onto Pakistani territory in the first place. Few cared to remember that it was Pakistani support for the Taliban, and Taliban protection of the perpetrators of 9/11, that had led to this situation. As 9/11 receded into the past, popular support for the alliance with the United States in the war on terrorism had plummeted and with it the popularity of the person with whom it was most identified, Pervez Musharraf. He desperately needed political relief, and peace accords with the Pakistani Taliban offered it. A similar agreement with Fakir Mohammed in Bajaur the following March completed the round of deals and brought relative peace to the tribal areas. But there was a price. The region had effectively passed out of Pakistani government control. It was the Pakistani Taliban who were in charge.

The United States supported the North Waziristan deal at first. President Bush personally endorsed it at a joint press conference with Musharraf two weeks after it was signed. This may partly have been out of politeness to his guest, since it is difficult to believe anyone in the U.S. government could have thought it would produce positive results. The prohibition on infiltration into Afghanistan depended exclusively on the goodwill of the Taliban. It contained no enforcement mechanism, and the primary malefactors, the Afghan Taliban, were not even parties to the agreement. The provision covering Al Qaeda and other foreign fighters should have been even more troubling. It suggested they leave North Waziristan but permitted them to stay so long as they promised to behave. Why would the United States even pretend to support such a deal? One possible explanation is that the two sides had reached agreement on other means of pursuing Al Qaeda militants in the tribal areas. Twice in the previous year, first in November 2005 and again in January 2006, the United States had launched Predator missile strikes against high-value Al Qaeda targets there. The first succeeded in killing Abu Hamza Rabia, at the time the third ranking person in Al Qaeda. The second targeted Ayman al-Zawahiri, the Al Qaeda number two. In that attempt, a residential compound was struck, killing at least eighteen people, some of them women and children. Due to bad luck or faulty intelligence, al-Zawahiri was not there, although two lower-ranking Al Qaeda operatives numbered among the victims. This attack, which the United States admitted it had carried out, generated considerable outrage in Pakistan, not simply due to the loss of innocent life but also because of its violation of Pakistani territory. The uproar was so great that the Pakistani government felt obliged to condemn it.

While it is possible that these attacks were carried out without Pakistani knowledge or approval, it seems unlikely the United States would risk a relationship it still considered indispensible to its goals in the region. It is much more likely that the Pakistanis not only approved the strikes in advance but may even have provided the intelligence used to target the intended victims. These were both extremely high-value targets, and if the al-Zawahiri attack had succeeded, the payoff would have been considerable. The failure of that attack and the public uproar it caused highlighted the risks involved. But the Pakistanis may well have decided that Predator attacks were preferable to having the army go looking for trouble in the tribal areas. That policy had not only failed to deliver up any high-profile Al Qaeda operatives, it had managed to convert the Pakistani Taliban into enemies. The Pakistanis probably insisted the strikes be kept to an absolute minimum and that targeting be limited to only the most senior Al Qaeda officials. They almost certainly insisted that their own involvement be kept secret. They probably also made clear to the United States that they would have to vigorously condemn the strikes when they did occur in order to make their denials of involvement more credible. If this was their plan, it failed. Most Pakistanis, historically fond of conspiracy theories and long accustomed to Byzantine plotting within the feudal political establishment, persisted in believing almost from the very beginning that the government had to be involved.

Although the Predator option provided the United States with a potentially effective weapon in countering the Al Qaeda presence in the tribal areas, the North Waziristan agreement offered it no comfort at all in Afghanistan. It was a device the Pakistanis used to end the fighting in the tribal areas, not a serious effort to prevent the Taliban from using Pakistani territory to stage attacks across the Durand Line. And in fact, it had precisely the opposite effect. Freed from the necessity of engaging the army in the tribal areas, the Pakistani Taliban were able to turn their attention once more toward Afghanistan. Lieutenant General Karl Eikenberry, commander of U.S. forces in the country, told Ahmed Rashid that the number of insurgent attacks originating from the tribal areas had increased threefold in the aftermath of the North Waziristan deal. This, of course, suited the Pakistanis just fine. They wanted the Taliban to win in Afghanistan, or at least not to lose. And this is precisely what was happening. Five years after the launching of Operation Enduring Freedom, the Taliban were now in the ascendant. Half of Afghanistan had fallen more or less permanently under their control. The number of insurgent attacks was growing by the month. In March 2006, there had been three hundred attacks; by September the number had reached six hundred. Even the U.S. ambassador in Kabul felt obliged to tell Washington that the United States was no longer winning the war. A war that was supposed to have ended five years before.

The problem, as had been the case from the outset, was numbers, and the primary culprit, the Iraq war. The North Waziristan agreement came just as U.S. fortunes in its occupation of Iraq were descending to their lowest ebb. U.S. troop levels there had risen to more than 140,000, yet even this was not enough to stem the violence or bring anything resembling stability even to the capital, Baghdad. But the troop situation was far worse in Afghanistan. There were only twenty thousand U.S. troops on the ground at the time. Desperate for help, the United States had gone cap in hand to its NATO allies asking them to shoulder a larger share of the burden. Many of them were already on the ground in Afghanistan, having gone there as peacekeepers in the NATO International Security Assistance Force (ISAF) operation launched in August 2003, just as I was leaving the NATO office at State. But now the United States was pressuring its allies to become involved in combat operations. This was a tough sell, since most of them had opposed the war in Iraq and resented being asked to bail the United States out in Afghanistan. Even when allies were prepared to help, their nervous parliaments placed caveats on the use of their forces. There were seventy-one such restrictions in place in 2006. German soldiers, for example, were not permitted outside their bases at night, and ambulances had to accompany each of their daytime patrols. Nonetheless, by the fall of 2006, NATO allies were reinforcing or relieving U.S. forces in many parts of the country, and ISAF had actually taken over responsibility for military operations in the south. But it was a very long way from being enough.

As these events unfolded, a subtle but important shift seemed to be taking place in the way the United States viewed the Taliban. They had not been the original enemy. The United States had launched Operation Enduring Freedom to destroy Al Qaeda, not defeat the Taliban. The Taliban ended up in the line of fire because they were in the way. If Mullah Omar had agreed to turn over bin Laden before the bombs began to fall, it is possible they might never have been targeted. But by 2006, the situation on the ground in Afghanistan had changed considerably. Al Qaeda was no longer a significant presence there. Osama bin Laden and what remained of the Al Qaeda high command were hunkered down next door, presumably somewhere in the Pakistani tribal areas. Yet the United States was still engaged in combat operations against the Taliban in Afghanistan. Not only that, it had managed to get itself bogged down in the uncertain—some might say hopeless—enterprise of nation building. It had made reforming the hopelessly corrupt Karzai regime a priority and committed itself to turning the ragtag remnants of the Northern Alliance forces into a respectable Afghan army. It made stamping out the Afghan drug trade a critical goal even though it promised to drive Afghan poppy growers, threatened with the loss of their livelihood, into the arms of the Taliban. It was also under pressure from feminist groups in the United States to take steps to reverse the second-class status traditionally occupied by women in deeply conservative Afghan society. Afghanistan, it seemed, was becoming a classic case of mission creep. In the process of trying to reclaim their country, the Taliban had managed to transform themselves from the protectors of Al Qaeda into a genuine enemy. And for the United States, preventing the Taliban from succeeding was starting to become an end in itself. The real reason for staying the course in Afghanistan—to prevent a return to the situation that existed prior to 9/11, with the Taliban in charge and Al Qaeda able to operate freely—was hardly ever mentioned.

In the tribal areas, meanwhile, the Pakistanis were trying to enjoy the relative peace that reigned in the wake of the North Waziristan agreement. The word *relative* is appropriate here since there were periodic violations of the various cease-fires that were supposed to be in place throughout the region. One of the most notorious followed in the wake of an alleged Predator attack at Hamzola in South Waziristan in January 2007, when a suicide car bomber rammed into an army convoy near Mir Ali in neighboring North Waziristan. Baitullah Mehsud was blamed for the attack. There was also skirmishing around the town of Tank in the NWFP across the border from South Waziristan. Such incidents illustrated the basic fragility of the situation but remained the exception rather than the rule.

In the best Pakistani tradition, the authorities had gotten themselves into a difficult situation and found a way to avoid coming to grips with it. Or so it must have seemed to them at the time. They had lost effective control over the tribal areas, it was true, but they may have been able to persuade themselves that it was not really that much of a calamity since the tribal areas had never been fully incorporated into Pakistan in any event. The American problem was still there, of course. The United States had figured out that the North Waziristan agreement was primarily an excuse for inaction and had started breathing down the Pakistanis' necks to do more. Washington was pressing them to accept a sharp increase in the number of Predator attacks, any one of which had the potential to unravel one or more of the deals they had in place with the Pakistani Taliban. The important thing was to try to hold on. Someday the United States would leave Afghanistan and the situation in the tribal areas would begin to calm down. What the Pakistanis failed to realize was that their relationship with the Pakistani Taliban had already passed the point of no return. That realization would arrive with explosive suddenness the following summer. It would come not because of events in the tribal areas but due to an incident in the very heart of the Pakistani capital, Islamabad, at a place called Lal Masjid.

7. Lal Masjid, Army Failures, and the Domestic Terrorism Campaign

The Red Mosque—or Lal Masjid, to give it its Urdu name—lies in the very center of Islamabad, no more than a mile from where I used to live. The largest Deobandi mosque in the capital, it was run by two brothers, Abdul Aziz and Abdul Rashid Ghazi, known collectively as the Ghazis. In addition to the mosque, they managed two madrassas. One, the Jamia Hafsa for female students, was part of the mosque complex. The Jamia Faridia for males was located several miles away in prime real estate at the foot of the green Margalla hills, which form the northern perimeter of Islamabad. The Ghazi brothers were among the many Islamic fundamentalists who stridently opposed the Pakistani decision to support the U.S. war on terror after 9/11, even calling Pervez Musharraf a traitor. Two years onward they had organized protests following the murder of the Sipah-e-Sahaba leader Azam Tariq, who had been gunned down in Islamabad, presumably by Sipah-e Mohammed henchmen. The Ghazis had achieved further notoriety a year later when they issued a fatwa declaring that Pakistani soldiers who died fighting against the Pakistani Taliban were not martyrs. Although their presence in the heart of the capital was an embarrassment to the government, no actions were taken against them.

It was early in 2007 that events began to spin out of control. The issue was the building of Deobandi mosques on public land in Islamabad without government permission. Apparently worried by the pro-liferation of radical mosques in the capital, the local authorities had decided to crack down by tearing down two of the most notorious of-fenders. The justification given pulled no punches. "Intelligence agen-cies" had argued that they were ideally located for the launching of terrorists attacks. In protest over the action, and presumably at the in-stigation of the Ghazis, female students from the Jamia Hafsa stormed and occupied a government library for children next door to the Lal Masjid complex. Despite this brazen act, the authorities took no ac-tions against them. Emboldened by this, the Ghazis proceeded to set up "virtue squads" composed of students from both madrassas, who were sent out into the city to intimidate shop owners into stopping the sale of CDs, DVDs, and other symbols of Western decadence. This was the same kind of vigilantism that had surfaced in the NWFP the previ-ous decade and given rise to the first concerns about Talibanization in-side Pakistan. But now it was happening in the heart of the Pakistani capital under intense public scrutiny and media coverage. The au-thorities condemned the actions and threatened reprisals but still did nothing.

At the end of March, Zaffar Abbas, a leading Pakistani journalist, was moved to write a piece about Lal Masjid for the Pakistani newspa-per *Dawn* titled "The Creeping Coup." It appeared on the same day that Abdul Aziz gave the Pakistani authorities a week to implement sharia rule throughout the country or suffer the consequences. But still the authorities declined to rise to the bait. They sensed they were sitting on a powder keg and were worried that punitive action would only make things worse. The fact that young girls and women were directly involved was an important complicating factor. The Ghazis reinforced this concern by threatening nationwide suicide attacks if the government moved against them. In April, local Islamabad au-thorities took limited action by arresting eleven madrassa students for vigilante activities. A month later, madrassa students kidnapped four local policemen, who were held hostage at Lal Masjid in return for the release of the students. In late June, a virtue squad raided a massage parlor operated by Chinese nationals and held several of them briefly at the mosque complex. This provoked a protest from Beijing that was as angry as it was rare. The normally phlegmatic Chinese had also been dismayed by recent attacks against Chinese workers in other parts of Pakistan. Several engineers had been murdered in Baluchistan and several other Chinese kidnapped in the tribal areas. Chinese workers were being singled out due to Chinese efforts to crack down on radical Islamists among China's native Uighur population in Xinjiang province, some of whom had fled to Pakistan and made their way to the tribal areas. Chinese anger was serious business given the fact that Pakistan had long regarded China as its very best ally, the one country that—unlike the United States—had never let it down.

Events were hastening to their bloody conclusion. Alarmed by the Chinese protests and eager to prevent similar incidents, the Pakistanis threw up a security cordon around Lal Masjid at the beginning of July. Rumors were rife that the complex had been reinforced by foreign fighters from the tribal areas and armed militants from local Deobandi jihadist groups. Pervez Musharraf specifically mentioned Jaish-e-Mohammed involvement in an address to a military audience at the end of June. But he also expressed continuing reluctance to move against Lal Masjid due to the large number of female students and children that were living there. The first outbreak of violence occurred on July 3 when madrassa students attempted to overrun a neighboring government building. This provoked a firefight in which more than twenty people were killed. The authorities subsequently tightened the cordon and called in an elite army commando force to oversee the operation. Aware that the government now meant business, twelve hundred madrassa students evacuated the complex the next day. Among them was Abdul Aziz, who became an object of ridicule for trying to escape disguised in a burqa. Although additional occupants emerged in smaller groupings during the next several days, attempts to negotiate a solution with the remaining Ghazi brother failed, paving the way for a commando assault on July 10. After hours of room-to-room fighting in booby-trapped surroundings, the government forces prevailed. More than a hundred people lay dead, Abdul Rashid Ghazi among them. The death toll included women and children, who may have been held as hostages or used as human shields. In searching through the victims, the government claimed to have found ten foreign fighters as well as a letter of encouragement from Al Qaeda's number two, Ayman al-Zawahiri, addressed to the Ghazi brothers.

It is difficult to overstate the significance of the Lal Masjid episode. It demonstrated to a worldwide audience that Talibanization had spread well beyond the confines of the NWFP into the urban heartland of Pakistan. Although Lal Masjid was by far the most dramatic example of the phenomenon, it was by no means an isolated one. In the Seraiki belt of south Punjab there were numerous reports of radical Islamists intimidating shopkeepers who sold items associated with Western culture. A decade earlier, this had been a rare event there, but no longer. The steady proliferation of radical mosques and madrassas in the region had made it almost inevitable. But the phenomenon was not confined to the Seraiki belt either. The first signs of Talibanization had also reached Lahore, the capital of Punjab and the cultural heart of Pakistan, where shopkeepers had come under threat of retaliation if they refused to clear their shelves of items and artifacts deemed to be un-Islamic. Such threats actually drove local Lahore merchants to organize a well-publicized mass burning of CDs in the Hall Street market area of the city in October 2008.

In the immediate aftermath of Lal Masjid, Pervez Musharraf talked tough about cracking down on radical mosques and madrassas, but he was in no position to deliver. The death and destruction that resulted from the final assault had triggered a strong public backlash. Many who had criticized the government for showing weakness and irresolution at the beginning of the episode now condemned it for the bloody manner in which it had been brought to an end. The former prime minister Nawaz Sharif saw fit to condemn the government's handling of the siege from his London exile. The authorities, it was widely believed, had overreacted. Within three months, Lal Masjid was back in business by order of the Supreme Court. Chastened by the backlash, the government made no further attempt to tear down illegal mosques in Islamabad or anywhere else. During the year that followed Lal Masjid, seventy new mosques sprang up in the capital city alone. Abdul Aziz was finally released from custody in April 2009, once again by Supreme Court order. On his return to Lal Masjid, he mourned the hundreds he said had perished there but insisted they had not died in vain. "Today," he proclaimed, "the whole country is resounding with cries to implement Islamic law."

The impact of Lal Masjid on radical Islamists throughout Pakistan was even more electric. Any doubts that members of the radical Deobandi jihadist and sectarian community perceived themselves as part of a single movement sharing a common purpose and destiny were swept away by their violent reaction to Lal Masjid. Al Qaeda's number two, Ayman al-Zawahiri, released a videotape the day after the siege ended urging the faithful to take up jihad against the Pakistani state. The tribal areas and parts of the NWFP exploded in rage as the Pakistani Taliban renounced the North Waziristan agreement and disavowed the cease-fire arrangements in place between themselves and the army. Violence had broken out in the tribal areas and elsewhere even before the siege had reached its bloody conclusion. On July 4, a suicide car bomb killed six soldiers in North Waziristan. Two days later, armed gunmen tried to shoot down a plane carrying Pervez Musharraf as it took off from the military airport in Rawalpindi. On the same day, an improvised explosive device (IED) killed four soldiers at Dir in the NWFP not far from the Swat Valley.

The bloody end to the siege precipitated even more attacks, directed against army, police, and civilian targets. On July 12, seven people were killed in separate incidents in Swat. On July 14, twenty-three Frontier Corps troops died in a car bombing in North Waziristan. The next day, forty-nine army and police personnel were killed in attacks in Swat and Dera Ismail Khan, a district capital in the southern part of the NWFP. On July 17, the violence reached back to Islamabad, where a suicide bomber blew himself up at a rally for the suspended Supreme Court chief justice, Iftikhar Chaudhry, killing seventeen. Forty people died in separate attacks on July 19, including several Chinese workers at a site north of Karachi in Sindh province. On July 24, nine civilians were killed in a rocket attack on the town of Bannu in the NWFP, across the border from North Waziristan. Violence returned to Islamabad once again on July 27, when a suicide bomber blew himself up in a hotel in Aabpara Market just down the street from Lal Masjid. The domestic terrorism campaign had begun.

Domestic terrorism was not new. There had been a steady diet of it for more than twenty years. This included the attacks against Western targets and high-ranking Pakistani officials that had been orchestrated by Al Qaeda in the aftermath of 9/11. Although these attacks had diminished in frequency, they still occurred. A U.S. diplomat in Karachi had been killed by a suicide car bomber in March 2006, and there was an assassination attempt against the interior minister in April 2007. But the vast majority of terrorist attacks in Pakistan in the two decades prior to Lal Masjid had been sectarian in nature, perpetrated by groups such as Lashkar-e-Jhangvi and the Sipah-e Mohammed. They would continue after Lal Masjid, but would be increasingly overshadowed by attacks on Pakistani military, police, and civilian targets. The techniques used—IEDs, car bombs, and suicide vests—would mirror those employed by Al Qaeda in Iraq and by the Taliban in Afghanistan, demonstrating the contact and cross-fertilization between these various groups. Although the terrorist attacks that took place in the immediate aftermath of Lal Masjid were an explosive reaction to the storming of the mosque complex, the use of terror against domestic targets was destined to develop into a major weapon in the war between the Pakistani Taliban and the army that was about to begin.

The army reacted to the breakdown in the cease-fire arrangements in the region by moving in additional troops. It had begun to reoccupy long-abandoned checkpoints in North Waziristan even before the Lal Masjid siege ended, and there is some evidence it had begun building up its forces in the tribal areas even earlier. On July 19, just four days after the Pakistani Taliban renounced the North Waziristan agreement, Pervez Musharraf told senior Pakistani journalists he was sending in an additional two divisions. I learned from a senior Pakistani official that by the end of 2007 the number of troops deployed in the tribal areas and Swat far exceeded all previous levels. Within another year, total troop strength had reached the equivalent of six infantry divisions, divided between Frontier Corps forces and the regular army. At the beginning, the troop buildup appears to have been designed primarily as a show of force, for which the Pakistanis paid dearly. Based on press reporting at the time, it appears that the Pakistani Taliban greeted the new arrivals with attacks on army patrols and newly reopened outposts and checkpoints. The most dramatic incident—and also the most embarrassing—occurred on August 30 when a group of approximately twenty Pakistani Taliban militants loyal to Baitullah Mehsud halted an army supply convoy of just under three hundred soldiers and persuaded them to surrender without a shot being fired. The episode left the clear impression that Pakistani soldiers did not want to fight.

In November, the government decided to go over to the offensive. Its first target was the Swat Valley. As we saw in chapter 5, the founder of the radical TNSM organization in Swat, Sufi Mohammed, had been imprisoned on returning to Pakistan following the destruction of his forces during the opening phases of Operation Enduring Freedom. He had been succeeded by his son-in-law, Mullah Fazlullah, who set about rebuilding TNSM cadres. As part of his strategy, Fazlullah made extensive use of FM radio broadcasts, in which he stridently called for implementation of sharia law and vituperated against evil Western influences such as polio vaccinations and education for women. His broadcasts attracted considerable attention, along with plenty of new recruits, and won both him and his station the moniker of Mullah Radio. He had signed his own peace agreement with the government less than two months before Lal Masjid but began launching suicide attacks against Pakistani soldiers in Swat while the siege was still under way. By autumn, his forces had taken over government buildings and police stations in fifty-nine villages and established their own separate governing institutions. It was at this point that the army began to reinforce its presence in Swat, and in November it began to attack. The Swat offensive, code-named Just Path, represented a fundamental shift in Pakistani military objectives in the region. The army had originally gone into the tribal areas under strong U.S. pressure specifically to hunt down Al Qaeda militants. Its original clashes with the Pakistani Taliban were an unwanted by-product of this effort. But now the target had shifted. In Swat and in subsequent army operations in the tribal areas, its primary objective would be to seek out and engage Pakistani Taliban forces. The gloves had come at least partway off. The Pakistanis had drawn their own lessons from Lal Masjid.

Just Path, spearheaded largely by Frontier Corps forces, made early progress. The army succeeded in driving the TNSM out of most of its strongholds in the Swat Valley, and by early December 2007 it had retreated into the mountains. The army claimed victory, but the Fazlullah forces continued to launch hit-and-run strikes from the security of their mountain hideouts. Back in Islamabad, meanwhile, the man who had authorized Just Path was in deep political trouble. Pervez Musharraf's popularity had plummeted precipitously since the beginning of the year. Already weakened by his unpopular support for the U.S. war on terror, he had done further damage to his standing in March by suspending the Supreme Court chief justice, Iftikhar Chaudhry, on corruption charges. His true motive had been fear that Chaudhry would rule him ineligible to run for another term as president that fall. This move caused outrage in the legal community and had led to the creation of the Lawyers' Movement. The protests that followed helped further galvanize public opinion against Musharraf. In late July, only weeks after Lal Masjid, the remaining members of the Supreme Court had defied Musharraf by reinstating Chaudhry. The Lal Masjid massacre and the unprecedented terrorist violence that followed in its wake only served to weaken him further still. Although he managed to engineer his reelection as president in early October, he felt obliged to declare a state of emergency the following month out of fear the Supreme Court would overturn the results. The exploding Pakistani Taliban threat provided just the excuse he needed.

But still the pressure continued to mount. At the end of November, he tried to revive his fading fortunes by giving in to long-standing demands that he resign his post as army chief. But this cut the institutional links to the army that had been the real source of his power. In December, he suddenly lifted the state of emergency, having used it to fire Chaudhry and remove several of his colleagues from the bench. But it was no use. Pervez Musharraf was a beaten man. He would be forced out as president the following August and find himself obliged to leave Pakistan in order to avoid prosecution on treason charges. His replacement was Asif Zardari, husband of Benazir Bhutto, the two-time former prime minister of Pakistan. Wanted on corruption charges, she had returned to Pakistan in October 2007 after nine years of exile. Her return came two weeks after Musharraf was reelected president and just over two weeks before he declared his state of emergency. It was the result of several months of behind-the-scenes negotiations with the Musharraf government, mediated by the United States. Musharraf had agreed to let her return in the hope that she would support his continuation as president. To sweeten the deal, he had agreed to legislate away the corruption cases against her. This would permit her to lead her party into the upcoming national assembly elections scheduled for January, which the PPP was strongly favored to win. The National Reconciliation Ordinance, as it was named, granted amnesty to politicians who had been charged with corruption during the civilian interregnum that preceded the Musharraf coup. This took Benazir off the hook and paved the way for her final return. But it was to be a tragic homecoming. She was about to become the most prominent victim of the domestic terrorism campaign.

On her arrival at Karachi airport, Bhutto took her place in a motorcade for a triumphal procession through the city to the tomb of Mohammed Ali Jinnah. Tens of thousands of people lined the streets to see her. Among them were two suicide bombers, who detonated themselves just as her convoy was passing by. Benazir was unhurt, but more than 140 people were killed and more than 400 wounded. It was the largest single death toll so far in the domestic terrorism campaign. Although shaken by the event, she threw all her energy into the national assembly election campaign. She managed to keep a healthy distance from Musharraf, who was so weakened by this time that he even felt obliged to acquiesce in the return from exile of Nawaz Sharif, the man he had deposed eight years earlier. Despite the Karachi incident, Bhutto refused to abandon the large public gatherings that were part and parcel of Pakistani politics. It was a fatal mistake. On December 27, as she was leaving a campaign rally in Rawalpindi, a bomb exploded next to her motorcade. She had been standing in the open hatch of an SUV waving to the crowd, and the force of the explosion slammed her head back against the rim of the hatch. The person almost certain to become the next prime minister of Pakistan was dead.

The Pakistani authorities blamed the assassination on Baitullah Mehsud. The CIA director, Michael Hayden, later supported this contention, asserting that Pakistani Taliban operatives loyal to Mehsud had carried the assassination out with assistance from Al Qaeda. As for motive, Bhutto was not only the likely next prime minister, she was believed by many to be a Shiite like her father before her, providing a possible sectarian motive. Even more likely—and ironic in view of her role in the original rise of the Taliban—was the fact that she had become a highly visible critic of the Pakistani Taliban and of the forces of radical Islam in Pakistan more generally. She had been particularly vocal in her condemnation of the vigilantism associated with Lal Masjid and had sharply criticized the government for failing to move against it sooner. Other politicians, by contrast, had kept their silence or, like Nawaz Sharif, castigated the government for the carnage that resulted from the final assault. This had made his own return to Pakistan a month before the Bhutto assassination a much less risky undertaking. Benazir's combination of forthrightness and accessibility proved to be her undoing. She had failed to realize how much Pakistan had changed during the time she had been away.

As for Baitullah Mehsud, he had come together with the other major Pakistani Taliban leaders in the region just two weeks prior to the Bhutto assassination to form an umbrella group, the Tehrik-e-Taliban Pakistan. Mehsud was elected the overall leader of the organization, with Hafiz Gul Bahadur of North Waziristan appointed second in command and Fakir Mohammed of Bajaur the number three. There is no real evidence that this alliance resulted in increased cooperation on the battlefield or that it was even intended to have that effect. The formation of the group appears to have been designed more as a statement of political intent than an effort to integrate Pakistani Taliban forces under a single unified command. In its initial policy declarations, the Tehrik-e-Taliban demanded the imposition of sharia rule in the tribal areas and Swat, and called for offensive jihad against the U.S. forces in Afghanistan and defensive jihad against the Pakistan army. It also expressed its solidarity with the defenders of Lal Masjid and demanded the release of the surviving Ghazi brother, Abdul Aziz.

But the Tehrik-e-Taliban had begun to hemorrhage almost immediately after it was formed. By the middle of February—just two months later—Gul Bahadur had decided to go his own way, reaching a deal with the government reviving the North Waziristan agreement. Eager to preserve all his options, he had been negotiating the arrangement even as the Tehrik-e-Taliban was being formed. He had been encouraged to return to the North Waziristan deal by his Haqqani network neighbors, whose interest in having the Pakistani Taliban focus their efforts on Afghanistan remained as strong as ever. Mullah Omar reportedly also personally intervened. At the same time, Gul Bahadur started moving toward an alliance with Maulvi Nazir, who also had been persuaded to accept a cease-fire with the Pakistanis. The previous spring he had come to blows with Uzbek fighters trying to throw their weight around on his home turf, and this helped turn him back toward cooperation with the government. The two leaders formally announced their alliance in early July 2008. It was significant for two reasons. Two major Pakistani Taliban organizations had made peace with the government and they were also prepared to cooperate with each other. This left Baitullah Mehsud and the tandem of Fakir Mohammed of Bajaur and Mullah Fazlullah of Swat as the only major Pakistani Taliban leaders still at war with the state. It also potentially isolated Mehsud, whose forces were now sandwiched between them, with Gul Bahadur directly to the north and Nazir immediately to his south.

There is every reason to believe that ISI worked hard to encourage this result, almost certainly in the knowledge that if Gul Bahadur and Nazir stopped fighting the Pakistan army, they were likely to turn their attention to the west and end up fighting alongside their Afghan brethren in Afghanistan. They were, after all, jihadists and had pledged their personal loyalty to Mullah Omar. While there is no direct evidence that the Pakistani authorities actively encouraged Gul Bahadur and Nazir to focus their efforts on Afghanistan, they must have realized this would be the outcome. Given the choice they faced—between confronting a united Pakistani Taliban opposition or adding to the burden faced by U.S. forces in Afghanistan—it is perhaps not surprising that they opted for the latter.

With Gul Bahadur and Nazir moving to the sidelines, the Pakistanis decided to take the offensive against Baitullah Mehsud. He was not only the most powerful and intransigent of the Pakistani Taliban leaders but also the driving force behind the domestic terrorism campaign. One of his chief lieutenants, Qari Hussain, was an admirer of the Iraqi Al Qaeda leader Abu Musa al-Zarqawi and had already gained notoriety for establishing a series of training camps for suicide bombers. The Pakistanis launched their operation, code-named Earthquake, on January 24 not long after the Mehsud forces overran a major Frontier Corps in Sararogha in northern South Waziristan. It is unclear whether the operation was launched in retaliation for this attack or had been in the planning stages for some time. The latter explanation seems more likely. The army had concluded its efforts to drive the TNSM out of Swat the previous month, and this had presumably freed up troops for use in the South Waziristan operation. The army may also have been reluctant to take on more than one foe at a time and so waited until the operation in Swat had ended. Both factors suggest that the Pakistanis did not believe they had sufficient forces in the region to do more, despite the substantial buildup in force levels following Lal Masjid.

Operation Earthquake achieved only limited successes before the army felt obliged to begin withdrawing in May. The army had managed to drive Mehsud out of a number of areas but was unable to deliver anything resembling a knockout blow. As in Swat several months earlier, when outgunned by superior army forces, the Pakistani Taliban had simply melted away into the surrounding hinterlands. However, the army was considerably more successful in destroying property and alienating the local population. Four thousand homes were destroyed during the campaign and two hundred thousand people displaced. Whatever else the army may have been good at, it was not good at this kind of fighting. Local residents had a habit of getting caught in the middle. Frontier Corps forces were poorly trained and poorly motivated, and regular army soldiers had no experience conducting counterinsurgency operations. They had been trained to fight infantry battles in Kashmir and tank battles on the plains of Punjab, not to chase after guerrilla fighters in the barren, rugged terrain of the tribal areas. The Pakistan army was a very blunt instrument caught in circumstances that required much more skilled and nuanced handling. When they began pulling out of South Waziristan in May, the Mehsud forces simply moved back in.

In Swat, meanwhile, events were taking a similar turn. The army had succeeded in driving the TNSM into the mountains but was having difficulty keeping them there. By this time, a new government had come to power in the NWFP. The secular ANP, which had been the dominant party in the province prior to the backlash election of 2002, had reasserted its power by badly routing the JUI in the provincial elections held in February 2008. Its leaders had been appalled by the widespread suffering and destruction caused by the continuing fighting in Swat and decided to try to negotiate an end to it. They managed to reach a deal with Mullah Fazlullah in May in which the ANP agreed to the implementation of sharia law in Swat in return for TNSM agreement to lay down its arms. The agreement lasted about a month. Mullah Fazlullah, who was by now a member of the Tehrik-e-Taliban and considered his forces part of the broader Pakistani Taliban movement, refused to disarm his men until the army removed its forces from the valley. When the army failed to comply, Fazlullah backed out of the deal and began attacking government forces. The army responded by going back on the offensive in July.

This offensive was considerably less successful than its predecessor. Although there were fierce clashes in several major towns, the army found itself unable to repeat the success it had enjoyed just a few short months earlier. During the next several months, Fazlullah was able to destroy most of what remained of the once vibrant tourist infrastructure in the Swat Valley. One of the earliest casualties was the one and only ski resort in all of Pakistan. Local politicians, including officials of the ANP, were targeted, some killed and others driven from the valley. Schools for girls were systematically burned and destroyed. As the Pakistani Taliban took over increasingly large parts of the area, they introduced a combination of sharia law and rough Taliban justice so draconian it might have made Mullah Omar blush. "Crimes" such as watching television, singing and dancing, and failing to grow a beard became punishable by death. One man was shot for wearing the cuffs of his pants too low. Beheading became a favored form of execution. The bodies of the dead could frequently be found hanging from utility poles in the main square of Mingora, the largest town in the valley. Their names were read out daily on Mullah Radio as a warning to everyone else. Three hundred thousand people fled in fear for their lives. There were reports that Fazlullah forces had been reinforced by Pakistani Taliban from South Waziristan—freed up by the withdrawal of government forces there—as well as recruits from radical Deobandi groups in the Seraiki belt. One local journalist who chronicled the destruction of the Switzerland of Pakistan titled his article "Paradise Lost."

At some point it must have become clear to the army that it did not have enough troops in the Swat Valley to deal with the Pakistani Taliban threat. But there is no indication it sent for reinforcements. Local residents began to complain the army was hunkered down in its encampments and reluctant to come out. One possible explanation for this inaction is that even as Fazlullah and his allies were beginning their rampage, the army was gearing up for a separate operation in nearby Bajaur tribal agency. Although Bajaur was the smallest of the tribal agencies, it was home to the largest concentration of Pakistani Taliban and foreign fighters outside the Waziristans. It also enjoyed particularly close ties to Swat. As we saw in chapter 6, the Bajaur Tehrik-e-Taliban leader Fakir Mohammed had been a disciple of the TNSM founder, Sufi Mohammed, and remained close to the Swat Taliban. It is not clear why the army chose to move into Bajaur just as it seemed to be losing its grip in Swat. U.S. pressure may have played a role since Bajaur was a major staging area for attacks into Afghanistan. Given Fakir Mohammed's strong ties to Swat and the physical proximity between the two Pakistani Taliban strongholds, it is possible the army saw Bajaur as part of the same operation.

Whatever its motive, when the army launched Operation Lion Heart in August, it encountered difficult going. The Fakir Mohammed forces had constructed and manned an elaborate system of tunnels, which made them particularly difficult to root out. The tactics employed by the army were as blunt as ever, causing great destruction of property—five thousand homes were reportedly destroyed in Bajaur— and forcing three hundred thousand people to flee. After months of hard fighting, the army finally emerged on top, having succeeded in driving most of the Pakistani Taliban forces out of Bajaur. A peace agreement concluded on government terms was signed in March 2009. At the time it was regarded as the first really significant defeat of Pakistani Taliban forces. But the reality was different. In March 2010, almost exactly one year after this supposed victory, the army proclaimed yet another decisive win in Bajaur. It even took journalists on a tour of a cave system it had recently captured. What the army failed to explain was what happened to the widely heralded decisive victory of the previous year. Presumably, the Fakir Mohammed forces had not been destroyed at all but had simply fled into Kunar province in neighboring Afghanistan or to nearby Swat, where they may have bolstered the forces of Mullah Fazlullah. Unwilling to remain in Bajaur in strength after its first alleged victory, the army began pulling out its forces, allowing the Bajaur Taliban to move back in.

With the dubious exception of Bajaur, by early 2009 it was obvious that the various operations launched by the army against the Pakistani Taliban in the aftermath of Lal Masjid had been unsuccessful. While the army may have deployed significantly more troops to the region than ever before, they had not deployed enough. Much of the fighting was still being done by the Frontier Corps, which was not only the most poorly trained fighting force in the Pakistan army but also the one most reluctant to fight, given the Pashtun tribal roots it shared with the Pakistani Taliban. At the beginning of its offensive operations in the tribal areas and Swat, the army may simply have miscalculated how many forces would be needed. But it seems to have been unwilling to send in more troops even when its operations started bogging down. More glaringly still, on those occasions when the army did succeed in seizing territory, it failed to leave sufficient forces in place to prevent the Pakistani Taliban from moving back in.

Why did the army fail to provide the necessary manpower? There were many reasons. Although the Pakistanis felt they had to respond to the gauntlet thrown down by the Pakistani Taliban in the wake of Lal Masjid, the fighting there remained highly unpopular both inside

Pakistan and within the ranks of the army itself. The United States continued to be regarded as the villain for having driven Al Qaeda and the Taliban onto Pakistani territory after 9/11 in the first place. Worse still, it had been U.S. pressure on Musharraf that forced the Pakistanis to send the army into the tribal areas, precipitating the disastrous war against their fellow citizens. Now ordinary Pakistanis were being killed in suicide bombings in the urban heartland of the country. This made them even more resentful of continuing U.S. efforts to pressure them. This resentment was on clear display in the uproar that followed an attack by U.S. commandos on a compound used by Al Qaeda in South Waziristan in September 2008. This was the first planned U.S. ground operation inside Pakistani territory and, until the May 2011 attack on Osama bin Laden, the last. Pakistanis of all stripes were outraged. Predators were one thing, but boots on the ground were beyond the pale. General Ashfaq Kayani, who had succeeded Musharraf as army chief, felt compelled to publicly warn the United States that Pakistan would defend its sovereignty at all costs. The army was well aware of just how unpopular the war was and Kayani reacted accordingly. It is very difficult for an army so concerned about its public image to vigorously prosecute an unpopular war.

The reliance on the Frontier Corps to do most of the fighting also suggests a reluctance to commit the regular army to the fray. In part this may have reflected a belief that fighting fellow Pakistanis on Pakistani soil is not a proper task for the regular army, whose primary role is to defend the country against foreign threats. The army may also have been concerned about the impact on morale. Unhappy Frontier Corps soldiers are one thing, unhappy regular army troops are quite another. Concern about collateral damage was an additional consideration. The devastation done to civilians and their property by the current levels of fighting was bad enough. Pumping in more troops would only have increased the destruction and further alienated the local population. Perhaps the most important factor was the opposition of the army leadership to stripping forces from the Indian frontier, which they would have had to do in order to more effectively meet the Pakistani Taliban threat. But the Pakistanis were also unwilling simply to abandon the tribal areas and Swat to the Pakistani Taliban. Who could say what that might lead to in time? There was also the U.S. reaction to worry about. The United States wanted more action, not less. Even though the Pakistanis deeply resented U.S. pressure, they were not prepared to risk the consequences of jeopardizing their relationship with Washington. So the Pakistanis ended up doing something, but not enough. Rather than teaching the Pakistani Taliban a lesson, they ended up giving them plenty of incentive to keep pushing for more.

At the same time that the army was locked in this unhappy struggle with the Tehrik-e-Taliban, the Pakistanis were continuing to pursue a much different policy toward the Afghan Taliban. As was the case before Lal Masjid, there is no indication they ever targeted the Haqqani network or troubled the councils of Mullah Omar in Baluchistan. Simply leaving them alone would have been one thing—the Pakistanis had their hands full with the Pakistani Taliban—but there is considerable evidence that there was more to it than this. Ahmed Rashid claims that not long after the Afghan Taliban were driven into the tribal areas, ISI was tasked to put together an underground organization staffed by retired ISI officers to work with them. The first public indication that the United States possessed evidence that ISI was collaborating with the Afghan Taliban came in a *New York Times* article that appeared shortly after the July 2008 bombing of the Indian embassy in Kabul. Unnamed U.S. officials told the *Times* that ISI had planned the bombing and enlisted members of the Haqqani network to carry it out. The following March, U.S. officials went even further, telling *Times* reporters that ISI support for the Afghan Taliban consisted of "money, military supplies and strategic planning guidance." An even more damning account was contained in a study by Matt Waldman of Harvard University, who conducted interviews with several Afghan Taliban commanders. They claimed their forces received extensive support from ISI and even asserted that the Pakistani military intelligence service was represented on the Quetta Shura.

Assuming that at least some of this is true, what exactly is its significance? As we have seen, shortly after 9/11, the Pakistanis made the decision to support the U.S. war on terrorism. They interpreted this as helping the United States bring members of Al Qaeda to justice, and they were, in fact, as good as their word, helping the United States capture many important Al Qaeda operatives, particularly those who had taken refuge in Pakistani cities. Despite strong reluctance to do so, they had finally agreed to send the army into the tribal areas to look for Al Qaeda militants. As they feared, this got them entangled in a very messy war with the Pakistani Taliban, who had retaliated by launching the suicide-bombing campaign that had brought terror to the urban heartland. They had also allowed the United States to use Predator missiles against Al Qaeda targets on Pakistani territory. These actions, and their consequences, had proved increasingly unpopular with virtually all segments of Pakistani society and had been a key factor in weakening Pervez Musharraf to the point where the scandal over his attempt to remove the Supreme Court chief justice was able to bring him down.

But Pakistani support for the United States did not end here. The Pakistanis allowed the United States and its NATO allies to use overland routes through Pakistan to supply their forces in Afghanistan. More than 80 percent of the container cargo and 40 percent of the fuel used by allied forces in Afghanistan reached their destination in this way. This was not simply a nice gesture on the part of the Pakistanis; it was indispensible to Western operations in Afghanistan. There was and is no satisfactory alternative means of supplying Western forces stationed there. Yet, at the very same time the Pakistanis were doing all these very helpful and, in their view, very hard things for the United States, they were providing safe haven to, and collaborating with, the Afghan Taliban forces who were killing U.S. soldiers in Afghanistan. They were, in other words, playing both sides of the street, supporting the forces who were killing the soldiers they were helping to provision. The fact that the Pakistanis felt compelled to act in such a duplicitous manner reflected the importance they attached to the future makeup of Afghanistan. They did not want to abandon their relationship with the United States but were unwilling to accept the consequences of an Afghan Taliban defeat. In their view, this would speed the departure of U.S. troops, leaving behind a fragile Afghan government, inherently hostile to Pakistan, which they were convinced would seek to forge at least an informal alliance with India. This could be used by India to threaten them from the rear in any future conflict. So it was that they found themselves in the position of being both a helpful ally of the United States and one of its most determined foes. It was a double game—full of risks, to be sure—but they felt they had no choice but to play it. "To hunt with the hound and run with the hare" is one of the most popular of Pakistani aphorisms.

But there was no double game being played in the urban heartland, where the Pakistanis continued to pay a heavy price for their operations against the Pakistani Taliban. Not only had their military offensives in the tribal areas and Swat been turned back, but they had failed to put any kind of dent in the domestic terrorism campaign. There was a steady drumbeat of attacks throughout 2008 and early 2009, most of them carried out by suicide bombers. Many were directed at army and police targets far from the battlefield. The largest death toll came in a double suicide bombing in August 2008 near the gates of the Pakistan Ordnance Factory at Wah just outside Islamabad. More than seventy people were killed at this army-run weapons production complex. Political gatherings were another favored target. A suicide bombing claimed twenty-five lives at an ANP election rally in February 2008. Four more people died when another suicide bomber tried to assassinate the ANP leader Asfandyar Wali in October as he was receiving visitors during Eid celebrations at his home. An ANP provincial assemblyman was killed by an IED the following February. The most notorious attack against a civilian target was the bombing of the Marriott Hotel in Islamabad in September, which destroyed much of the facility, killing more than 50 people and injuring more than 250. The Marriott, the best hotel in the capital, was also a gathering place for local political, diplomatic, and cultural elites. The biggest and most important wedding receptions in Islamabad were usually held here. It was also where the United States and other embassies housed their temporary visitors. Two Americans staying at the hotel were among the dead, as was the Czech ambassador.

The most sensational attack of all occurred in March 2009, when twelve men armed with machines guns opened fire on a bus convoy ferrying the Sri Lanka national cricket team to a match against Pakistan at the Lahore cricket ground. The Sri Lankan cricketers were lucky to escape with relatively minor shrapnel injuries, thanks to the quick thinking of their bus driver, who floored his vehicle and managed to escape the machine gun fire. But eight people were killed in the attack, including six policemen and the driver of a minivan carrying the match umpires. The gunmen got away scot-free. The attack created a scandal in Pakistan. Cricket is the only truly major national sport, and it attracts a massive, passionate following. Test matches between national teams—one side hosting, the other visiting—were its most important venues. But the domestic terrorism campaign had already scared off the rest of the cricketing world. National teams from other countries refused to play in Pakistan. The only country still prepared to do so had been Sri Lanka. The Pakistanis had given the Sri Lankans solemn guarantees they would receive the kind of protection usually accorded to visiting heads of state, but the police escort assigned to accompany the convoy proved inadequate to the task. The incident was an unqualified fiasco for the Pakistani authorities and drove an even bigger nail into the coffin of Pakistani cricket. Now no one would visit. Suspicion for carrying out the attack initially fell on several groups, but it would eventually be blamed on an entirely new group, one that had not been heard from before: the Punjabi Taliban.

The late winter and early spring of 2009 represented a true nadir in Pakistani fortunes, not just in cricket but in the tribal areas and Swat as well. The Tehrik-e-Taliban controlled most of the region. Its overall leader, Baitullah Mehsud, reigned supreme in South Waziristan, from where he and Qari Hussain continued to orchestrate their suicide-bombing campaign. The attack on the Sri Lanka cricket team, together with several other successful attacks in Punjab, strongly suggested they had received considerable help from within the province itself. That February, Mehsud had also succeeded in resolving his differences with Hafiz Gul Bahadur and Maulvi Nazir. Their joint statement singled out Obama, Karzai, and Zardari as their common enemies. The reference to Zardari reflected the fact that the government of Pakistan was now back in civilian hands. The PPP had won the parliamentary elections held in February 2008, two months after the assassination of Benazir Bhutto. Her widower, Asif Zardari, had replaced her as head of the party, and he had become president of Pakistan when Musharraf finally resigned in August. But the change in government changed nothing on the ground. Although the army had enjoyed some success in Bajaur, it had paid dearly for it in Swat, which had spun totally out of its control. The failure of the army in Swat caused something resembling panic in the ranks of the ruling ANP in the NWFP. Its supporters had been driven out of the valley by the Pakistani Taliban, and its leaders were being increasingly targeted by suicide bombers. By early 2009, amid rapidly fading expectations that the army would be able to reverse their fading fortunes, they decided they had little choice but to try to negotiate another deal.

They reached back into the past to choose Sufi Mohammed as their negotiating partner. He had been released from prison the previous year in the hope he might be able to wean support away from his even more fanatical son-in-law, Mullah Fazlullah. This had not happened, but the ANP leaders managed to convince themselves that if they could reach an agreement with him he might be able to sell it to Fazlullah. In the negotiations that ensued, the TNSM founder drove a hard bargain. His ANP interlocutors found themselves obliged to agree to the imposition of sharia law, not just in the Swat Valley, where the Fazlullah forces held sway, but throughout Malakand division, of which the Swat Valley was only a relatively small part. This was a big deal since Malakand made up one-third the total territory of the NWFP. For their part, the Fazlullah forces would lay down their weapons and return control of local government institutions to NWFP authorities. This agreement, which was reached in the middle of February, was publicly endorsed by the army shortly after it was announced. Asif Zardari, who, as president, had to sign the agreement for it to take effect, took his own sweet time doing so. He was under considerable pressure from the United States not to sign at all. It is easy to see what the United States disliked about the agreement. It gave the Pakistani Taliban what they wanted—sharia law—but provided no mechanism for delivering what the government wanted—disarmament of the Fazlullah forces and the restoration of government authority in Swat. Every agreement the Pakistanis had negotiated with the Pakistani Taliban over the previous half decade had left the latter in control of the areas in dispute. There was absolutely no reason to believe this time would be any different, particularly given the fact that the ANP was negotiating under duress.

That was how it looked to me and other experts on Pakistan at the time. It made me wonder whether the Pakistani political establishment, civilian and military, would ever be able to summon up the will to resist the rapidly spreading radical Islamic threat. After all, if the Pakistanis were not prepared to defend the most valuable piece of outdoor tourist real estate in the country, what would they defend? In deal after deal, they had sought to take the easy way out, to kick their problems farther down the road. But now they were beginning to run out of road. I laid out my concerns in an article titled "The Unravelling of Pakistan," which appeared early that summer in the British foreign affairs journal *Survival*. I suggested that the weakness the Pakistanis had demonstrated in confronting the Pakistani Taliban had only served to whet their appetite for more. They would continue to push until they were stopped. In mid-April 2009, just before my article went off to the printer, Asif Zardari finally got around to signing the Swat agreement. He had been insisting on evidence that peace had actually returned to the valley, but his hand had been forced by Sufi Mohammed, who threatened to renege on the entire deal. In order to cover his political backside, Zardari insisted that the national assembly also ratify the agreement. This it did, unanimously.

But even as Zardari was signing the agreement, Mullah Fazlullah was sending forces into Buner, a district in Malakand division just to the south of Swat. Within days of his signature, hundreds more started pouring in. Islamic courts were set up to impose Pakistani Taliban justice, and outside political parties were banned. The local ANP administration was driven out. Exactly one week after Zardari signed the agreement, a Fazlullah spokesman proclaimed that the Fazlullah forces in Swat did not consider themselves bound by it. The move into Buner demonstrated that Mullah Fazlullah had no intention of limiting his reach to the Swat Valley. The Pakistani authorities had agreed to bring all of Malakand division under sharia law and he would see to it that this happened. But it would be on his terms, not theirs. His choice of Buner as his next target was almost certainly meant to convey a message. It was the next district down from Swat in the direction of Islamabad, a scant sixty miles from the Pakistani capital. The barbarians were literally at the gates. The Pakistani political establishment, civilian and military, had been humiliated. Their policy of concession had been shown to be bankrupt. It suddenly seemed possible that the Pakistani Taliban would bring all the Pashtun lands west of the Indus under their sway.

But that, unfortunately, was only the half of it.

8. Mumbai, the Buner Moment, and Troubles with the United States

It was the evening of November 26, 2008, two months before the ANP concluded its deal with Sufi Mohammed and four months before Mullah Fazlullah moved into Buner. Ten heavily armed young men emerged from Zodiac boats in a dockland neighborhood of south Mumbai and quickly left the area, some by taxi, others on foot. Over the course of the next sixty hours, they would move purposefully through the city, stopping at preselected points to toss grenades and spray automatic weapons fire into terrified crowds. By the time their journey was over, they had taken the lives of more than 160 people and wounded more than 300. Their stops included the central railway station, a local hospital, a popular café, two downtown luxury hotels frequented by Westerners, and an obscure Jewish community center. Some of the Jews taken captive at the center were tortured before being executed. Indian security forces were caught totally off guard by the assault and took the better part of three days to root the last of the terrorists out of the Taj Mahal Hotel. The attack on Mumbai was the most spectacular act of international terrorism since 9/11, its impact intensified by its duration and the saturation coverage it received on global television. It affected Indians in much the same way that 9/11 had traumatized Americans. The perceived similarity between the two events is reflected in the expression they use to refer to it. It is known, simply, as 26/11.

Nine of the terrorists were killed in the assault. The lone survivor was a young man by the name of Ajmal Kasab. He turned out to be a Pakistani, hailing from the small Punjabi village of Faridkot, sixty-five miles south of Lahore. As he was soon to confess, he was also a member of the Lashkar-e-Taiba, which had planned and carried out the attack. Mumbai brought India and Pakistan once again to the brink of armed conflict, much as the attacks on the Indian parliament in New Delhi and on Indian army dependents in Jammu had done in late 2001 and early 2002. The primary difference was the context. The earlier attacks had occurred during a period when the Pakistanis were actively involved in trying to infiltrate jihadists into Kashmir. Relations between the two countries had been at a low ebb and memories of Kargil were still fresh in Indian minds. Mumbai was a completely different story. It took place more or less completely out of the blue, during a period of relatively good relations between India and Pakistan, and brought an abrupt and sour end to a peace process the two countries had begun with some hope and more than a little fanfare five years earlier.

The peace process had itself emerged from the crisis of late 2001 and early 2002. The Bush administration had helped pull the two sides back from the brink by convincing Pervez Musharraf to pledge that Pakistan would permanently terminate its support for jihadist infiltration into Kashmir. In return, the United States promised it would try to bring the two sides back to the negotiating table. A former senior army officer who closely follows events in Kashmir told me that the Pakistanis had fulfilled their side of the bargain by ending what he called their "positive support" for the jihadists. This claim appears to be supported by casualty statistics from Kashmir, which show a marked decline in fatalities beginning in 2002 and continuing up to the present. This did not mean that infiltration into Kashmir, or attacks by jihadist groups, ceased altogether; they continue to occur and are frequently reported in the Indian press. Most attacks today are carried out by the same groups that were responsible for them a decade ago, the Hizbul Mujahideen, the Lashkar-e-Taiba, and the Jaish-e-Mohammed. But without active Pakistan army support, they have found the logis-

tics of crossing the Line of Control into Kashmir considerably more difficult. Artillery duels along the LOC apparently continued sporadically
until November 2003, when Indian and Pakistani negotiators reached
agreement on a cease-fire that silenced the guns. This also brought
a halt to the fighting on the Siachen Glacier to the north. The move
toward renewed peace talks culminated two months later, in early
January 2004, when both sides agreed to resume their composite
dialogue.

U.S. efforts played a key role in getting the peace process going.
The breakthrough occurred at precisely the same time the Bush administration was putting heavy pressure on the Pakistanis to send the
army into the tribal areas to search for Al Qaeda. The Pakistanis saw
these moves as coordinated. A former senior Pakistani official in government at the time told me that Washington wanted the Pakistanis to
improve relations with India so they would be free to focus their efforts on the tribal areas. As an inducement, the United States promised to remain engaged on the Kashmir issue and to be helpful in
trying to move negotiations in a positive direction. The official told me
the Pakistanis had used this alleged U.S. commitment to placate the
various jihadist groups fighting in Kashmir, who had not taken kindly
to the end of active army support for their infiltration efforts. But the
government made no attempt at all to shut down the jihadist training camps in Azad Kashmir, where the Lashkar-e-Taiba and Jaish-e-
Mohammed continued to prepare their militants for infiltration across
the Line of Control. A year after the peace process had begun, I asked
a former senior army officer, the one with the Kashmir pedigree, why
the Pakistani authorities had not moved to close down the camps. His
reply was simple and direct. The government was letting them stay in
business as insurance against the breakdown of the peace process.
Didn't that make sense? After all, the jihadists were the only real card
that Pakistan had to play in Kashmir.

Although the launching of the peace process represented a genuine breakthrough in relations between the two adversaries, it produced
few visible results. During the five years leading up to Mumbai, they
failed to reach agreement on any of the major issues in dispute. All
they could agree on was a short list of relatively innocuous confidence-
building measures, topped by the initiation of a bus service between
Srinagar and Muzaffarabad, the capital of Azad Kashmir. Or so it

seemed to outside observers at the time. But in March 2009, four months after Mumbai, the journalist and author Steve Coll reported in a *New Yorker* article that India and Pakistan had come very close to settling the Kashmir issue in early 2007. The near breakthrough had allegedly occurred during renewed back-channel negotiations, which, like their Lahore Summit predecessor in 1999, had been conducted in secret while the less productive composite dialogue played out on a more public stage. The two negotiators this time around were Tariq Aziz, a longtime friend and advisor to Pervez Musharraf, and Satinder Lambah, a veteran Indian diplomat. According to Coll, the draft agreement would have extended substantial autonomy to the Muslim majority in Kashmir while permitting Kashmiris on both sides of the Line of Control to move freely across the border. Indian and Pakistani military forces would gradually withdraw from the region, while a joint mechanism, composed of Indian, Pakistani, and Kashmiri representatives, would address political and economic issues affecting both sides of the LOC.

Significantly, the proposed deal contained no provisions on the territorial issues that were at the heart of the Kashmir dispute. There was no effort to permanently divide Kashmir along the Line of Control, the Chenab River, or anywhere else. The subject was simply too hard. Since the Pakistanis were unwilling to accept any outcome that appeared to concede permanent Indian sovereignty over the Vale of Kashmir, they insisted that the agreement be kept strictly interim in nature. Provision was made to review it after fifteen years. The Pakistani foreign minister at the time, Khurshid Kasuri, later confirmed most of the details originally reported by Coll. He had told Coll in an interview for the *New Yorker* article that by early 2007 the two sides came so close to finalizing the deal that it had come down to differences over semicolons. A senior Indian official made a similar assertion. The deal was never consummated, reportedly, because by this time Musharraf did not feel politically strong enough to rally his nation behind it. He was already in trouble over his alliance with the United States and was in the process of sinking even deeper over his suspension of the Supreme Court chief justice. But this does not appear to have been the whole story.

Although Kasuri told Coll that the army supported the deal, I have been told this was not the case. As the two sides were nearing the semicolon stage of the negotiations, Tariq Aziz briefed the top leadership of the army, its corps commanders, on the proposed deal. Musharraf was also present. A former senior Pakistani diplomat, who had spoken to one the participants, told me that although Musharraf had enthusiastically endorsed the deal, the corps commanders had emerged unpersuaded and concerned. Most of them harbored serious doubts as to whether India could be trusted to live up to the terms of the agreement. They were probably most concerned about the issue of troop withdrawals, since there is no indication the proposed agreement contained any mechanism for monitoring withdrawals or ensuring their permanence. As we saw earlier, the Pakistanis had refused to pull their forces out of Azad Kashmir during the earliest days of the Kashmir dispute, as called for by the UN plebiscite resolution, because they feared India might take advantage of it by moving its forces into the territory they had vacated. With no enforcement mechanism in place to monitor the Indian withdrawals, the Pakistani lieutenant generals probably feared the Indians would be inclined to do so again.

But the army was not the only problem. The Pakistanis also had difficulties selling the agreement to the Kashmiri Muslims. The primary opposition groups in Kashmir had been secretly consulted as the negotiations reached their endgame, and most were prepared to go along. But one of the key players was not. This was Syed Ali Geelani, a longtime leader of the Kashmir wing of the Jamaat-e-Islami. As Kasuri later admitted, Geelani steadfastly refused to accept any outcome that did not include a territorial settlement ceding the Muslim areas of Kashmir to Pakistan. His hard-line rejection was important, not simply because of his following in the valley but also for what it revealed about the likely response within Pakistan itself. There would be opposition from the Jamaat-e-Islami for certain, as well as from the secular nationalist Kashmir screamers, many of them close to the army, for whom achieving Pakistani territorial objectives in Kashmir had long since become an idée fixe. And what would be the Pakistani jihadist groups' response? The Lashkar-e-Taiba and Jaish-e-Mohammed had been told to cool their heels in anticipation of a favorable settlement. How would they react to one that would be certain to produce no forward movement on their transcendent issue for at least the next fifteen years?

The reality was that the proposed agreement was a vehicle for conceding sovereignty over Kashmir to India but without having to spell it out. The idea was not a new one. The heart of it was first outlined to me in 2000 by the bookish former Pakistani lieutenant general whose comments on Pakistan's use of nuclear weapons and the impending Karamat resignation I cited in chapter 2. He said he had concluded, reluctantly, that Pakistan was never going to be able to prevail in Kashmir, but needed a graceful way to back down. His idea, which he said he had been shopping around in small-group discussions, was to negotiate an agreement that would restore full autonomy to the Kashmiris and create an open border along the Line of Control, but take no position on territorial issues. His proposal was, in its basic thrust and many of its details, identical to the deal subsequently worked out in the back-channel negotiations. I do not know whether the general had the opportunity to share his thinking with Musharraf, whom he knew extremely well, but I thought at the time that some such arrangement probably constituted the only realistic way to move forward on the Kashmir issue. The difficulty, then as now, is selling it inside Pakistan itself. Musharraf, who was a hard-liner on Kashmir when he first came to power, was eventually able to accommodate himself to the idea, but others most assuredly have not. Maybe Musharraf would have tried to push it through had he been stronger politically at the time, but he would still have encountered formidable opposition.

It is unclear whether the Lashkar-e-Taiba was aware of these developments prior to Mumbai. With a wink and a nod from the authorities, its leader, Hafiz Saeed, had changed the name of the organization to Jamaat-ud-Dawa shortly after the Lashkar was formally banned in early 2002. Although the Lashkar continued its efforts to infiltrate Kashmir without active army support, it spent much of its time tending its garden inside Pakistan. It continued to cultivate an image of respectability and a position of influence through its charitable activities. This paid big dividends during the devastating Kashmir earthquake of October 2005, when the infrastructure provided by its training camps in Azad Kashmir enabled it to deliver relief supplies and medical assistance to victims. Its performance, which far outstripped that of the relatively ineffectual Pakistani authorities, earned it both respect and popularity among ordinary Pakistanis. There is also some evidence the Lashkar may have shifted some of its activities to the Afghan theater during this period, in order to pursue jihad there. Nonetheless, it appears to have become increasingly frustrated at the failure of the peace process and the withdrawal of Pakistani support for its efforts in Kashmir. India accused the Lashkar of collaborating with a radical Indian Islamic group in bombing a series of trains near Mumbai in July 2006, which killed more than two hundred people. But this event, although it claimed more lives, failed to generate anything near the same drama as 26/11, which was clearly designed by its planners to be a media extravaganza.

The Pakistanis appeared to be caught off guard by the Mumbai massacre and by Ajmal Kasab's early confession that the Lashkar-e-Taiba was behind it. They were also stung by Indian accusations, most prominently from India's prime minister, Manmohan Singh, that elements in the Pakistani government—he was clearly referring to ISI—were involved in the attack. These were accompanied by thinly veiled threats of retaliation. As in previous such incidents, the United States quickly went into crisis management mode in an effort to prevent events from spiraling out of control. The Pakistanis reacted defensively at first, denying that the attackers had been Pakistani. But they finally conceded the point and the following February arrested the Lashkar operational commander Zaki-ur-Rehman Lakhvi and several of his associates. In November, Lakhvi and seven others were formally charged with planning the Mumbai attacks. The move came almost exactly a year after 26/11. The Pakistanis also placed the Lashkar leader Hafiz Saeed under house arrest, although they claimed to have uncovered no evidence linking him to Mumbai. This supposed lack of evidence prompted the Lahore High Court to order his release in early June 2009. The authorities also carried out raids against Lashkar facilities in Muzaffarabad and several Pakistani cities but, as in 2002, made no serious effort to crack down on the organization as a whole.

In the spring of 2010, the Indians repeated their charges of Pakistani involvement. This time they claimed to have evidence provided by a Pakistani American named David Headley. He had recently been sentenced by a U.S. court for assisting the Lashkar by traveling to Mumbai to identify possible targets for the attacks. He reportedly told Indian investigators sent to interview him that ISI had been deeply involved in all aspects of the operation. While his allegations cannot be dismissed out of hand, it is difficult to believe that General Kayani, the Pakistan army chief and former head of ISI, would have authorized an attack that deliberately targeted sites known to be frequented by Westerners. I mention General Kayani here because, given the magnitude of the planned operation, ISI would have felt compelled to seek his personal approval. It seems clear that Mumbai was designed by its perpetrators to be a media spectacle and equally clear that Pakistan would be blamed and universally condemned for it. It is easy to see why the Lashkar-e-Taiba would have wanted to stir up trouble between India and Pakistan but hard to see what the Pakistanis stood to gain by it. The Indians later suggested that the Pakistanis did it to prevent the Lashkar from hemorrhaging members or from gravitating toward Al Qaeda and the Pakistani Taliban. But if this really were a serious motivation, they would have been much better off by simply reopening the floodgates into Kashmir. Yet there is no indication this has occurred. Nonetheless, even without ISI involvement in Mumbai, the fact that a jihadist group based in Punjab and known to have links to ISI was able to plan and carry out an operation like Mumbai was damning enough. It demonstrated yet again that the Pakistanis did not exercise anything like complete control over the jihadist groups they had chosen to support.

Equally damning is the fact that, even though the Lashkar-e-Taiba had just carried out the second most sensational terrorist attack in history, the Pakistanis made no effort to dismantle it. By limiting their response to the arrest of a handful of perpetrators, the Pakistanis seemed to be insinuating that Lakhvi and a small renegade faction of the Lashkar had been responsible, not Hafiz Saeed or the organization as a whole. This insinuation, never spelled out by the Pakistanis themselves, makes little sense. It seems highly unlikely that the operational commander of Lashkar forces could have carried out such an incendiary mission without the knowledge or approval of his immediate superior without precipitating a major breach within the organization. Yet no such breach seems to have occurred. Lakhvi, instead, seems to have been offered up as a sacrificial lamb to protect the integrity of the organization as a whole. The Pakistanis, meanwhile, managed to get themselves largely off the hook through vehement denials and by hiding behind legalisms, dismissing Headley as a liar and shrugging their shoulders at the alleged lack of evidence against Saeed and the Lashkar.

But why continue to protect the Lashkar in the wake of an event like Mumbai? There is, of course, their long history of cooperation in Kashmir. As we have seen, even after the army ended its active support for infiltration efforts, the Pakistanis still viewed the Lashkar as an insurance policy. Despite the risk of future incidents like Mumbai, it is difficult to sacrifice the only real chips you have to play in what you regard as your most important game. But there is more to it than this. With the possible exception of remnants of the heavily splintered Jaish-e-Mohammed, the Lashkar-e-Taiba is the only domestic jihadist group that has never turned against the state. The Pakistanis would like to keep it that way, and for very good reason. The Lashkar is the largest and most formidable radical Islamic group in the Punjabi heartland of the country. A midlevel ISI officer told *The New York Times* in 2009 that it had 150,000 members. He suggested that together with the Jaish-e-Mohammed, it had the ability to send Pakistan "up in flames." A considerably more senior former Pakistani official, one who was in a significantly better position to know what ISI really thought about the Lashkar, told me he believed this figure was too high. He said its trained cadres probably numbered somewhere between twenty and twenty-five thousand. Nonetheless, it was a formidable organization, far and away the best-organized jihadist group in Pakistan. Even the army was afraid of it. The sense of menace generated by the Lashkar was reflected in the comments of a well-known Lahore journalist, who told me that if the Lashkar wanted to it could send five thousand men into the Punjab capital and take it over within a day. The police, he insisted, would be nowhere to be found.

By the spring of 2009, in the immediate aftermath of Mumbai, Pakistani fortunes in dealing with the radical Islamists in their midst had reached their lowest ebb. The Mumbai attacks had brought the once promising peace process with India over Kashmir to a sudden end and further besmirched Pakistan's tattered international reputation. In the west of the country, they had all but abandoned the tribal areas to the Pakistani Taliban yet continued to suffer from a steady drumbeat of terrorist attacks administered by their victorious foes. Perhaps most embarrassing, they had virtually signed away their right to govern the Swat Valley only to be further humiliated by Mullah Fazlullah, who had reneged on the deal before the ink on the agreement was dry and menacingly marched his forces southward into Buner, in the direction of Islamabad.

It was at this point that the Pakistanis finally began to stir themselves to action. The Pakistani Taliban had finally overreached. A senior former Pakistani diplomat with close ties to the army told me the move into Buner had convinced the government, army and civilians alike, that the Taliban would continue to push until they were stopped. The time had come to push back. Importantly, the authorities also sensed that public opinion had at last turned against the Tehrik-e-Taliban. Up to this point, most Pakistanis placed the blame for their problems in the tribal areas and Swat squarely on the United States, or on Pervez Musharraf for having agreed to support the United States in its war on terror. It had been their actions that had turned the Pakistani Taliban into enemies of the state. The conventional wisdom was that these problems would go away just as soon as the United States departed the region, an event that could not come soon enough. While these anti-American attitudes had not changed, attitudes toward the Pakistani Taliban had. The domestic terrorism campaign, orchestrated by the Tehrik-e-Taliban leader Baitullah Mehsud, played a major role. But ordinary Pakistanis were also repelled by the brutal nature of Pakistani Taliban rule, which attracted increasing media coverage inside Pakistan itself. A video showing a teenage girl in Swat being savagely whipped generated particular outrage. Her crime had been to be seen walking in public with a man who was not her husband. The tone-deaf Fazlullah forces had released the video as an example of what their brand of sharia justice had to offer. As the Pakistani Taliban began to draw nearer to Punjab, ordinary Pakistanis began to feel threatened. What had been a distant abstraction now loomed on the horizon as something very real. This was not the way most Pakistanis, the majority of them Barelvi followers of Sufi Islam, wished to be governed. The Pakistani Taliban were a threat to their way of life.

At the end of April 2009, the army moved into Buner and started driving the Fazlullah forces out. At the same time, they began gearing up for a major operation in Swat itself, which they decided to name Right Path. Mindful of the civilian casualties that had plagued their earlier efforts here and in the tribal areas, the army began urging the civilian population to leave. They did—in prodigious numbers—some finding shelter with friends and relatives elsewhere in the NWFP, but many ending up in hastily constructed refugee camps set up by the government outside the Swat Valley. By some accounts as many as three million people fled the fighting in Swat and adjacent areas, a mind-boggling number. In early May, the army began moving into Swat in earnest. By the end of the month, it had driven the Pakistani Taliban out of Mingora, the largest city in Swat, and began methodically moving up the valley, driving the Fazlullah forces from town after town. Pakistani Taliban casualties were reportedly high, although Fazlullah himself managed to elude capture. By the end of July, the army had succeeded in clearing the entire valley and was engaged in mop-up operations against isolated Fazlullah forces. Swat residents began returning to their homes. Sufi Mohammed was rearrested and thrown back into jail. The army had won.

Why did the army win? Evacuating the civilian population played an important role, since it eliminated the burden of having to worry about civilian casualties. But the main reason the army won was that it committed far more troops to the effort than it had ever done before. In mid-June, by which time the offensive was well under way, a Pakistani commanding general in Swat told reporters that the army had devoted forty thousand troops to the operation. This, he said, was four times the number the army had deployed in its earlier efforts to drive the Fazlullah forces out of Swat in the aftermath of Lal Masjid. Mindful that it had abandoned captured territory to the Taliban in the past, the army announced it would stay in Swat as long as the Pakistani Taliban remained a threat. On July 15, just as the operation was winding down, the government announced that it intended to follow up its efforts in Swat by moving into South Waziristan. The plan was to root out Baitullah Mehsud and put an end to his domestic terrorism campaign once and for all. The Pakistanis were signaling that Swat was not an isolated effort but the first stage of a broader campaign to destroy all the Pakistani Taliban forces that had taken up arms against the state.

Although the July 15 announcement created expectations that a South Waziristan offensive was imminent, the operation ended up being delayed for three months, raising eyebrows along the way. Part of the problem was logistical. Since the army was committed to garrisoning Swat, it needed to identify and transfer additional forces into the region to ensure it had sufficient forces on hand for the South Waziristan operation. But another difficulty also seems to have played a role. The army plan of attack was to move against the Mehsud forces from both the north and the south, through territory controlled by Hafiz Gul Bahadur and Maulvi Nazir. The catch was that in late June both these Pakistani Taliban leaders had abandoned their alliance with the government. The main reason they had done so was anger at the recent dramatic increase in U.S. Predator attacks in the tribal areas.

The Obama administration had taken office in January 2009 promising a tougher line on Afghanistan and the tribal areas. During the campaign, candidate Obama had said he would not approve military aid to Pakistan unless it made progress in preventing the Afghan Taliban from using Pakistan as a staging area for attacks into Afghanistan. But the newly minted President Obama found himself confronting a Pakistan that seemed incapable of handling even the Pakistani variety of Taliban. The most the Pakistanis would agree to was a substantial increase in the number of Predator attacks in the tribal areas. The groundwork for this had actually been laid the previous September, when the outgoing Bush administration secured Pakistani agreement to a substantially broadened Predator program. The expanded target set included not only the hardy Al Qaeda perennials but also both varieties of Taliban, including the Haqqani network that the Pakistanis were alleged to support. There had been a noticeable uptick in the number of drone attacks even before Obama took office. In the first eight months of 2008, there had been only twelve attacks. But during the final four months of the year, there were twenty-two. The Obama administration picked up where the Bush administration had left off. During the first half of 2009, both Afghan and Pakistani varieties of the Taliban came under Predator attack. This included groups that were on good terms with the Pakistanis, including the Haqqani network and the forces of Hafiz Gul Bahadur and Maulvi Nazir. There were, in fact, far more attacks against Taliban targets during this period than against Al Qaeda. This demonstrated increasing U.S. preoccupation with Afghanistan, where the struggle against the Taliban insurgency was not going well. But the drone campaign also targeted Pakistani public enemy number one, Baitullah Mehsud. A New America Foundation survey of Predator strikes counted fourteen separate drone attacks against Mehsud forces through July 2009.

The drone attacks against Mehsud suggest why the Pakistanis agreed to the widened target set in the first place. The September 2008 agreement with the Bush administration came at a nadir in Pakistani fortunes in the tribal areas. As we have seen, Mehsud had beaten back army efforts to drive him from his South Waziristan stronghold and was continuing to orchestrate the domestic terrorism campaign with impunity. Predators offered the Pakistanis a relatively low-cost opportunity to target Mehsud. But there was a price. The United States was prepared to help, but only if the Pakistanis acquiesced in targeting their Haqqani network allies and the forces of Gul Bahadur and Maulvi Nazir. This was a price the Pakistanis were reluctant, but ultimately willing, to pay. It helped them rebut allegations they were supporting these groups, but without actually threatening their existence. Drones could kill individuals but not take down an entire organization. The Pakistanis, who were no more troubled about double-dealing with the Taliban than they had been with the Americans, were prepared to live with the consequences. The fact that they disavowed and condemned the Predator attacks provided them with the deniability they needed in confronting the complaints of their Taliban allies. But the Pakistanis still had their limits. They drew a firm line between the tribal areas, where drone attacks were permitted, and Baluchistan and the NWFP, where they were not. Although there were plenty of potential targets in both provinces—Mullah Omar comes to mind—no Predator attacks have ever taken place there. These are settled areas of Pakistan, regular provinces, no different in the Pakistani imagination from Punjab or Sindh. Drone strikes in the tribal areas were bad enough, but allowing the Americans to target these areas would require the Pakistanis to surrender far too much of their sovereignty. The country would not stand for it.

On the evening of August 4, 2009, the Pakistanis received their single biggest payoff of the drone campaign. Baitullah Mehsud was spotted by Predator cameras on a rooftop in South Waziristan. According to press reports, he was on a glucose drip for diabetes and receiving a leg massage from his recently acquired second wife. Moments later, missiles slammed into the house, killing the newlyweds along with several others. The death of Mehsud provided the Pakistanis with a strong psychological boost. This was reinforced by reports of dissension among his possible successors, although his deputy, Hakimullah Mehsud, eventually emerged on top. Meanwhile, the Pakistanis had managed to smooth the ruffled feathers of Gul Bahadur and Nazir, setting the stage for the army's long-awaited move into South Waziristan. As had happened in Swat in the run-up to Right Path, local residents fled the area, more than two hundred thousand in all. The operation itself was finally launched on October 17 and bore the name Path to Salvation. As planned, the path to this salvation passed through the territories of Hafiz Gul Bahadur and Maulvi Nazir, enabling the army to attack the Mehsud forces on two fronts. Press reports at the time indicated the army had committed thirty thousand troops to the operation. There was fierce fighting for the first two weeks, but rather than stand and fight, as many of the Fazlullah forces had done, the Mehsud forces began quietly slipping through gaps in the army lines, taking advantage of local knowledge and the rugged terrain. The army soon found itself in possession of the Mehsud lands in South Waziristan but without really having destroyed the Mehsud forces.

The Swat and South Waziristan offensives may have been successful in reclaiming lost territory, but there were consequences in the urban heartland. In a replay of the aftermath of Lal Masjid, there was an upsurge in terrorist spectaculars, scattered among the drumbeat of more minor attacks that frequently numbered two or more a week. On May 27, a car bomb exploded outside the regional headquarters of ISI in Lahore, ripping the outer wall off the building and killing twenty-seven and injuring more than three hundred. The Pakistani Taliban claimed credit for the attack, stating that it had been in retaliation for the army offensive in Swat. On June 9, a massive truck bomb destroyed the five-star Pearl Continental hotel in Peshawar, killing seventeen. The United States had been planning to buy the hotel to serve as the site for a new, allegedly less vulnerable, consulate in the NWFP capital. The tempo of attacks intensified in October in anticipation of the imminent army move into South Waziristan. On October 9, more than fifty people were killed in a car bomb attack on a crowded bazaar in the heart of Peshawar. Terrorist violence returned to Lahore on October 15, as three separate teams of terrorists attacked two police training academies and the regional headquarters of the civilian Federal Investigation Agency, killing thirty-eight.

The most spectacular attack of all occurred on October 10, just a few days before the army move into South Waziristan. Ten terrorists dressed in army fatigues burst into the Pakistan army headquarters in Rawalpindi, guns blazing. They cut down several bystanders on the way in, including a brigadier general. Before long they had commandeered a building and managed to corral more than forty hostages. They held them in a standoff that lasted through the night until army commandos burst in and overwhelmed them. The death toll would have been considerably greater if a suicide vest worn by one of the attackers had not failed to detonate. Nine of the terrorists were killed in the attack, but the ringleader survived. His real name was Mohammed Aqeel but he went by the alias Dr. Osman. A former member of the army medical corps and a native Punjabi, he may have passed through several radical Deobandi groups before finally making his way to South Waziristan. There he formed the Amjad Farooqi brigade, named after the former Jaish-e-Mohammed militant who had taken part in the Daniel Pearl kidnapping and an assassination attempt against Pervez Musharraf. Dr. Osman was already well-known to the Pakistani authorities. He was believed to be the mastermind behind the attack on the Sri Lankan cricket team in March.

The attack on army headquarters and capture of Dr. Osman helped make clear what had been suspected for some time. Many of the terrorist attacks taking place in Punjab were being carried out not by Pashtuns affiliated with the Pakistani Taliban but by native Punjabis, many of them hailing from the Seraiki belt of south Punjab. Even before the attack on army headquarters, these militants had begun to be referred to in the press as Punjabi Taliban. They were not members of a single organization that went by that name or any single organization. Many were current or former members of groups such as the Jaish-e-Mohammed, the Lashkar-e-Jhangvi, and the Sipah-e-Sahaba. They had made their way to the tribal areas where they joined up with the Pakistani Taliban and honed their terrorist skills before returning to their home bases to plan and carry out attacks. Nor were they a new phenomenon. As we saw earlier, members of these groups had collaborated with Al Qaeda in carrying out attacks against Western targets and Pakistani government officials in the aftermath of 9/11. What had changed was the size and character of the phenomenon as more and more radically inclined Punjabis made their way to the tribal areas.

It is interesting to read contemporary press reporting on Dr. Osman. He is variously described as having previously belonged to the Lashkar-e-Jhangvi, the Jaish-e-Mohammed, and the 313 Brigade of the former HUJI leader Ilyas Kashmiri. This may simply reflect confusion or a lack of reliable information, but the increasing use of the name Punjabi Taliban also reflected the fact that the organizational distinctions among these groups were breaking down. A senior State Department official familiar with the subject told me that recruitment for terrorist operations in Pakistan functioned much like a terrorist Craigslist, with organizers trolling the radical Deobandi community for both foot soldiers and individuals possessing specialized skills. It is not clear whether some of these groups even existed anymore. Consider the Jaish-e-Mohammed. It has been hemorrhaging members for years, many of whom can now best be described as Punjabi Taliban, yet it continues to conduct operations in Kashmir. The Pakistani authorities routinely refer to it as a hostile organization, and its leader and founder, Masood Azhar, has disappeared. Nevertheless, it maintains a highly visible headquarters in Bahawalpur in south Punjab, which is reportedly expanding. One possible explanation is that although the organization has badly splintered over the years, a loyal core, still prepared to cooperate with the Pakistani authorities, remains. Those who know for certain are not saying.

What the emergence of the Punjabi Taliban does seem to reflect is a gradual collapse in the organizational distinctions between the Pakistani Taliban and the various Deobandi jihadist and sectarian groups based in Punjab. They have gravitated increasingly toward one another, forming a collective of individuals and groups who are committed to overthrowing the Pakistani state and bringing their own uncompromising brand of Islamic fundamentalism to power in the country. It is still far from becoming a monolithic organization. There does not appear to be one person or group that can be said to be in charge overall, but the trend is definitely toward increasing collaboration and unity of purpose. A retired senior army officer, who has also served in some of the most important positions in the Pakistani government, told me that this development constituted the single greatest threat to the long-term stability of Pakistan. He was speaking in the summer of 2010, more than eight months after the army managed to drive the Mehsud forces out of South Waziristan, where most terrorist training camps had been located. But during those eight months there had been little or no diminution in the frequency and magnitude of terrorist attacks, either in Khyber Pakhtunkhwa, as the NWFP was renamed in April, where members of the Tehrik-e-Taliban were the likely perpetrators, or in the Punjab, where the Punjabi Taliban held sway.

More than one hundred people were killed by a car bomb in a crowded bazaar in the center of Peshawar in late October 2009. In early November, a suicide bomber detonated himself outside a bank in Rawalpindi where army personnel and civilian army employees were cashing paychecks, killing thirty-five. A month later, forty people were killed, including a major general and sixteen children, when another suicide bomber attacked a Rawalpindi mosque frequented by army families. One of the children killed was the son of the Peshawar corps commander. In January 2010, more than a hundred people were killed at a volleyball match in the NWFP, when a suicide bomber drove his explosives-laden SUV into the crowd. In the months that followed, such attacks continued, week in and week out, with seemingly no end in sight. During 2010, there were more than forty terrorist attacks in Pakistan that claimed five or more lives. Although overshadowed by the dramatic increase in attacks against secular targets following Lal Masjid, purely sectarian attacks, most of them against Shiite targets, continued to occur. Processions commemorating the Shiite holy day of Ashura were hit particularly hard. More than forty Shiites were killed in an attack on an Ashura procession in Karachi in late December 2009, one of several such incidents in Pakistan on that day. Four months later, more than forty Shiites who had fled the fighting in the tribal areas were killed by suicide bombers at a refugee camp near Kohat in the NWFP. A decade earlier, there had been a clear distinction between jihadists and violent sectarians. But as radical Deobandis turned against the state and began to congeal into the Punjabi Taliban, that distinction had begun to collapse. The same groups and individuals were now carrying out attacks against both secular and sectarian targets.

In late May 2010, radical Deobandi gunmen moved beyond their traditional Shiite target list to attack members of the controversial Ahmadi sect. They burst into two Ahmadi mosques in Lahore crowded with worshippers, killing more than eighty people. Three days later, they attacked a hospital where many of the wounded survivors were being treated, killing five more. An even more incendiary attack took place just over a month later, on July 1, when two suicide bombers deto-

nated themselves in a crowd of pilgrims worshipping at the Data Durbar shrine in Lahore. The attack killed fifty people and injured two
hundred. The shrine, dedicated to the legendary Sufi saint Data Ganj
Bakhsh, is the largest in Pakistan. This was not the first major attack
by radical Deobandis against a Barelvi target. Fifty-seven people had
been killed and more than eighty injured at a Barelvi ceremony to
mark the birthday of the Prophet Mohammed in Karachi in April 2006.
Three members of the Lashkar-e-Jhangvi were later charged with responsibility for what at the time was an isolated attack. Nor was it the
first attack against a Sufi shrine. The Pakistani Taliban had bombed a
shrine in Peshawar in March 2009. But that attack occurred at night
when no one was around and also proved to be an isolated incident.
The Data Durbar bombing was the first against a Sufi shrine crowded
with worshippers and, more important, the beginning of a trend. A
Sufi shrine in Karachi was hit in early October, killing nine people.
The Pakistani Taliban claimed credit for the attack. This was followed
by the bombing of the shrine of the famous Sufi saint Baba Farid at
Pakpattan in Punjab later in the month, claiming seven lives. Another
Sufi shrine in Lahore was hit in February 2011. A suicide bombing
during an urs celebration at the famous Sakhi Sarwar shrine in Dera
Ghazi Khan in south Punjab in early April killed fifty worshippers.
These attacks threatened to raise sectarian conflict in Pakistan to a
new and more dangerous level. Radical Deobandis may not have liked
the religion practiced by most of the their fellow Pakistanis, but they
previously had managed to refrain from picking a fight. The shrine attacks demonstrated their growing willingness to take up arms against
any group or government, secular or sectarian, Sunni or Shiite, that
failed to embrace their militant brand of Islamic fundamentalism.

Equally disturbing were growing signs of increasing politicization
within the Barelvi community itself. Barelvi religious organizations
were in the vanguard in agitating against changes to the blasphemy
laws that were being mooted by the Zardari government in late 2010.
In early January 2011, Salmaan Taseer, the governor of Punjab province and a vocal proponent of the changes, was assassinated by a
Barelvi member of his elite security guard detail who admitted he had
acted from religious motives. The largest Barelvi group in Pakistan, the
Jamaat-e-Ahle Sunnat, subsequently praised the attack and warned
Muslims not to attend Taseer's funeral.

The seemingly endless cycle of terrorist attacks in Punjab provoked increasing unease within the feudal political class. At first, neither the Zardari government nor the provincial Punjab government headed by the rival PML-N was willing to admit that most of the terrorist violence was being carried out by native Punjabis. Their reluctance was understandable. If they acknowledged the problem, they would come under pressure to do something about it. It was far easier to pretend that the domestic terrorism campaign was being orchestrated by the Tehrik-e-Taliban in the tribal areas. At least something was already being done about that. The Zardari government finally broke the ice in early June in the aftermath of the attack against the Ahmadis, when the interior minister conceded that terrorist groups based in south Punjab had become well entrenched and posed a serious threat to the state. His turnabout followed controversial remarks made in March by Shahbaz Sharif, the chief minister of Punjab and younger brother of Nawaz. He had urged the terrorists to stop targeting Punjab because the PML-N government currently in power had shared with them a common opposition to Pervez Musharraf and his alliance with the United States. After admitting the problem, the Zardari government hinted it might be willing to send the army into the Seraiki belt, but later distanced itself from the idea. After all, what good could troops do against groups operating in secrecy underground? Rooting out the Punjabi Taliban on their home turf required good intelligence and police work, both of which were in short supply. A former senior army officer familiar with the situation told me that most ISI intelligence assets were being targeted on the tribal areas. There were simply not enough to go around. Nor was there any serious discussion of moving against the radical mosques and madrassas that served as feeder organizations for the Punjabi Taliban, this despite the fact that their ranks were increasing every year. The Zardari government had announced plans to take them on two years earlier but the proposal had never gotten off the ground.

As I followed these events from afar, I was reminded of a conversation I had ten years earlier with Tariq Aziz, at that time the chief civilian advisor to Pervez Musharraf. I asked him why the government was reluctant to move against the radical Islamic groups, who even then were causing serious problems for the state. He told me the Pakistanis feared becoming another Algeria. His reference was to the terrorist campaign, replete with massacres and other terrorist acts, that had been carried out by radical Islamists in the North African country during the previous decade, claiming many thousands of lives. In the ten years since my conversation with Aziz, the Pakistanis have still not moved against the sources of radical Islam in the Punjabi heartland. But Pakistan has become another Algeria nonetheless.

The steady persistence of the domestic terrorism campaign, particularly in Khyber Pakhtunkhwa, reflected the fact that the Pakistani Taliban had not been comprehensively defeated. The bulk of the Hakimullah Mehsud forces had managed to slip away, taking their terrorist training capabilities with them. One of their destinations was the Orakzai tribal area to the north, where Hakimullah had earlier had his home base. The army appears to have followed close behind, since by early 2010 the Pakistani press was full of daily militant body counts in Orakzai that appeared to exceed those from the earlier fighting in South Waziristan. This fighting also spilled over into the neighboring tribal areas of Kurram and Khyber. Although the army claimed victory in Orakzai in June, local residents insisted that pockets of resistance remained. The weight of evidence would seem to be on their side since deadly attacks on Pakistani forces in the area continued through the remainder of the year. In early 2011, news reports indicated the army was engaged in a major offensive against Pakistani Taliban forces in the Mohmand tribal area farther to the north.

The one tribal area that seemed to be largely unaffected was North Waziristan. This was not because the Mehsud forces fleeing South Waziristan had avoided the area. There was ample evidence that Hafiz Gul Bahadur had granted them safe haven despite an earlier pledge to the Pakistanis not to do so. His motives remain unclear, but it is possible he felt unable to turn them away, given the Pashtunwali requirement to provide sanctuary even to unwanted guests. The army was reluctant to launch operations into North Waziristan because it did not want to risk coming to blows with either Gul Bahadur or the Haqqani network, who shared the same territory. This was clearly the U.S. assessment of the situation. Although it praised the Pakistanis for their operations in Swat and South Waziristan, it sharply criticized them for not moving against the Haqqanis. U.S. concern was driven primarily by its own strategic interests in the region. The Haqqani network was the principal Afghan Taliban force fighting against U.S. troops in eastern Afghanistan. U.S. success in the area depended on neutralizing it. Not surprisingly, the United States was angered not simply by the Pakistanis' recalcitrance in confronting the Haqqanis but also by their willingness to support and even collaborate with them. In an effort to ratchet up the pressure while trying to foreclose Pakistani options, the United States added the Haqqani network to its list of terrorist organizations. By the summer of 2010, Pakistani support for the Haqqani network had become the most divisive issue in U.S.-Pakistani relations.

The Pakistani take on the situation in North Waziristan was somewhat different. A former senior officer close to the army leadership told me that the primary problem facing the Pakistan army was one of capacity. It had already moved a substantial percentage of the regular army into the region and simply could not spare any more. There was some truth to this. I learned from a high-ranking Pakistan army source, who spoke on condition of anonymity, that by the spring of 2010 the total number of troops deployed in the tribal areas and Swat had reached nearly 150,000. Ninety thousand were regular army, deployed in eighty-eight battalions, the equivalent of nine divisions. The remainder were Frontier Corps. By contrast, in normal times the regular army maintains two divisions in the region, headquartered at Peshawar. This meant the Pakistanis had moved the equivalent of seven additional regular army divisions into the region. The total commitment represented almost one-third the unit strength of the regular Pakistan army. I was a bit taken aback when I first heard these numbers. One of the main reasons why earlier army forays into the tribal areas and Swat had failed was Pakistani unwillingness to move forces away from the Indian frontier. What, I wondered, had changed? I asked my former senior army officer contact this very question. He said it was simple. The government had concluded that the Pakistani Taliban threat had become so serious it justified the risk.

It is worth bearing in mind here that the number of Pakistani troops that began to flow into the tribal areas and Swat beginning in the spring of 2009 far exceeded the number of U.S. troops in all of Afghanistan at the time. U.S. troop levels there did not reach the one hundred thousand mark until August 2010, in the wake of the Obama surge. Yet the former officer I spoke to appeared genuinely worried that the Pakistanis did not have enough troops in the tribal areas and Swat to deal with the current Pakistani Taliban threat, much less the Haqqani network and the forces of Hafiz Gul Bahadur. The army had driven the Pakistani Taliban out of Swat and northern South Waziristan, but he was far from confident it could defeat the forces that had managed to escape while continuing to hold on to the territory it had brought under its control. He said the army was frustrated by the inability of civilian security forces to take up the slack but saw no clear way out of its dilemma. Although we did not directly discuss the possibility of operations in North Waziristan, his message was clear enough. If the army did go into North Waziristan, it risked losing its grip elsewhere, while making powerful new enemies of the Haqqani network and Gul Bahadur. It could, of course, send even more forces into the region. But how much would be enough? Half the regular army? Two-thirds? The army was clearly unwilling to find out. It had already moved far more forces from the Indian frontier than it believed wise.

There was, of course, more to it than just this. Pakistani aims in Afghanistan had always differed sharply from those of the United States. As we have seen, for most of the past decade, the Pakistanis had viewed the Afghan Taliban as a hedge against an Afghanistan it feared would be dominated by India once the United States left. This was not unlike the way they had viewed the Lashkar-e-Taiba during the peace process with India, as a hedge against a breakdown in the talks. It might appear from this that the Pakistanis had learned nothing from their experience with the forces of radical Islam. But this was not completely true. It had begun to dawn on them even before 9/11 that they could not completely control the Afghan Taliban. Their experience with the Pakistani Taliban in the years following 9/11, and their sufferings under the domestic terrorism campaign, had brought home to them just how dangerous such forces could be. By early 2010, the army had suffered almost nine thousand battlefield casualties and become the primary victim of terrorist violence outside the war zone itself. Nor had ISI been exempt. Seventy-three ISI officers had lost their lives in terrorist attacks since Lal Masjid. The former officer whose comments I cited above told me the army had come to the painful realization that it was in the nature of radical Islamists to push until they were stopped. He insisted that Pakistan no longer saw the Afghan Taliban as an ideal solution to its problems in Afghanistan. A former senior Pakistani diplomat who often reflects army views made the same point to me. But the Pakistanis also had reality to contend with.

In late 2009, the Obama administration decided to send an additional thirty thousand troops to Afghanistan, bringing the overall total to one hundred thousand. It hoped the additional troop commitment would help turn the tide of battle so that the Afghan army could hold its own once U.S. forces began to depart. The United States was not opposed to negotiating with the Afghan Taliban but wished to do so from a position of strength. However, in announcing the surge, the administration also set July 2011, a bare eleven months after the surge would be complete, as the date when U.S. forces would begin drawing down. This decision was reportedly taken to forestall public criticism that the United States was becoming bogged down in yet another endless war it could not win. The Pakistanis' reaction was guarded, but the early date set for beginning the drawdown spoke volumes to them. After several years of chasing the Pakistani Taliban across the tribal areas, they were convinced it would take many more years of sustained effort, and perhaps even larger numbers of troops, for the United States to turn the tide decisively against the Afghan Taliban. Twelve months was not going to cut it. Nor did they believe there was much chance the Afghan army would be able to take up the slack. In the spring of 2010, I heard a very senior Pakistan army officer heap scorn on the idea. Not wanting to criticize the Afghan army directly, he simply noted that it took the Pakistan army six months to train a new recruit but thirty years to groom a senior officer. His implication was clear. The Afghan army was not well enough led to compete with the Afghan Taliban on a level playing field once U.S. forces began to depart.

The Pakistanis concluded from this that the Afghan Taliban were unlikely to be defeated. This, of course, was due in no small measure to their own policies, driven by their fear of an Indian foothold in Kabul and by what they regarded as the absence of any better alternative. By the summer of 2010, however, they had begun to show the first signs of interest in pursuing a negotiated settlement in Afghanistan. This may have reflected a desire to hedge their bets in case the U.S. surge proved more effective than they thought likely. It may also have been designed simply as a time waster, aimed at creating an impression of forward movement when, in fact, nothing significant was taking place. But it could also have reflected a desire to try to limit and control the extent of Afghan Taliban influence in the country once U.S. forces did begin to depart. A strong Taliban presence in Kabul would help keep the Indians out as well as free the Pakistanis from the burden of having to deal with an Afghan government run exclusively by radical mullahs. They had experienced that before, and it had led them straight down the garden path to 9/11. Their unlikely ally in this endeavor was Hamid Karzai, who by this time had drawn similar conclusions about U.S. staying power in Afghanistan. Both sides lined up in favor of negotiating with at least some elements of the Afghan Taliban.

For the Pakistanis, this appeared to mean, first and foremost, the Haqqani network. As we saw, the ISI connection to the Haqqani patriarch Jalaluddin extended back to the days of the anti-Soviet jihad. He was a mujahid by background, not a hard-core Taliban, and had joined the movement only in 1995 when they were at the gates of Kabul. ISI had continued the relationship after the Haqqanis had retreated into North Waziristan in the rout that followed 9/11. This was familiar territory for them since Jalaluddin had made it his Pakistani base of operations during the anti-Soviet jihad. But he had become increasingly bedridden by this time and had begun turning control of the network to his eldest son, Sirajuddin, who was cut more in the Taliban mold. As we saw earlier, the younger Haqqani had been strongly supportive of Pakistani interests in the region, having played an active role in efforts to persuade the Mehsuds and others to end their war with the Pakistan army. Haqqani operatives had also collaborated with ISI in carrying out attacks against the Indian embassy in Kabul in July 2008 and October 2009. The Pakistanis believed that Haqqani was their man and might be persuaded to accept a power-sharing arrangement with the Karzai government.

It was less clear what role the Pakistanis foresaw for Mullah Omar. Other Taliban leaders, whether Afghan or Pakistani, at least pretended to acknowledge the Taliban founder as their leader. His Quetta Shura, meanwhile, was responsible for managing Taliban operations in southern Afghanistan. A former senior army officer familiar with Pakistani thinking conceded to me in the summer of 2010 that Pakistan would welcome Haqqani participation in an Afghan coalition, but he was much less sure about Mullah Omar. His uncertainty may have been linked to the mysterious arrest of Omar's chief deputy, Mullah Baradar, in Karachi several months earlier. Many analysts at the time thought the arrest might be a signal that the Pakistanis had finally decided to take action against the Afghan Taliban. But this appears not to have been the case. Pakistani security officials told *The New York Times* in August they had arrested Baradar because he had been negotiating with the Karzai government behind their backs. If this is true, it suggests that Pakistan and the Karzai government may have been working at cross-purposes in pursuing a negotiated settlement. Whatever the truth of the matter, by April 2011 they had agreed to form a high-level joint commission to promote negotiations with the Afghan Taliban. As part of this process, they had also endorsed a Turkish proposal to have the Taliban open an office in Turkey.

Although the United States conceded the necessity of negotiating with the Afghan Taliban at some point, it had drawn a firm line in the sand opposing a role in Kabul for any Taliban group that continued to support Al Qaeda. The Pakistanis were well aware of this and had tried to convince the Haqqanis to break with the Arabs, but apparently without success. The United States also wanted to negotiate from a position of relative strength. This had been a large part of the impetus behind the Obama surge: seriously weaken the Taliban and then see if you can bring them to the negotiating table on more favorable terms. There was also a Predator component to this stepped-up U.S. presence on the ground. Faced with continuing Pakistani reluctance to launch an offensive in North Waziristan, the United States had pressured Islamabad into agreeing to yet another increase in the tempo of drone attacks. Beginning in late 2009, their frequency increased from an average of approximately three a month to between five and ten. The overwhelming majority were directed at targets on territory occupied by the Haqqanis in North Waziristan. Mohammed Haqqani, a younger brother of Sirajuddin, was killed in one such attack in February 2010. Then, beginning in September 2010, the tempo was stepped up yet again. By the end of the year, Predator strikes were taking place approximately every other day, with some days witness to multiple attacks.

But the sharp increase in drone attacks was not enough to satisfy the United States. This was made clear in late September when the United States decided to test Pakistani limits by sending attack helicopters across the border into Pakistan in hot pursuit of fleeing Haqqani network militants. There were three such attacks, one of which resulted in the deaths of three Frontier Corps soldiers, who had fired into the air in an effort to warn the helicopters off. These attacks violated a long-standing prohibition against U.S. combat operations on Pakistani territory. The Pakistanis reacted with considerably more anger than the United States had anticipated, closing down one of the two routes used by the United States to supply its forces in Afghanistan. This was followed almost immediately by attacks against U.S. supply convoys stalled at various points along the route by the border closure. Although the Tehrik-e-Taliban took credit for the attacks, it seems highly unlikely that their forces could have found and targeted the convoys so quickly. Some of the attacks occurred in areas such as interior Sindh, where the Pakistani Taliban did not even operate. A much more likely explanation is that the Pakistanis carried out the attacks themselves in order to help drive home their point. They were apparently successful, since within a few days the United States felt compelled to issue a public apology, paving the way for the Pakistanis to reopen the Khyber Pass route to U.S. and NATO supply convoys.

Late in 2010, reports began to surface that elements of the Haqqani network were moving into Kurram agency, which lies just to the north of North Waziristan. There was speculation in the Pakistani press that this was being done in an effort to escape the constant U.S. drone attacks that were taking place on the Haqqanis' home turf. But it is also possible the Haqqanis were moving out of harm's way in anticipation of a Pakistan army offensive in North Waziristan. Not only were the Pakistanis under relentless U.S. pressure to undertake such an operation, they had their own good reasons for doing so. As we saw earlier, many of the Mehsud forces had taken refuge in North Waziristan after being driven out of South Waziristan in the fall of 2009. It had quickly developed into the primary nerve center of Pakistani Taliban opposition to the state. Although the Pakistanis were still concerned about losing their grip elsewhere, they may have decided that going into North Waziristan was worth the risk. With the Haqqanis safely packed off to Kurram agency, most likely at their instigation, the army would feel free to move in. The United States would end up getting its North Waziristan offensive, but not the one it had bargained for. Nonetheless, Pakistani officials continued to deny they had any immediate plans to move into the contentious tribal area.

The sharp differences between the United States and Pakistan over what to do about North Waziristan were the most visible signs of the schizophrenic relationship that existed between the two ostensible allies. Pakistan had helped the United States bring a substantial number of senior Al Qaeda operatives to justice. It had permitted the United States to use Predator drones to attack hundreds of Al Qaeda and Taliban targets in the tribal areas despite withering criticism at home. As was revealed in early 2009, some of the drones even operated out of Pakistani territory from a remote base in the interior of Baluchistan. Many of them hit their targets thanks to intelligence provided by the Pakistanis. Pakistani support was also critical to U.S. operations in Afghanistan. As the Pakistani response to the U.S. helicopter incursions into the tribal areas clearly demonstrated, the United States was heavily dependent on Pakistani goodwill in supplying its forces in Afghanistan. But when it came to supporting U.S. goals in that country, the Pakistanis had proved to be far more of an adversary than a friend. They had also failed in their efforts to track down Osama bin Laden, despite the widely held belief that he was hunkered down somewhere on their territory. An exasperated Secretary of State Hillary Clinton had told Pakistani newspaper editors during an October 2009 visit that she found it hard to believe no one in the Pakistani government knew where bin Laden was.

The United States, for its part, had provided the Pakistanis with considerable material and financial support. In 2004, it had designated Pakistan a major non-NATO ally, one of only fourteen worldwide, making it eligible for the priority delivery of defense matériel. (India is not one of the fourteen.) By 2010, the United States was providing Pakistan with almost $2 billion in annual security assistance, much of it designed to defray the costs of Pakistan army operations in the tribal areas. The United States had also agreed to sell Pakistan advanced F-16 aircraft and unarmed surveillance drones, ostensibly for use against the Taliban, but which could potentially be employed against India. The United States had flattered the Pakistanis by agreeing to establish a wide-ranging "strategic dialogue" featuring regular meetings at the foreign minister level. A former senior Pakistani diplomat told me the Pakistanis liked it because it provided them with a forum in which the United States had to listen to what they had to say.

On the civilian side, assistance to Pakistan had reached $1.5 billion a year, thanks to the Kerry-Lugar Bill passed in 2009. Despite the largesse involved, the final passage of Kerry-Lugar had actually ignited a firestorm of protest inside Pakistan. The problem was not the money; the Pakistanis found the language in the bill condescending and accusatory, calling on them to end their support for terrorism and requiring the Obama administration to certify that the army was not trying to subvert "the political or judicial processes" of the country. The situation only worsened when the United States announced plans to significantly expand its diplomatic facilities in Islamabad and nearly double the size of its embassy staff. This helped generate wild rumors that the United States was sending in a thousand additional marine guards and had hired the Blackwater security firm to perform various nefarious deeds. It turned out that many of the new staffers were being brought in to monitor how the Kerry-Lugar money was being spent— justified, perhaps, but hardly a vote of confidence in the honesty of Pakistani end users. This development played directly into Pakistani stereotypes about the United States and its ultimate intentions in Pakistan. The Americans really were moving in and trying to take over. A Pew Research poll taken several months later revealed that almost 60 percent of Pakistanis regarded the United States as an enemy.

The Pakistani authorities had also been angered by these events. They took the money but, in a foretaste of the border-closing incident, refused to issue visas to incoming embassy personnel. They also began harassing U.S. diplomats as they drove around the capital, pulling them over and insisting on searching their vehicles. This unseemly spectacle went on for months. It was a relatively small payback for what they regarded as chronic U.S. insensitivity to Pakistani sensibilities and concerns. As always, the Pakistanis were most unhappy at the unwillingness of the United States to respond to their concerns about India. The Americans hammered them over Mumbai but refused to do much of anything about Kashmir. They were well aware that the Obama administration had initially planned to give Richard Holbrooke, the former UN ambassador appointed to serve as senior envoy for Pakistan and Afghanistan, a Kashmir mandate, but had backed off in the face of Indian opposition.

Just as frustrating was U.S. refusal to take Pakistani concerns about the Indian presence in Afghanistan seriously. Far from telling the Indians to cool it, U.S. officials continued to praise the Indian role there, denying that it posed any real danger to Pakistan. As far as the United States was concerned, the best way for Pakistan to address its Afghan security concerns was to cozy up to the Karzai government. This was a hard sell given the chronic suspicions and animosity that the Pakistani authorities and Karzai harbored toward each other. At the end of the day, neither the United States nor Pakistan was prepared or able to satisfy the other on the issues they regarded as most important. They had done a lot for each other, but not nearly enough. Suspicion and mistrust continued to cast deep shadows over the relationship.

In December 2010 the CIA withdrew its station chief from Islamabad after death threats were made against him. U.S. officials told *The New York Times* they believed that ISI had blown his cover. Then, in late January 2011, relations took an even more dramatic turn for the worse when a U.S. diplomatic-passport holder named Raymond Davis was taken into custody in Lahore after shooting to death two Pakistanis he claimed were trying to rob him. The incident inflamed public opinion in Pakistan, which was further outraged by subsequent U.S. assertions that Davis enjoyed diplomatic immunity and should be immediately released. It was later revealed that Davis was a contractor working for a mysterious CIA team in Lahore whose activities were previously unknown even to ISI. This seemed to confirm the worst Pakistani suspicions about what the Americans were up to in their country. Pakistani officials claimed that the CIA team had been engaged in surveilling the activities of local Islamic radicals. They also asserted that the two men killed were not robbers but ISI informants detailed to follow Davis. Although the Pakistanis did not say so directly, the Islamic radicals who were under CIA surveillance were almost certainly members of Lashkar-e-Taiba, which is the only radical Islamic group based in the Lahore area. Given the sensitive nature of Pakistani relations with the Lashkar, this is not something that ISI would have taken kindly to. It also raised the specter that the CIA might be engaged in similarly unfriendly activities elsewhere in Pakistan. The local Punjabi provincial authorities, led by the opposition PML-N, decided to bring murder charges against Davis despite U.S. insistence that he possessed diplomatic immunity. The Zardari government, already badly weakened by a host of domestic failings and unnerved by the intense public anger over the affair, proved reluctant to intervene.

The matter was finally settled in March, after ISI obtained a CIA commitment to seek its permission prior to setting up operations of the Lahore variety. A face-saving deal was arranged in which the United States agreed to pay the relatives of the two victims *diyat* (blood money) in return for their acquiescence in having the charges dropped. Davis was on a plane out of Pakistan before the Pakistani public even knew he had been released. The use of diyat, a rarely invoked element of sharia law, to resolve the matter helped to dampen down protests led by the Jamaat-e-Islami.

Any improvement in relations that might have flowed from the conclusion of the affair was dashed the very next day when U.S. missiles claimed forty-eight lives in an attack in North Waziristan, one of the highest body counts of the Predator war. Although the United States insisted that the victims were terrorists, the Pakistanis vehemently denied this. A senior Peshawar journalist who investigated the incident claimed that the missiles had struck a local tribal *jirga* called to discuss leasing arrangements for a local chromite mine. General Kayani led the chorus of shrill Pakistani protests in what appeared to be an effort to force the United States to end or sharply curtail its Predator campaign. After more than two years of sullen acquiescence in the face of ever more frequent drone attacks, the Pakistanis were beginning to act as if they had had enough.

But even worse was yet to come. On May 1, 2011, in what will no doubt linger as one of most audacious and successful commando raids in military history, the United States sent special forces deep into Pakistani territory on a mission to kill Osama bin Laden. He was not hunkered down in some cave in the tribal areas as had previously been thought, but was finally run to ground in a massive compound on the outskirts of Abbottabad, a city in Khyber Pakhtunkhwa only thirty miles north of Islamabad. Abbottabad was not just any city. It was an army city, home to the Pakistan Military Academy at Kakul, the Pakistani counterpart to West Point. The bin Laden compound was situated only a short distance away, in an affluent neighborhood where many retired army officers also lived. The commando operation, conducted by a Navy SEAL strike team ferried in by helicopters from Afghanistan, was reportedly carried out without the knowledge or consent of the Pakistani authorities. Although Secretary of State Hilary Clinton declared that intelligence provided by Pakistan had helped put the United States on bin Laden's trail, the Pakistanis were deeply embarrassed by the incident. Not only had they not been trusted with advance knowledge of the operation, it had been conducted under their very noses. There was no glossing over the fact that bin Laden had chosen to hide out in a city dominated by the Pakistan army. The army either knew nothing about his presence, suggesting incompetence, or was aware of the fact he was there and did nothing.

These explosive events, coming almost a full decade after 9/11, served to highlight the competing interests and chronic mistrust that drove U.S.-Pakistani relations. They were allies, not by choice but of necessity, who found it difficult to resist viewing each other as adversaries. It seemed like the only real glue left holding the relationship together was fear of the consequences of letting it fall apart.

9. The Shape of Things to Come

It had begun with good intentions. Pakistan had first used religiously motivated fighters, the legendary mujahideen, to promote its foreign policy goals during the Soviet occupation of Afghanistan. The United States had wholeheartedly supported this effort and was Pakistan's primary ally and benefactor in the decade-long struggle to drive the Soviets from the country. The two sides had seen eye to eye on Afghanistan back then. And it had worked. It worked so well the Pakistanis decided to continue using radical Islamists as low-cost weapons of war. And why not? They had been able to control them in Afghanistan. Surely they could control them now. And, once again, it had seemed to work quite well at first. The jihadists made life miserable for the Indians in Kashmir, and their Taliban surrogates quickly swept to power in Afghanistan. The Pakistanis were on a roll. But then it had all started to unravel. These groups were prepared to cooperate, but only up to a point. They were driven by religious zeal, not by any desire to help the feudal Pakistanis, most of whom practiced a form of Islam they despised. The Taliban would not turn over bin Laden. The jihadists kidnapped and beheaded young Western backpackers in Kashmir and attacked the Indian parliament in New Delhi. After 9/11, many of these former instruments of Pakistani foreign policy would turn increasingly and ruthlessly against the state. By then they had gained a powerful foothold inside Pakistan itself, where they continued to grow and spread, year after year, like some inexorable metastasizing cancer. It began with good intentions. But how is it going to end?

A good deal could depend on what eventually happens in Afghanistan. If the Pakistanis could wave a magic wand, they would conjure up an Afghanistan dominated by reliably pro-Pakistani secular Pashtuns. But there are no such animals. There is only Hamid Karzai, and he is hardly their friend. They see themselves forced to choose between an Afghanistan dominated by the Tajik and Uzbek descendants of the Northern Alliance, whom they are convinced will make common cause with India, and one dominated by the Afghan Taliban. This is not a happy choice for them, but it is not a difficult one either. Despite everything that has happened since 9/11, they continue to regard India as the more serious threat. The Indians, after all, are certainly their enemy, while the Afghan Taliban are only potentially so. In their minds it may not even be a matter of choice anymore. They seem to have concluded that the Afghan Taliban are not going to be defeated, either by the United States, while it remains in Afghanistan, or by the Afghan army once the United States leaves. Although the Pakistanis may be amenable to a negotiated settlement, their interests could be served just as well by a continuing stalemate. As long as the Afghan Taliban maintain their insurgency, Indian ambitions in Afghanistan are blocked, yet they do not have to face the consequences of an Afghan Taliban regime in Kandahar or Kabul.

And those consequences do worry the Pakistanis. They could not bend the Afghan Taliban to their will before 9/11, and there is little reason to believe they could do so now. This is why they may favor negotiating a power-sharing arrangement in Kabul that might possibly serve to constrain the Taliban. On the other hand, it has probably also occurred to them that a coalition government might be only a way station on the road to a complete Taliban takeover. In coalition or not, they undoubtedly hope that a Taliban regime restored to power in Kabul would be a friendly one or, at least, not develop into an adversary and make common cause with their Pakistani Taliban enemies. This hope rests on the fact that they provided Mullah Omar and the Haqqanis with safe haven and material support when they could just as easily have abandoned them. The Afghan Taliban have repaid this kindness by trying to help the Pakistanis with their Pakistani Taliban problem.

As we have seen, the Haqqanis, in particular, have consistently pressed their Pakistani counterparts not to make war on the Pakistani state. This has paid real dividends with the likes of Hafiz Gul Bahadur and Maulvi Nazir. But Afghan Taliban efforts have also been self-serving, since their primary objective has not been to help the Pakistanis but to persuade their Pakistani brethren to refocus their efforts on Afghanistan. So what happens if and when they do return to power in Afghanistan? Many Pakistanis believe the Afghan Taliban will inevitably turn against Pakistan and support the Pakistani Taliban in their war against the state. I heard a well-known Pakistani journalist make just such a prediction at a public lecture, treating it as if it were a foregone conclusion. But the people who actually run Pakistan must hope, and may even believe, that the Afghan Taliban would have little choice but to cooperate with them, since their alternative would be almost total global isolation.

The United States, for its part, will continue its sometimes heavy-handed efforts to pry the Pakistanis away from their support for the Afghan Taliban. But the United States has never been able to paint a picture of an alternative Afghan end state that the Pakistanis find attractive. In Hamid Karzai it backed a known Pakistani foe. It has done nothing to respond to Pakistani concerns about the Indian presence in Afghanistan, and almost certainly would be unable to do much about it even if it tried. The United States is unwilling to jeopardize its expanding relationship with the nascent South Asian superpower, and the Indians would not take kindly to any U.S. effort to pressure them on Afghanistan. Unable to satisfy Pakistani concerns about the Indian presence there, the United States has instead offered substantial financial and military support and a pledge to remain permanently engaged in the region, and with Pakistan itself. The ministerial-level strategic dialogue between the two countries that was launched in March 2010 was meant to demonstrate this enduring commitment. The implicit message is that the Pakistanis do not need to worry about the Indian presence in Afghanistan, Northern Alliance domination of the Afghan government and army, and the fact that Hamid Karzai does not like them, because the United States will not allow anything bad to happen. The problem is that even if the United States is sincere, it has been far too much of a fair-weather friend in the past for the Pakistanis to trust its assurances.

Although the Pakistanis may doubt U.S. sincerity and staying power, it is hard to imagine the United States abandoning the region altogether so long as Al Qaeda retains a significant presence there. This will remain true even if the United States begins withdrawing forces from Afghanistan without having dealt a decisive blow to the Afghan Taliban or before negotiating a power-sharing arrangement in Kabul. The United States will almost certainly want to continue its Predator campaign so long as there are Al Qaeda targets to be had in the tribal areas. Nonetheless, the Pakistanis may believe that with the death of Osama bin Laden, U.S. interest in who ends up running things in Kabul will inevitably begin to wane. As the Pakistanis see it, the United States was already anxious to leave Afghanistan, and the death of bin Laden will only serve to accelerate the process. This would clearly work to their advantage, since they would find it much easier to play their Afghan Taliban card against the dreaded Indian presence. This is probably the best reason for believing that the Pakistanis really didn't know that bin Laden was encamped in Abbottabad, although the possibility that some in the army or government knew about it but did nothing cannot be completely ruled out. The Pakistanis may also hope that the death of bin Laden will help loosen the ties that have bound the Afghan Taliban to Al Qaeda. As we saw in the previous chapter, they would like to see the Haqqanis rid themselves of Al Qaeda once and for all as part of negotiations leading to a coalition arrangement in Kabul. This is an outcome that the United States could almost certainly live with if it resulted in the destruction of Al Qaeda or its permanent expulsion from the region.

But the Pakistanis have more reasons than just this for wanting to see Al Qaeda depart. Al Qaeda was a major catalyst in turning the Pakistani Taliban against them, and despite the death of bin Laden, it continues to operate as a shadowy presence in the tribal areas, collaborating with the Tehrik-e-Taliban and its Punjabi allies in orchestrating the domestic terrorism campaign. Its presence on Pakistani soil also constitutes a time bomb ticking away at the heart of U.S.-Pakistani relations. What, after all, would happen if there were another 9/11, similar in magnitude to the first, and traceable back to Al Qaeda in the tribal areas? In the aftermath of the first 9/11, the United States attacked and occupied Afghanistan, driving the Taliban out of power and forcing the leadership of Al Qaeda to flee into Pakistan. If another 9/11 were to occur, the political pressure in the United States to retaliate with a response of similar magnitude would be overwhelming. The best the Pakistanis could hope for in such circumstances might be an offer to conduct joint operations aimed at ridding the tribal areas of Al Qaeda once and for all. Drones would no longer be enough. The United States would want to undertake a far more substantial effort, featuring U.S. boots on the ground and combat aircraft in the sky. Lots of them.

No one can say with complete confidence how the Pakistanis would respond. Given the dramatic circumstances that would, by definition, accompany another 9/11, it is possible, perhaps even likely, they would acquiesce. This, after all, was the course they chose after the first 9/11. They have no more reason now to make an enemy of the United States than they had back then. The difference is that this time around Pakistani territory would itself serve as ground zero for U.S. military operations. We have already seen how adamantly the Pakistanis object to violations of their sovereignty and how mistrustful they are of U.S. intentions. Some Pakistan watchers believe that the presence of U.S. troops on Pakistani soil could precipitate a mutiny in the Pakistan army, with soldiers deserting to join the Pakistani Taliban in confronting the U.S. forces. Although some Pakistanis might feel sympathy for the United States in the immediate aftermath of another 9/11, this would almost certainly prove to be a rapidly wasting asset. Unless there were immediate successes on the ground accompanied by early U.S. withdrawal from Pakistani territory, opposition to the U.S. presence could be expected to accelerate rapidly. At any step along the way, from uneasy acquiescence at a U.S. presence at the outset to growing demands that the U.S. withdraw later on, the situation could begin to spiral out of control. This is not a road the Pakistanis want to go down.

For this reason, they must surely hope that if the Haqqanis prove unwilling to jettison Al Qaeda, they will at least take it with them. This is the other benefit the Pakistanis foresee in trying to broker a deal to bring the Afghan Taliban back into government in Afghanistan. The Haqqanis would no longer need to remain in North Waziristan and could move their forces permanently back across the Durand Line. As we have seen, one of the primary reasons the Pakistanis have not seriously gone after the Mehsud forces taking refuge in North Waziristan is fear of coming to blows with the Haqqanis. If the Haqqanis left, this would no longer be an issue. If the Mehsud Taliban were to decamp for Afghanistan along with them, so much the better.

This, or something like it, seems to be the Pakistani plan. But the reality will almost certainly be different. The Pakistanis have kept the Afghan Taliban on their good side for a decade now, and their bottom-line goal is to keep it that way. Their nightmare scenario, on the other hand, would be to see them return to power in Afghanistan only to make common cause with the Pakistani Taliban and Al Qaeda against them. It is no small testament to their animus toward India that they are prepared to risk this outcome in order to preclude the possibility of India emerging as the dominant outside power in Afghanistan. Much will obviously depend on the ultimate success of U.S. efforts there. So long as the Afghan Taliban remain dependent on Pakistani protection and support, they are unlikely to add to the radical Islamic threat facing Islamabad. But if they are able to shake free of that dependency at some point down the road, all bets are off. As the former senior army officer cited in the previous chapter said to me in insisting that the Afghan Taliban were not an ideal solution to Pakistan's problems in Afghanistan, "a mullah is still a mullah."

While the Afghan Taliban constitute a potential threat, the Pakistani Taliban and their Al Qaeda mentors remain a very real one. The army has managed to drive them out of Swat and South Waziristan and has engaged in major fighting in many of the remaining tribal areas, with the exception of North Waziristan. As we have seen, the Pakistanis have employed almost a third of the unit strength of their regular army and most of the Frontier Corps in the effort. But the Pakistani Taliban, by themselves, do not pose an existential threat to the Pakistani state. There was never any danger they could move beyond the tribal areas and Khyber Pakhtunkhwa into the Punjabi heartland. The Pakistan army is far too determined and formidable a force to permit that to happen. The question was whether the Pakistani Taliban would be able to permanently wrest control of some or all of the Pashtun areas of Pakistan from the state. The robust Pakistani reaction to Buner, jointly agreed to by the civilian and army leadership, demonstrated that the people who govern Pakistan were not prepared to abandon them. Now that the army has managed to take back much of the ground that had originally been lost, it remains to be seen just how far it will be able, or willing, to go.

A former senior army officer who remains well plugged in to current army thinking told me he had serious doubts the army would be able to defeat the remaining Pakistani Taliban forces while holding on to the territory it had already liberated. He seemed to suggest the army had sent all the troops into the region it felt it could reasonably spare and still defend the country against the Indian threat. He also voiced considerable frustration, bordering on despair, at the failure of civilian security forces to pick up the slack. This is a common army complaint. The feudal politicians want the army to protect them against the depredations of the radical Islamists but are unwilling to help ease the pressure the army is facing by building up civilian security forces. That would be expensive. It could also prove dangerous to their political health, since larger and more professional police forces might threaten the kleptocratic practices that are a necessary concomitant of patronage politics. Such attitudes are symptomatic of a wider abdication of responsibility by the civilians in the face of the growing radical Islamic threat. Unprepared to come to grips with the predicament facing their country and unwilling to fundamentally alter their feudal ways of doing business, they have tried to turn the whole sorry mess over to the army. One sure sign of this was the almost unprecedented decision taken by President Zardari in the summer of 2010 to extend the term of Ashfaq Kayani as army chief for an additional three years.

If the army is willing, and able, to maintain something like its current troop strength in the tribal areas and Swat, it probably can keep the Pakistani Taliban on the run. Whether it has the ability to comprehensively defeat them is quite another matter. Many of the Pakistani Taliban who once ruled over Swat and South Waziristan have simply fled elsewhere. Those who fled into the Orakzai and Mohmand tribal agencies were subsequently attacked in their turn, but many of the fleeing forces appear to have made their way into North Waziristan. As we have seen, the army has been reluctant to launch an offensive into the region because the Haqqani network is based there. But this is also where the strongest concentration of Taliban forces, both Afghan and Pakistani, currently resides. Even if the Haqqanis attempt to get out of harm's way by moving to Kurram agency, the army worries that it lacks the ability to defeat the Pakistani Taliban in North Waziristan while holding on to the territory it has captured elsewhere. Despite the earlier army victories, these areas remain something less than totally secure. Although the army continues to garrison them and most of the civilian population has returned, so have the Pakistani Taliban, not in the strength necessary to contest army control but in sufficient strength to launch hit-and-run attacks against army forces, harass and intimidate selected communities, and carry out assassinations and other terrorist attacks.

The Pakistani Taliban have been able to do this despite the fact that almost a third of the unit strength of the regular Pakistan army is deployed in the tribal areas and Swat. But there is no guarantee the army will be prepared or able to stay in these areas in this kind of strength indefinitely. Although the army has said it will remain for as long as necessary, outside events, such as a major crisis with India, could compel it to withdraw forces from the region. The Pakistani Taliban would be certain to take advantage of this, and the Pakistanis could quickly find themselves back at square one. Even if this does not happen, recent events suggest that the Pakistani Taliban should be able to hang on indefinitely as a potent insurgent force. Despite their substantial loss of territory since Buner, they remain capable of launching guerrilla attacks against army forces throughout most of the region, and their ability to prosecute their domestic terrorism campaign in Khyber Pakhtunkhwa appears undiminished. In this they seem to be following in the footsteps of their Afghan Taliban brethren, who were swept from power in Afghanistan only to return with a vengeance as a potent insurgent foe. The outcome of this struggle is also of considerable importance to the United States. The assassination of Baitullah Mehsud in August 2009 by Predator missiles appears to have had the unintended consequence of converting his forces into committed enemies of the United States. His successor, Hakimullah Mehsud, was directly responsible for the suicide bombing that killed seven CIA operatives at a remote base in eastern Afghanistan only three months later. This act of apparent revenge was followed in May 2010 by a failed car bombing in Times Square. It was carried out by Faisal Shahzad, a naturalized Pakistani American, who had traveled to the tribal areas of Pakistan to pursue jihad and been recruited and trained by the Pakistani Taliban to carry out the attack.

Despite the formidable challenge the Pakistani Taliban continue to pose, as a military force they remain a purely regional threat, essentially confined to the Pashtun areas of northwestern Pakistan. By themselves, even with the assistance of their Al Qaeda mentors, they cannot contend for state power in Pakistan. A much greater danger lies in their growing collaboration with their like-minded Punjabi counterparts, drawn from Deobandi groups headquarted in the Seraiki belt, who, as we have seen, have increasingly been grouped together under the nom de guerre of Punjabi Taliban. It is Punjabi Taliban who have carried out the most audacious attacks in the Pakistani heartland, including the attack on the Sri Lankan cricket team in Lahore and the assault on army headquarters in Rawalpindi. As we have seen, many of these Punjabi Taliban cut their terrorist teeth in the tribal areas, fighting and training alongside their Pashtun and Al Qaeda comrades. They also benefit from a seemingly inexhaustible pool of potential recruits, drawn from the Deobandi mosques and madrassas in the region, which remain unmolested by the Pakistani authorities. But these forces have not yet congealed into a single operational entity, either among themselves or in cooperation with the Pakistani Taliban. Should this ever occur, they would pose a much more serious threat.

Nonetheless, the extent of this threat needs to be kept in perspective. No one has any firm grasp of the overall size of Punjabi Taliban forces, but there appear to be far fewer of them than of the Pashtun variety. Estimates of the number of Pakistani Taliban in the tribal areas and Swat themselves vary widely, but I have seen figures ranging from thirty to more than fifty thousand. The Mehsud forces in South Waziristan, for example, were believed to number between ten and twenty thousand men at the beginning of Operation Path to Salvation. But the Lashkar-e-Jhangvi, one of the major component groups of the Punjabi Taliban, is many times smaller than this and may number no more than a few hundred militants. No one knows for sure how many Punjabis have made their way to the tribal areas for training and to fight alongside their Pashtun counterparts, but one report attributed to Pakistani intelligence sources estimated that two thousand Punjabis had joined the Mehsud forces between 2005 and 2007. The Pakistani interior minister, Rehman Malik, told reporters in the spring of 2010 that the government had put 729 militants from south Punjab on its wanted list. This is certainly only a fraction of overall Punjabi Taliban strength, but they still probably add up to no more than ten thousand militants in total and quite possibly a good deal fewer.

The Punjabi Taliban have been responsible for the majority of the most spectacular terrorist attacks in Pakistan since Lal Masjid, but these remain relatively few in number and are at best monthly rather than weekly occurrences. This suggests that only a small handful— hundreds at most—are directly involved in planning and carrying out attacks. The majority of terrorist attacks in Pakistan continue to take place in Khyber Pakhtunkhwa and are presumably perpetrated by the Pashtun variety of Taliban, thanks to their greater numbers and the general chaos existing in the region. Nonetheless, the Punjabi Taliban, with their more sensational attacks, have succeeded in terrorizing the civilian population and roiling the feudal political class. They have created an impression of threat that exceeds their actual accomplishments. The fact is that they have not seized any territory, taken over any government buildings or institutions, or increased the frequency and destructiveness of their attacks to the point where it disrupts the rhythm of daily life. Whether this reflects their relatively small numbers or simply a lack of ambition is not completely clear. But it seems safe to conclude that, for the moment at least, the Punjabi Taliban, by themselves, or in conjunction with the Pakistani Taliban and their Al Qaeda allies, do not constitute a mortal threat to the state. They can make life miserable for ordinary Pakistanis caught in their path and worry the councils of the great, but they cannot contend for state power. The threat they pose remains far more potential than real. But if they continue to grow in number and succeed in developing a more unified organizational structure, they will undoubtedly present an increasingly serious threat. For the moment, most Pakistanis will tell you that being another Algeria is bad enough.

The threat would increase substantially if the radical Islamic forces that have not yet turned against the state someday decided to do so. This includes, first and foremost, the Lashkar-e-Taiba. But it also includes the surviving remnants of Jaish-e-Mohammed, as well as the Sipah-e-Sahaba, some of whose members continue to contest local elections in south Punjab, occasionally with the support of the mainstream political parties. As we have seen, the Lashkar-e-Taiba, as the best-organized and most professionally run radical Islamic group in Pakistan, with trained cadres numbering twenty thousand or more, currently poses the most serious potential threat to the state. Although Mumbai precipitated a crisis in confidence between Lashkar and the authorities, the two sides appear to have weathered it with their relationship relatively intact. As has been true from the beginning, the future well-being of the relationship will depend in large part on developments in relations between Pakistan and India, particularly over Kashmir. Mumbai can be viewed as a Lashkar shot across the government bow, warning it away from a peace process with India that appeared to be going nowhere.

The Lashkar succeeded in bringing the peace process to an end but left the Pakistanis wondering what to do next. Mumbai made clear they needed to find some kind of gainful employment for the Lashkar or face the prospect of future unpleasantness. This is why it came as little surprise when evidence began to mount of an increasing Lashkar presence in Afghanistan. It was blamed for several attacks against Indian officials and relief workers, including suicide bombings of two guesthouses in the heart of Kabul frequented by Indians in the spring of 2010. U.S. forces have also encountered Lashkar fighters in eastern Afghanistan, suggesting they may be operating alongside the Haqqani network. What better way to wean the Lashkar away from contemplating another Mumbai than to enlist them in countering the Indian presence on the far side of the Durand Line? This also relieved the Pakistanis of any early need to contemplate the most obvious alternative: to renew their active support for jihadist infiltration into Kashmir.

As matters stood, things were going badly enough for the Indians in Kashmir even without the jihadists. The years immediately following 9/11 had been relatively quiet ones in the valley as war-weary Kashmiris retreated into themselves. But this began to change in the summer of 2008 when massive protests erupted over an Indian decision to transfer a hundred acres of Kashmiri land to a Hindu group that needed housing for pilgrims visiting a local shrine. The largest demonstration attracted a half million people, and sporadic clashes with security forces resulted in several dozen deaths. Protests continued the following summer after Indian investigators absolved local police of responsibility in the rape and deaths of two Kashmiri women. The summer of 2010 saw the situation worsen, as tens of thousands of Kashmiris came together in demonstration after demonstration against Indian rule. Most featured angry stone-throwing youths, more than one hundred of whom were killed for their efforts when Indian paramilitary forces fired into the crowds using live ammunition. The reawakening of the Kashmiri intifada suggested that the Muslim majority of Kashmir remained resolutely opposed to Indian rule. This was borne out by a Chatham House poll conducted in the autumn of 2009. The percentage of people in the various districts that make up the Vale of Kashmir who favored independence from India ranged from a low of seventy-four to a high of ninety-eight. Most of the naysayers were presumably supporters of the pro-Indian collaborationist government of Omar Abdullah, grandson of the Lion of Kashmir.

The other interesting result of the poll was the fact that no more than 7 percent in any district favored becoming part of Pakistan. Most Kashmiris were aware of what was going on inside its Islamic neighbor—chronic poverty, feckless feudal rule mixed with military dictatorship, radical Islamists on the rampage—and did not like what they saw. Nor were they impressed by the jihadist infiltrators the Pakistanis had sent their way. No more than 14 percent in any valley district believed that militant violence played a positive role in solving the Kashmir dispute. The plain fact of the matter is that no matter what they do, the Pakistanis are never going to get more out of the Indians on Kashmir than was put on the table during the negotiations that came close to succeeding back in 2007. It is simply a question of whether they will ever step up to the plate. Many in the Pakistani political establishment continue to dream of a Kashmir integrated into Pakistan, despite the fact that the Kashmiris themselves are overwhelmingly opposed to it. The passion that still lurks behind the Pakistani attitude, and the unfortunate consequences that continue to flow from it, was brought home to me in a conversation with a well-known, very senior former Pakistani official in the spring of 2010. In what struck me as an unguarded moment, this native Punjabi civilian with close ties to the army told me in a voice full of defiance that Pakistan would never move against the Punjabi jihadist groups who were active in the valley until Pakistan received satisfaction on Kashmir.

This, of course, is a recipe for continued tension between the two South Asian nuclear powers. The Pakistanis may have farmed the Lashkar-e-Taiba out to Afghanistan for the time being, but they could easily decide to resume their active support for jihadist infiltration into Kashmir at some point, particularly if relations with India do not significantly improve. One of the main reasons they have not done so, even after Mumbai, is continuing U.S. pressure. Refraining from actively supporting infiltration is one of the things the Pakistanis do for the United States. Although they will probably try to keep the Lashkar distracted and on a tight leash, they may prove no more successful than they were prior to Mumbai. The senior army officer I cited earlier in the chapter told me that ISI did not have the resources to monitor everything the Lashkar was doing since so many of its assets were directed toward the tribal areas. Unfortunately, any repetition of Mumbai could provoke a crisis that would force the army to shift forces back to the Indian frontier, putting at risk all its hard-won gains in the tribal areas and Swat. It could also lead to another war between India and Pakistan. How much, after all, can the Indians take? It might begin with Indian air attacks against suspected Lashkar training camps in Azad Kashmir. Although the United States would work hard to defuse the crisis, in a worst-case scenario events might spiral out of control. Inconclusive infantry skirmishing in the mountainous terrain along the Line of Control could give way to mechanized warfare across the broad Punjabi plains to the south. If the more numerous Indian tank divisions succeeded in breaking through Pakistani defenses, the Pakistanis could find themselves forced to choose between humiliating defeat and the first use of nuclear weapons in anger since Nagasaki.

These are just some of the calamities the Lashkar-e-Taiba could bring to Pakistan and the region even if it does not turn against the state. It has refrained from doing so in large measure because the Pakistanis continue to support its anti-Indian agenda, however much they may try to limit or channel it. The Lashkar may also share the Pakistanis' reluctance to risk a test of strength. It is certainly not obvious what the outcome would be. At the very least, turning against the state would force the Lashkar to move underground. Hafiz Saeed and company would have to abandon their headquarters complex at Muridke, jettison the charitable activities that have provided them with more than a veneer of respectability within Pakistani society, and evacuate their many training camps in Azad Kashmir. Their jihad against India would have to be put on the back burner. These consequences are certain to give its leadership pause. Nonetheless, many observers believe that conflict between Lashkar and the state is inevitable. A Pakistani journalist who has studied the Lashkar stressed to me that its ultimate goals are globalist in nature, similar to those of its Wahhabist cousins in Al Qaeda, and only temporarily and tactically directed at India. He was convinced that sooner or later it would conclude it had gotten all it was going to from its strange bedfellowship with the Pakistanis and would decide to move against the state.

Some analysts believe the Lashkar is already moving toward realizing its global ambitions and could in time pose an even more dangerous threat than Al Qaeda. The U.S. national intelligence director, Dennis Blair, told the Senate Intelligence Committee in February 2010 that the Lashkar already had European targets in its sights. This would take matters well beyond Mumbai. Although the Lashkar deliberately attacked hotels frequented by Westerners in the Indian financial capital, it was still at root an attack against Indian interests aimed at embarrassing the Indians. If the Lashkar were to begin carrying out terrorist spectaculars in Europe or the United States, on the other hand, the Western reaction would be swift and intense. The Pakistanis would no longer be able to respond by putting Hafiz Saeed under house arrest or prosecuting a few sacrificial lambs. They would have little choice but to move decisively or see their relationship with the United States come to a sudden and possibly violent end. Lashkar attacks against Western targets, therefore, would be the functional equivalent of the Lashkar turning against the state.

If the Lashkar did decide to turn against the state, it would prove a formidable foe, all the more so if it made common cause with the radical Deobandis and their own Wahhabist cousins in Al Qaeda. Although the Lashkar might not be able to take over Lahore in the span of a single day, as the Lahore journalist cited in chapter 8 would have us believe, it could pose a substantial threat, particularly if it succeeded in mobilizing a significant percentage of the twenty thousand or more militants it is believed to have trained. No one can say with any confidence how events would play out in such a scenario. Presumably, there would be a dramatic increase in the number of major terrorist attacks in Punjab, designed to terrify and demoralize the civilian population. Since the Punjab is a politician-rich environment, there would probably be a sharp increase in the number of assassination attempts against political figures and high-ranking government officials, designed to terrify and demoralize the civilian feudal class. This might be followed by assaults on police stations and the seizure of public buildings in cities and towns in the Seraiki belt and other areas of the province. Besieged here and there, would the police be able to cope with the situation, or would they flee as the Lahore journalist believed they would, and as so many of them actually did in the towns and villages of Swat?

There seems little doubt the civilian organs of government would quickly turn to the army if events threatened to get out of hand. But it is considerably less certain how the army would fare if driven from pillar to post in the urban landscapes of Punjab. The army is already overstretched on the far side of the Indus. Could it hang on in the tribal areas and Swat, provide what it regards as adequate coverage on its Indian border, while staging major operations in the Punjab? The answer obviously depends on the magnitude of the threat and the level of resources that would need to be diverted to the region. At some point it becomes something of a numbers game. The army cannot be everywhere. If there are too many bad guys doing too many bad things in too many places, even the army would be unable to cope. It is anybody's guess how the Pakistanis would react in such circumstances. There would no doubt be attempts at deal making, offers to implement sharia rule here and there in an effort to hold back the tide. I could foresee a Jamaat-e-Islami stage, in which the authorities, with the blessing, or at the instigation, of the army, turned to the Jamaat as a more respectable alternative to a complete jihadist takeover. Is there a point at which the army itself gives way, as the vaunted Iranian army did during the revolution in Iran? The army is the most powerful and professional organization in Pakistan, but every army has its breaking point. The key question is whether the forces of radical Islam could ever become strong enough to make good on something resembling the above scenario and actually take over the state.

The fact of the matter is that no one really knows and no one wants to find out. As bad as things now look to Pakistanis and outsiders alike—as bad as things are—these forces are still a very long way from being able to seriously contend for state power. The Lashkar-e-Taiba lacks the inclination while the radical Deobandi groups lack the strength. But this is the situation as it exists today. What happens in the years, and even decades, to come if these forces continue to strengthen, unchallenged by the state? The Pakistani authorities managed to put a temporary check on Pakistani Taliban ambitions following the humiliation of Buner, but they have done nothing to stop the spread of the radical mosques and madrassas that serve as recruiting centers for the radical Deobandi groups. A retired senior army officer I know well, the same individual whose concerns about the growing collaboration between the Pashtun and Punjabi Taliban were cited earlier, told me he had visited army headquarters shortly after the Musharraf coup and had raised this very subject with the top army leadership. He asked if the threat posed by radical Islamic groups had worsened during the preceding five years. They conceded that it had. He asked if they believed the threat was likely to increase during the next five years. They conceded that it was. Then why, he asked, didn't they do something about it? They told him it would be too difficult and they didn't have the resources to get the job done.

Maybe so. But this does not mean the army has not at least considered the matter. Several months after the Musharraf coup, I paid a visit to another former very senior army officer—someone who was indisputably in a position to know what he was talking about—who told me that Nawaz Sharif, during his second term as prime minister, had asked the army to put together a contingency plan to dismantle the radical groups. The general told me that the plan that emerged involved providing specialized training to selected army units. He was unwilling to say more, but he left me with the strong impression he was referring to something like a Night of the Long Knives, in which army commandos would swoop down on the major groups to decapitate their leadership. The plan, of course, has never been implemented and is presumably gathering dust somewhere out at army headquarters. It has, in any event, long since passed its sell-by date since most radical Deobandi leaders are now in hiding, many of them having taken refuge with the Pakistani Taliban. Tracking down those who remain in Punjab requires good intelligence and police work, both of which are lacking. As noted earlier, the army has most of its intelligence assets engaged in the tribal areas and may lack the resources even if they were tasked. Matters have not been helped by the fact that the Punjabi Taliban have singled out ISI for special treatment, car bombing ISI headquarters in Lahore as well as its offices in Multan, the largest city in south Punjab.

Perhaps even more worrisome over the longer term is the continuing unchecked growth in the number of radical mosques and madrassas. In the spring of 2010, the Pakistani interior minister admitted that the number of madrassas in the country had grown to more than twenty thousand. He said that almost half—44 percent—were located in the Seraiki belt. While many of these may not be feeder organizations for the radical Deobandi groups, there is probably a higher percentage of radical madrassas here than anywhere else in the country. Unlike the Punjabi Taliban, who have gone underground, these mosques and madrassas operate out in the open and are there for the taking. The barrier to action is fear. As one of my former senior army officer contacts told me, the government is reluctant to go after them because it fears creating more Lal Masjids. One such experience was bad enough, but what would happen if the authorities tried to shut down dozens, or even hundreds? This is another question that no one is eager to have answered. The tendency yet again, therefore, is to avoid conflict now and try to muddle through. But the longer nothing is done, the worse the problem becomes. There are worrying signs that a radical Islamic underclass has already begun to emerge in major Pakistani cities. I was particularly struck by an editorial in the Pakistani English-language newspaper the *Daily Times* in September 2009 asserting that the urban poor of Islamabad had become Talibanized, many no doubt suborned by these very mosques. If this is happening in Islamabad, it is also happening elsewhere. This is born out by the veteran Pakistan watcher Anatol Lieven, who noted a similar attitude among the urban poor during his own travels through the Seraiki belt and other parts of Punjab in 2009. The vast majority of these rootless men may not have joined any radical organizations, but they constitute a potentially mobilizable mass that could take to the streets if the country ever does begin lurching toward an Iranian solution.

As 2010 was drawing to an end, a new development raised further concerns about the extent of religious radicalization in Pakistan. It appeared in the form of a strident campaign organized by the traditionally tolerant Barelvi clergy to oppose changes in the draconian Zia-era blasphemy laws that were being mooted by the Zardari government. As we saw in chapter 8, Salmaan Taseer, the governor of Punjab and a strong proponent of changing the laws, was assassinated in early 2011 by a Barelvi member of his own security guard, who admitted he had acted out of religious motives. The assassination was subsequently praised by prominent Barelvi religious leaders and endorsed by the largest Barelvi organization in the country. But it was not just the

Barelvi clergy that supported the action. Lawyers at the Islamabad court where the perpetrator was arraigned strewed rose petals in his path as he was led in, and other seemingly Westernized Pakistanis also supported the killing. It is not yet clear what lies behind this development or whether it indicates the beginning of a major shift in attitudes within the Barelvi community. Blasphemy is a hot-button issue for most pious Muslims regardless of sectarian affiliation, and not necessarily or even probably linked to radical or political Islam. The Barelvi clergy may have seen the blasphemy issue as a cause it could use to rally its troops in the face of ongoing assaults on its ranks by more aggressive Deobandi proselytizers. Whatever the motivation, the episode sent shock waves through a secular political establishment that had failed to appreciate the intensity of popular attitudes on the blasphemy issue. It demonstrated that although political life in Pakistan is secular and feudal, it operates within an underlying culture that is as deeply religious as any in the world. The South Asian brand of Sufi Islam that is practiced in Pakistan is probably no less tolerant than it has ever been, but the blasphemy issue amply demonstrated that even it has its limits. Do ordinary Barelvis constitute a mobilizable mass that could someday be harnessed to a radical Islamic solution? The real danger here would be if the pirs who constitute the spiritual leadership of the Barelvi community ever decided to go down this path. Opposing changes in the blasphemy laws, even to the point of violence, is still a far cry from embracing radical Islam. Needless to say, if the mainstream Barelvi community ever did give way to widespread militancy, Pakistan, as a secular state, or perhaps as any kind of state at all, would be finished.

So where does it all end? Will the Punjab reach its own Buner moment, when the powers that be finally decide that enough is enough, or will events be allowed to play out according to something like the scenario laid out earlier in this chapter, with Punjab slowly but inexorably transforming itself into another Swat? The logic of the situation suggests that nothing much will be done anytime soon. Things are bad but not critical. The Punjabi Taliban can wreak a certain amount of havoc and destruction but cannot contend for state power. The radical mosques and madrassas that churn them out have learned their own lessons from Lal Masjid and are going about their business under the radar. The Lashkar-e-Taiba has not yet turned against the state. The situation in the tribal areas and Swat is better than it was before. The Pakistani Taliban have been driven from many of their strongholds and, although far from destroyed, do not loom as the imminent threat they once did. This is hardly a clarion call for decision makers whose default setting is inertia.

Although the Pakistanis may be reluctant to pick a fight in the Punjab, there are other things they could do to fend off the day of reckoning. The feudal politicians who purport to run the country could start taxing themselves and pump the money into a crash program to improve public education as an alternative to the madrassas. Increased investment in human capital could also help to modernize the economy and begin the long process of whittling away at the endemic poverty that makes the embrace of radical Islam an attractive alternative for many of the poor and dispossessed. These are long-term solutions, of course, and would take many years, perhaps decades, to produce meaningful results. But it makes no difference since the Pakistanis will do none of these things. They could at least spend some real money on increasing the size and professionalism of the police, but they are unlikely to do this either, unless the army forces them to. As I indicated earlier, the feudal politicians have tried to foist the whole sorry mess onto the army, which resents it. Needless to say, transferring even more power and responsibility to the army, while earning even more of its contempt, is hardly likely to enhance prospects for democracy in Pakistan.

The Pakistanis have already reached the point where they cannot move against the radical Islamist presence in Punjab without making things worse, at least in the short run. But the longer they wait, the more difficult the task is likely to become. If they do not begin closing down radical mosques and madrassas in some reasonable time frame, they may well end up having to fight the radical Deobandis, and eventually the Lashkar-e-Taiba, in the major cities of Punjab. But given their predilection for kicking serious problems down the road, it is hard to be optimistic that they will act anytime soon. Nonetheless, even if they do not act, I suspect a Buner moment will eventually come to the Punjab, when the incidence of domestic terrorism finally reaches intolerable limits or militant groups start to seize property. The Pakistanis may actually find themselves fortunate if this happens sooner rather than later, with the radical Islamists overreaching themselves, as they did at Buner. The longer these forces have to build up their strength, the more formidable their challenge will be. And even if the Pakistanis do someday move against them, the outcome may not be decisive. The government could easily find itself in a protracted conflict, with much destruction and suffering but no ultimate victor.

Will Pakistan eventually fall to the forces of radical Islam? I confess that a very large part of me finds it impossible to believe this could happen. This attitude is shared by most, if not all, of the veteran Pakistan watchers I know. How, after all, could a nation of 160 million people, most of whom espouse a relatively tolerant, nonthreatening brand of Islam, fall to a relatively small group of hard-core religious fanatics? Surely the army will prevent it from happening. The Pakistanis, as always, will find some way to muddle through. But we are viewing the question from the perspective of the present. Things may look considerably different five years, or ten years, or twenty years from now. The Algerians defeated their Islamic extremists but the shah of Iran fell victim to his. Russia gave way to a small group of Bolsheviks and Germany was handed over to the Nazis by conservatives who thought they could control Hitler. Each situation is unique, but the precedents are there. It is wise never to say never.

What seems far more certain is that Pakistan will be infected with radical Islam for a long time to come, regardless of any steps the Pakistanis may take to eradicate it. The events that followed Buner are revealing here. The army was able to chase the Pakistani Taliban from Swat and South Waziristan, but like a bad penny they keep turning up elsewhere. If the army cannot comprehensively defeat them, as seems likely, it may have to content itself with keeping them perpetually on the run. When and if the government does decide to move against the radical mosques and madrassas in Punjab, or is forced to confront a rising Punjabi Taliban tide in the urban landscapes of the Seraiki belt, resource constraints suggest the result could be more or less the same. There is also little reason to believe the Pakistanis will pick a fight anytime soon with the radical Islamic groups they continue to support, the Afghan Taliban and Lashkar-e-Taiba preeminent among them. As we have seen, whatever foreign policy advantages they may hope to gain from continuing to maintain relations with these groups, they are equally fearful of converting them into enemies.

This all points to one inescapable conclusion: whatever else happens, Pakistan is likely to occupy a position very near the center of the radical Islamic universe for years and even decades to come. The threat is likely to end, here as elsewhere, only when the descent into religious radicalism that has roiled parts of the Islamic world for the better part of the last three decades finally comes to an end. But that is an even larger subject and the topic for another book.

Little did the Pakistanis realize, when they began to run the mujahideen into Afghanistan thirty long years ago, that this was the future that awaited them. The Afghan mujahideen were religious fundamentalists, it was true, but their primary goal was to drive the Soviet invaders out of their homeland. They had a Jamaat-e-Islami view of the world, not a jihadist one. The fundamental mistake the Pakistanis made was failing to take account of the differences between the two. They were victims of bad luck when Osama bin Laden turned up in Afghanistan and befriended Mullah Omar, and victims of bad judgment in believing they could control the jihadists they had unleashed against their foes. They had learned some lessons along the way, but not nearly enough. As their clever plans began to unravel on the steps of the Indian parliament, in the rubble of the World Trade Center, and in the barren, unforgiving landscape of the tribal areas, so too did their hold on their improbable state. Pakistan had been founded in the dying embers of the British Raj amid great hope and enthusiasm. Yet little more than sixty years on, its survival as something that resembles the secular state for South Asian Muslims that its founder, Mohammed Ali Jinnah, had intended remains very much in doubt. It began with good intentions. But no one can say for certain how it will end.

10. The Final Unraveling

The forces of radical Islam in Pakistan may not be able to challenge the feudals and the army for state power just yet, but what if they did succeed in seizing the reins of power someday? What would happen then? One thing seems certain. If no one tried to do anything about it, Pakistan would quickly become a magnet for jihadists around the world. Al Qaeda would have an entire country to plan and exercise in, as well as ready access to international air and sea travel. There would be no more hunkering down in Pakistan for the remaining Al Qaeda leadership. Yes, it would be bad. But what would make it even worse, infinitely worse, is the fact that Pakistan has nuclear weapons. What would the jihadists do if they had the bomb?

Pakistan currently has more than one hundred warheads in its nuclear arsenal. These weapons, which are capable of causing damage on a Hiroshima scale, can be delivered by F-16 jet aircraft or by ballistic missiles, the most formidable of which may be able to hit targets up to fifteen hundred miles away. This would bring all the major cities of India within reach. Whether the jihadists would actually be able to make use of them, however, is another story. Marrying nuclear warheads to their delivery systems and then delivering them to their targets requires considerable manpower and technical expertise. In Pakistan, these resources are exclusively in the hands of the military.

If the Pakistani armed forces melted away in the process of a radical Islamic takeover, as happened to the Iranian army during the Islamic revolution, the jihadists might find themselves in possession of a nuclear arsenal of distinctly limited utility. This would probably be only a temporary setback since the army could be rebuilt and its nuclear expertise reconstituted. In the interim, the jihadists could still pose a serious threat to India and the West by smuggling individual warheads out of the country. In any event, this would be the only way they would be able to attack the United States in any reasonable time frame since Pakistani nuclear delivery vehicles cannot reach anywhere near that far.

India is not so lucky. If the Pakistan army and air force did not collapse and were prepared to cooperate with a jihadist regime, the Indians could find themselves in immediate jeopardy. The U.S.-based National Resources Defense Council estimated in a study released during the war scare that followed the May 2002 Jammu massacre that more than a million and a half Indians would die, and more than two million would be injured, if Pakistan were to drop Hiroshima-sized warheads on only five major Indian cities. This scenario posited that the warheads would be detonated far aboveground as was the case at Hiroshima. But ground burst weapons are easier to detonate and produce considerably more lethal radiation. In a second scenario, which posited the use of twelve ground burst weapons on seven Indian cities, it was estimated that more than ten million people would die from radiation alone. Attacks on this scale would not destroy India; the overwhelming majority of the population would survive. But the destruction of its major business and industrial centers could reduce India to a miserable backwater for decades. More bombs dropped on more targets would produce that much more misery. It is just these kinds of calculations that have helped deter India following jihadist spectaculars such as Mumbai. Even if India looked like it were decisively winning a conventional war with Pakistan, what good would it do them if the Pakistanis responded by attacking them with nuclear weapons?

One thing that might protect India from nuclear attack in the event of a jihadist takeover in Pakistan is its substantial Muslim population. Even the Lashkar-e-Taiba might think twice about killing tens or hundreds of thousands of its coreligionists. Their stated goal, after all, is to liberate the Muslim population of India, not to decimate it. Nonetheless, events could easily get out of hand. A nuclear ultimatum over Kashmir might have to be carried out if India decided to resist. The Lashkar might be able to persuade itself that its religious brethren in India were being martyred in a glorious cause. After all, its actions would be likely to result in the deaths of even larger numbers of Muslims inside Pakistan itself. But for this scenario actually to play itself out, the Pakistani military would have to go along and it would almost certainly balk at the prospect of deliberately committing nuclear suicide.

I find it difficult to believe the Pakistan army would do the bidding of jihadists in any event. While there are undoubtedly some officers who harbor jihadist sympathies, they are far too few to form anything like a critical mass. Whatever sympathies the army may have had toward the Pakistani Taliban and other radical Deobandis have long since been swept away by their battlefield casualties and the terrorist attacks they have suffered at their hands. Even more important, it is difficult—I am tempted to say impossible—to believe the army would ever willingly take orders from a jihadist regime. It may be willing to do business with the Lashkar-e-Taiba, but not to do its bidding. The army sees itself as the ultimate arbiter of Pakistani national security. It would not execute policies it regarded as disastrous to the future of the nation. Only a broken shell of an army would meekly do as it was told. At the end of the day, it would be the Pakistan army calling the shots. This is why any credible jihadist takeover of Pakistan would have to take place in the context of an army collapse.

The one gray area might be if a more radicalized version of the Jamaat-e-Islami were to emerge as a stopgap to a jihadist takeover. As we have seen, Zia was close to the Jamaat, and several high-ranking army officers, including the former ISI head Hamid Gul, have joined it following their retirement. To the extent that officers of a fundamentalist disposition are drawn to politics, they are drawn to the Jamaat. An academic expert who has written about the group told me there is pressure among its members to move in a more radical direction. Its leadership has pointedly refrained from criticizing the radical Deobandi groups for the domestic terrorism campaign, preferring instead to blame India or to conjure up conspiracy theories involving the Blackwater security firm. As far as the Jamaat is concerned, everything bad that has happened since 9/11 is the fault of the United States. Nonetheless, even a more radicalized Jamaat would be unlikely to pursue nuclear suicide. There is little doubt that its policies would be more bellicose toward India, and the possibility of confrontation over Kashmir would almost certainly be heightened, but the people who run the Jamaat are not fanatics, they do not engage in terrorism, and they can be deterred.

The real danger to the United States and its Western allies would be if radical Islamists who could not be deterred came to power in Pakistan. Al Qaeda, the radical Deobandi groups, and the Lashkar-e-Taiba have all committed multiple acts of terrorism and shown a penchant for great brutality and a callous disregard for human life. Given their propensity for suicidal and fidayeen attacks, and their belief that martyrdom in a jihadist cause will gain them accelerated entry into paradise, it is at least an open question whether they could be deterred. As we have seen, the greatest single threat that a jihadist regime would pose would be that of nuclear terrorism. Should such a government suddenly come to power in Pakistan, the United States would be faced with a mortal choice. It could seek to deter such an attack through the threat of massive retaliation, or it could strike quickly, attempting to seize or destroy the Pakistani nuclear arsenal before it could be diverted to terrorist ends.

There is speculation that the United States is already training Special Operations forces to deploy into Pakistan in a crisis to attempt to take control of its arsenal. The possibility has been raised most frequently in the context of concern that terrorists might be able to seize a nuclear warhead, possibly with the help of sympathetic army officers who have access to the material. But this concern is based on speculation rather than grounded in fact. Nuclear warheads are the most highly guarded artifacts in all of Pakistan. They are the crown jewels of the state. The army almost certainly invests far more resources in guarding them than its does in any other single activity. It is simply not credible that the army would store warheads at any location that might conceivably come under serious threat of terrorist attack or permit soldiers or civilian personnel suspected of harboring even the remotest sympathies for radical Islam to get anywhere near them.

This is the situation as it exists today. But if the army were to disintegrate in the face of a jihadist takeover, all the existing safeguards would presumably melt away. If there are concerns today that terrorists might be able to seize a warhead and either use it for nuclear blackmail or seek to detonate it somewhere in the United States, imagine the level of concern that would exist if jihadists were actually running the show in Islamabad. A nuclear armed Iran might be deterrable, but a jihadist Pakistan very likely would not be. It is easy to imagine that confronted with such a circumstance the United States would decide to strike first, deploying its specially trained commando units, if they exist, or attempting to bomb Pakistani warhead storage facilities, if they can be located. But even if the United States believed its efforts at securing or destroying Pakistani warheads had been largely successful, it could not be certain it had run the entire arsenal to ground. Nor could it, in any event, easily tolerate a jihadist regime, led by Al Qaeda or groups sympathetic to its cause, remaining in control of the sixth most populous country on earth.

The logic of the situation would seem to demand that the United States attempt to liberate the country from the jihadists. The challenge here is that the United States does not possess a large enough army to occupy and hold a country the size of Pakistan, which, by stipulation, would be inundated with jihadist forces. It could probably destroy all that was left of the Pakistani armed forces through the use of air power. But it would need considerable help to wrest physical control of the state away from the radical Islamists. In such circumstances, the obvious move would be to collaborate with India, whose own interest in driving the jihadists from power would be at least as strong. An Indo-American alliance could see the experience of Operation Enduring Freedom repeated on a much larger scale, with the United States providing the air power and India the bulk of the ground forces. This would be far from an easy task, particularly if, as seems likely, the jihadists retreated into the urban jungles of Punjab and Sindh, there to reinvent themselves as insurgent forces. In order to avoid catastrophic casualties to their own troops, the Indians might be tempted to use draconian methods, including siege tactics or artillery in urban settings, that would generate enormous suffering among the civilian population.

It is difficult to speculate on how far into Pakistan the Indians might feel inclined to push. Would they attempt to occupy the entire country, or perhaps call a halt at the Indus? Much could depend on what Afghanistan looked like at the time. At the very least they would want to bottle up the remaining jihadist forces and deny them ready access to the sea. This could militate in favor of seizing Punjab, Sindh, and the coastal areas of Baluchistan, while leaving the Pashtun areas on the far side of the Indus as a kind of jihadist no-man's-land. Once the dust had settled, the Indians and their U.S. allies would then face a critical political question: what to do about the areas of Pakistan that had been brought under their control. Should they attempt to reconstitute Pakistan politically, handing power back to civilian feudals while trying to reconstruct a less hostile Pakistani military? Or would they decide to incorporate the occupied territories into India, bringing about the final unraveling of the Pakistani state?

It would be the greatest of ironies if Pakistan ended its existence by being reabsorbed into India. As I have tried to make clear, it is not sympathy for radical Islam but animus toward India that has driven the Pakistanis to use jihadist groups for state ends. Although the idea itself initially emerged during the anti-Soviet jihad in Afghanistan, when the first of these groups was formed, it was the decision to employ them in support of the Kashmiri intifada that transformed what could have been an isolated phenomenon into a full-blown industry. Continuing Pakistani support for the Afghan Taliban in the wake of 9/11 has also been driven by concerns about the substantial Indian presence in Afghanistan and what it might mean for future Pakistani security. Nonetheless, if Osama bin Laden had never returned to Afghanistan, driven there by U.S. pressure on Sudan, the Taliban might still be the dominant power in that country and Pakistani support for radical Islamists might have remained a purely regional phenomenon, a bitter issue in Indo-Pakistani relations but little more. The Pakistanis, it is fair to say, have had their share of bad luck.

Bad luck or not, the Pakistanis now find themselves occupying center stage in what has become a global struggle between the forces of radical Islam and the West. Pulled this way and that, Pakistan has ended up becoming the most conspicuous victim of the jihadist forces whose rise to prominence it did so much to foster. Yet in spite of it all, the Pakistanis have been unwilling to completely abandon their relationship with radical Islamic groups, as their continuing ties to the Afghan Taliban and Lashkar-e-Taiba clearly demonstrate. Although it is true that the Pakistanis fear converting these groups into enemies, they persist in regarding them as strategic assets in their adversarial relationship with India. This has had enormous consequences for U.S. interests in the region. The safe haven the Pakistanis extended to the Afghan Taliban in the tribal areas and Baluchistan has directly contributed to current U.S. woes in Afghanistan. The Afghan Taliban have used these areas as staging grounds for mounting attacks and as sanctuaries into which they can retreat. Pakistani reluctance to go after the Afghan Taliban in the tribal areas may also have played a major role in enabling Al Qaeda central to survive relatively intact in the years since 9/11. After all, if the Pakistanis had gone after the Taliban from the very beginning, there might have been no safe place for Osama bin Laden to hide. The United States, in an effort to wean the Pakistanis away from the Afghan Taliban, has offered financial assistance and assurances of continuing engagement in the region. But it has not addressed Pakistani concerns about the Indian presence in Afghanistan. And this is why it has come up short. Like it or not, for the Pakistanis, concerns about India trump all others.

To be fair, there is probably very little the United States can do to satisfy the Pakistanis on Afghanistan. The Indians have justified their strong presence there on the grounds that they are helping to combat the spread of radical Islam in the region. The irony here is that their presence in Afghanistan has helped ensure continuing Pakistani support for the Afghan Taliban. However, even if the Indians could be persuaded to substantially lower their profile there, the Pakistanis would still worry that a Karzai-led, Northern Alliance–backed Afghan government could invite them back in once U.S. forces have left. The one development that might be able to change this basic calculus would be a fundamental improvement in Indo-Pakistani relations. This would require finding some kind of mutually agreeable resolution on Kashmir. The United States, however, has been extremely reluctant to intrude itself directly into the Kashmir dispute or to undertake any major diplomatic effort aimed at improving Indo-Pakistani relations. It has limited its involvement primarily to shouting encouragement from the sidelines or resorting to crisis diplomacy whenever the two sides begin lurching toward another war. The primary impediment to U.S. involvement has been Indian opposition. The Indians do not want outsiders meddling in their affairs and have clung tenaciously to their interpretation of the 1972 Simla agreement that their disputes with Pakistan must be settled through bilateral negotiations. As we saw in chapter 8, Richard Holbrooke, the senior envoy for Afghanistan and Pakistan until his death in December 2010, was originally supposed to be given an Indian and Kashmir mandate, but this was dropped in the face of strong Indian resistance.

Of course, if the United States wanted to, it could try to pressure the Indians into changing their position on outside involvement. But there is no evidence it has ever attempted to do so. The United States has worked hard to develop good relations with India, which it does not wish to jeopardize. India is a nascent superpower and a potential U.S. ally in contesting Chinese hegemony in Asia. A senior U.S. official with long experience working on Indian affairs confessed to me that there was also an element of romanticism in U.S. attitudes toward India that went beyond cold calculations of national interest. Even if this is an exaggeration, it speaks to the fact that, while U.S. relations with Pakistan are currently driven by necessity and riven with animosities and double-dealing, the U.S. relationship with India rests on much firmer ground. On the key issues that really matter to Pakistan, such as outside help in resolving the Kashmir dispute and the Indian presence in Afghanistan, the United States has always seemed to tilt in the direction of New Delhi. This is certainly how the Pakistanis perceive matters, and they resent it. If the United States had been willing to bend just a little in the direction of Pakistan, by making at least of show of pressing the Indians on Kashmir and Afghanistan, it might have succeeded in generating a modicum of good will with the Pakistanis and helped moderate some of the virulent anti-Americanism that is rampant in the country. But it has chosen not to do so.

That said, there is little reason to believe India would be amenable to U.S. pressure in any event, given the strength of its feelings on these issues and the absence of any obvious U.S. leverage. Even the U.S.-Indian nuclear deal, the centerpiece of recent U.S. efforts to reach out to the Indians, had plenty of critics in India. This lack of leverage also plagues the United States on the Pakistani side, given U.S. dependence on the use of Pakistani territory to supply its troops in Afghanistan. There is also justifiable concern that bringing too much pressure to bear on the Pakistanis could convert them into genuine adversaries and end up making matters a whole lot worse. What would the Pakistanis do if the United States started using Predators against Afghan

Taliban forces in Baluchistan or sent ground forces and manned combat aircraft into the tribal areas? This could lead the two sides down a
slippery slope toward armed confrontation and even war. Who knows
where it might end? The United States worries about radical Islamic
groups gaining control of a Pakistani nuclear warhead. But what if the
Pakistanis decided to give them one?

Short on leverage and confronted by a fanatical and stubborn foe,
the United States could be facing a very bleak future in Afghanistan.
Unless the Obama surge succeeds in fundamentally altering the situation on the ground, the United States may find itself forced to choose
between maintaining a permanent military presence in the country or
abandoning all or a significant part of it to the Afghan Taliban. The
latter outcome would risk a return to the situation that existed before
9/11, with Afghanistan once again serving as home base for Al Qaeda
as well as a magnet for disaffected anti-Western young Muslims from
around the world. India, for its part, also faces an uncertain future. In
the three decades that have passed since Simla, it has failed to resolve
its differences with Pakistan, and its stubborn refusal to accept outside
involvement seems guaranteed to perpetuate the status quo. Kashmir
is now in the throes of a second intifada and India controls it only by
the application of overwhelming force. If relations between India and
Pakistan fail to improve or deteriorate further, it is possible that Pakistan could decide to renew its active support for jihadist infiltration.
With the Lashkar-e-Taiba still intact and the ability of the Pakistanis
to rein it in as uncertain as ever, the Indians face the very real prospect
of future Mumbais. They are also left with the knowledge that any attempt at retaliation, such as attacking Lashkar training camps in Azad
Kashmir, carries with it the risk of war and nuclear confrontation with
Pakistan.

To add one final complication, even if Pakistan and India were
somehow able to compose their differences, the Pakistanis might not
profit from the exercise, at least in the short run. If they decided to
finally move against the Afghan Taliban, they would add one more
enemy to their mix. A peace deal with India on Kashmir along the lines
of the proposed 2007 agreement could end up being the catalyst that
drives the Lashkar-e-Taiba over the edge into outright opposition to
the state. In such circumstances, there would probably be very little the
United States or their newfound Indian friends could do to help them

in their distress. It is the Pakistanis who gave life to these forces and it will be up to them to root them out. The future is uncertain, and the fundamental question still lingers: Will they make the hard choices their circumstances demand of them, or will they continue dissembling until they are swept away?

Notes

Introduction

4 *finally landed*: I was serving at the U.S. embassy in Islamabad at the time of President Clinton's visit. Although I did not go out to the airport to greet the presidential party, I heard about the multiple aircraft and the unmarked business jet later in the day. But the exact number of aircraft and their landing sequence remained unclear to me and others at the embassy. As I started working on this book, I talked to Bruce Riedel, who was the special assistant to President Clinton responsible for South Asia at the time of the Islamabad visit and a passenger on the small unmarked business jet that actually carried the president. He worked closely with the Secret Service in making arrangements for the trip and was able to clarify for me the number and type of aircraft involved as well as their landing sequence.

1: An Improbable State

20 *division along communal lines*: The text of the Lahore Resolution, which emerged from the meeting, actually calls for the creation of independent states and does not even mention the name Pakistan. The operational paragraph reads as follows:

> Resolved that it is the considered view of this Session of the All-India Muslim League that no constitutional plan would be workable in this country or acceptable to the Muslims unless it is designed on the following basic principles, viz., that geographically contiguous units are demarcated into regions which should be constituted, with such territorial readjustments as may be necessary, that the

areas in which the Muslims are numerically in a majority as in the North Western and Eastern Zones of India should be grouped to constitute Independent States in which the constituent units should be autonomous and sovereign.

20 *form of confederation*: This view is persuasively argued by Ayesha Jalal in her book on Jinnah, *The Sole Spokesman*. Shorter treatments of her analysis appear in two of her later works, *The State of Martial Rule*, pp. 9–24, and *Democracy and Authoritarianism in South Asia*, pp. 12–16.

20 *substantial Hindu populations*: Punjab also had a substantial Sikh population.

20 *"mutilated and moth-eaten"*: Jalal, *Sole Spokesman*, p. 121. The language is taken from a speech given by Jinnah to the Muslim League Council in Lahore in July 1944.

20 *very viability*: Ibid., p. 179.

22 *horrific retreat*: A classic account of the British failure in Afghanistan can be found in Hopkirk, *The Great Game*. The events leading up to and during the tragic retreat of the British garrison from Kabul are depicted in chapters 18–19.

22 *neighboring Bombay*: For a discussion of British motives in moving into the areas that constitute present-day Pakistan, as well as their approach to governance, see Talbot, *Pakistan*, pp. 54–64.

22 *Government of India Act*: Ibid., p. 68. As Talbot mentions, the Unionist Party also included Hindus and Sikhs in its ranks.

22 *similar in Sindh*: Ibid., p. 76.

23 *New Delhi, Calcutta, and Bombay*: Waseem, "Causes of Democratic Downslide," p. 4532. Also see Talbot, *Pakistan*, p. 106.

23 *remained behind*: Jalal, *Sole Spokesman*, p. 2.

23 *new capital of Karachi*: Waseem, "Democratic Downslide," p. 4537.

23 *senior civil servants*: Jalal, *Democracy and Authoritarianism*, p. 36.

24 *to the vote*: Waseem, "Democratic Downslide," p. 4532. See also Waseem, *Politics and the State in Pakistan*, p. 32. Also Talbot, *Pakistan*, p. 111.

24 *summarily dismissed*: Jalal, *Democracy and Authoritarianism*, p. 52.

24 *Objectives Resolution*: Cohen, *The Idea of Pakistan*, p. 57. The text of the Objective Resolution, available at www.pakistani.org/pakistan/constitution/annex _objres.html, was later incorporated into the Pakistani constitution.

24 *street fighting*: This is the Muttahida Quami Movement (MQM), formed in 1984 by the former student leader Altaf Hussain.

25 *under Indian control*: Bose, *Kashmir*, p. 30.

25 *installed Gulab Singh*: Allen, *Soldier Sahibs*, pp. 81–83.

26 *in their direction*: Bose, *Kashmir*, p. 33.

26 *flying Indian troops*: There are a number of good accounts of how Hari Singh acceded to India. See Ibid., pp. 30–36, and Jamal, *Shadow War*, pp. 45–57.

26 *Azad (free) Kashmir*: Bose, *Kashmir*, pp. 40–41.

26 *mandated a plebiscite*: Jamal, *Shadow War*, pp. 60–61.

26 *right to do*: Ibid., p. 65.

27 *material and financial assets*: Talbot, *Pakistan*, pp. 98–99.

27 *flow to the army*: Ibid., pp. 118–19.

27 *their venality*: Ibid., pp. 151–53.

27 *formula for national elections*: Ibid., p. 142.

27 *seized the reins of power*: Ibid., p. 146. For a comprehensive account of the first years of Pakistan and the ascent of the army to the apex of power, see Jalal, *The State of Martial Rule*.

27 *secular orientation*: Talbot, *Pakistan*, p. 157.

28 *Basic Democracies*: Ibid., pp. 153–56.

28 *advocacy of full independence*: Bose, *Kashmir*, pp. 64–65.

28 *security threat*: Ibid., p. 66.

28 *returned him to prison*: Ibid., pp. 78–83.

29 *general Muslim uprising*: Jamal, *Shadow War*, p. 79.

29 *successful insurgencies*: Cohen, *Idea of Pakistan*, pp. 104–105.

29 *Muslim insurrection*: Jamal, *Shadow War*, pp. 82–83. See also Bose, *Kashmir*, pp. 83–84.

29 *spare parts*: Talbot, *Pakistan*, pp. 176–79. The United States imposed the spare parts embargo on both Pakistan and India, but only Pakistan was materially affected since most of its equipment was of U.S. origin while that of India was not.

29 *originated with Bhutto*: Ronny Data, "1965: An Indian Officer's View," *Daily Times*, November 17, 2003.

29 *a more secular desire*: This seems clear from the accounts provided in both Jamal, *Shadow War*, p. 79, and Bose, *Kashmir*, p. 84.

30 *without a heart*: Jalal, *Sole Spokesman*, p. 179.

30 *"rural slum"*: Ibid., p. 256.

30 *overwhelming predominance*: Talbot, *Pakistan*, p. 162. The tables displayed show the overwhelming preponderance of West Pakistanis in the military and the civil service, at the time the two key institutions of the state.

30 *Dacca in 1952*: Ibid., p. 141.

31 *failed to benefit*: Ibid., p. 163.

31 *virtually undefended*: Ibid., p. 189.

31 *Six Points*: Ibid., p. 188.

31 *absolute majority*: Ibid., pp. 199–201.

32 *forced to resign*: For an authoritative account of these events, see Sisson and Rose, *War and Secession*. Talbot draws heavily on this in his own summary account in *Pakistan*, pp. 201–13.

32 *apex of political power*: In fairness, Feroz Khan Noon, who also came from a feudal background, had served as prime minister during the year leading up to the Ayub coup. But this was the second-ranking position in the government after that of president.

32 *he needed bureaucrats*: Talbot, *Pakistan*, 227–28.

32 *confidence and its power*: Ibid., pp. 224–27.

32 *nuclear weapons program*: Federation of American Scientists, "Pakistan Nuclear Weapons."

32 *never recovered*: Cohen, *Idea of Pakistan*, pp. 81–83.

33 *source of political patronage*: Talbot, *Pakistan*, pp. 233–34.

2: The Feudals and the Army

35 *Malik Asif*: Lyon, "Power and Patronage in Pakistan," 2002, pp. iv–vii. This is from Lyon's Ph.D. thesis at the University of Kent, available online in its entirety at http://sapir.ukc.ac.uk/SLyon/Lyon.pdf. This is by far the best study ever done on Pakistan's feudal culture.

36 *special times of need*: Ibid., pp. 97–123.

37 *as a biraderi*: Ibid., p. 73. See also Talbot, *Pakistan*, p. 30.

37 *Power relationships*: Lyon, "Power and Patronage," p. 2.

37 *The power and status*: Ibid, p. 88.

38 *befuddled opponents*: Talbot, *Pakistan*, p. 68.

38 *West Pakistani representation*: Waseem, "Democratic Downslide," p. 4532.

38 *viewed as patronage networks*: In "Power and Patronage in Pakistan," Lyon uses the expression "human resource network" rather than "patronage network." I have chosen the latter to refer specifically to political networks, whereas Lyon uses "human resource networks" to extend to a broader range of relationships, such as the one that exists among family members of a biraderi.

38 *Nawaz rose to prominence*: Cohen, *Idea of Pakistan*, p. 149.

39 *substantial industrial empire*: The Pakistani English-language newspaper the *Daily Times* published a short piece on Mian Mohammed Sharif, Nawaz Sharif's father, on October 31, 2004, www.dailytimes.com.pk/default.asp?page=story _31-10-2004_pg7_33. Although he did not go into politics himself, he was widely believed to be the real power behind the Nawaz throne.

39 *So too is Chaudhry Shujaat*: Lyon, "Power and Patronage," p. 198.

39 *joint heads of the party*: "Bhutto's Son, Husband, to Be Co-Leaders of Party," Reuters, December 30, 2007. See also "Bhutto's Son Named as Successor," BBC News, December 30, 2007.

40 *Mr. Ten Percent*: Cohen, *Idea of Pakistan*, p. 252.

40 *switching sides*: Talbot, *Pakistan*, p. 361.

41 *taxes on agricultural income*: See the lament of Mohammed Iskar in *The Daily IIJ*, June 14, 2009, the blog of the International Institute of Journalism, http://inwent-iij-lab.org/Weblog/2009/06/14/pakistans-agriculture-not-taxed-rather-subsidies/#more-697.

41 *1 percent of its tax revenue*: Zaidi, "Pakistan's Roller-Coaster Economy," p. 9.

42 *Nepal and Bangladesh*: Omer Farooq, "Education." Also reported by Khawar Ghumman, "Only Two Percent of GDP Spent on Education," *Dawn*, June 5, 2010.

42 *only 1 percent*: Barry Bearak, "Pakistan Battles Its Tax Scofflaws," *New York Times*, May 27, 2000.

42 *2 percent*: Zaidi, "Pakistan's Roller-Coaster Economy," p. 5. See also Sabrina Tavernise, "Pakistan's Elite Pay Few Taxes, Widening Gap," *New York Times*, July 18, 2010.

42 *lowest in the world*: Tarique Niazi, "Tax Offers Pakistan Escape from Poverty," *Asia Times Online*, November 20, 2009, www.atimes.com/atimes/South_Asia/ KK20Df03.html. See also Zaffar Khalid Farooq, "Fly on the Wall," *The News*, December 17, 2009. The World Bank has recently done a study of Pakistan's tax problems: Pakistan Tax Policy Report, Report No. 50078-PK, July 2009.

42 *five technology institutes*: Luce, *In Spite of the Gods*, p. 31.

42 *low-quality textiles*: Filipe and Miranda, "A Plea to Pakistan," p. 41.

42 *outdistanced that of China*: See Ishrat Husain, governor of the National Bank of Pakistan, in his keynote address to the 12th General Council and General Body Meeting of the Asia Oceania Tax Consultants Association, in Karachi, November 26, 2004, http://ishrathusain.iba.edu.pk/.

43 *how this process works*: Lyon, "Power and Patronage," pp. 199–202.

45 *Yellow Taxi scheme*: Cohen, *Idea of Pakistan*, p. 251.

45 *national defense*: "Half of the Budget Allocated to Defense, Debt Servicing," *Express Tribune*, June 6, 2010. The percentages quoted are for the 2010–2011 budget. See also Ashfaque H. Khan, "Unrestrained Borrowing," *The News*, October 13, 2009.

45 *renegotiate more liberal terms*: Meekal Aziz Ahmed, "A Road to Nowhere," *The News*, December 1, 2008.

46 *urban middle class*: Cohen, *Idea of Pakistan*, p. 109.

47 *broaden its recruitment base*: See Fair and Nawaz, "The Changing Pakistan Army Officer Corps," which shows the changing demographics of the officer corps from 1974 to 2005.

47 *rigorous examination process*: Cohen, *Idea of Pakistan*, pp. 97–98.

47 *have taken root in the institution*: Ibid., pp. 101, 107.

49 *unpromotable positions*: Ibid., p. 108.

49 *religious fundamentalists*: Lt. Gen. Mahmud Ahmed was commander of X Corps, located at Rawalpindi just outside Islamabad, while Lt. Gen. Mohammed Aziz Khan was chief of general staff, based at army headquarters in Rawalpindi. Musharraf was on a passenger airliner returning from a conference in Sri Lanka on October 12, 1999, when Prime Minister Nawaz Sharif fired him. Acting on their own initiative, the two generals immediately launched a coup, which Musharraf supported after he landed in Karachi.

49 *sported a beard*: I have it on good authority that Mahmud, who served subsequently as director of ISI and figures prominently later in this book, grew a beard after he was retired from the army in October 2001, just before the United States commenced offensive operations in Afghanistan in retaliation for 9/11.

49 *largest business conglomerates*: Siddiqa, *Military Inc.*, p. 2.

50 *stock brokering*: Ibid., pp. 119–22. See also the Fauji Foundation website at www .fauji.org.pk/Webforms/home.aspx for its own description of the various enterprises it oversees.

50 *Askari Leasing Limited*: Siddiqa, *Military Inc.*, pp. 122–23. The Army Welfare Trust website is www.awt.com.pk/.

50 *largest landowners*: Siddiqa, *Military Inc.*, pp. 174–85.

50 *Basic Democracies scheme*: Talbot, *Pakistan*, pp. 380–85.

51 *power to dissolve parliament*: Ibid., p. 262.

52 *boycotting the event*: George Iype, "Pak Military Chiefs Boycott Wagah Welcome," *Rediff on the Net*, February 20, 1999.

52 *backdrop for the Musharraf coup*: The best account of Kargil I have seen is by William Milam, who was U.S. ambassador in Islamabad at the time—and, therefore, my boss—in *Bangladesh and Pakistan*, pp. 155–58. Although we did not know it then, Milam later learned that the Kargil operation had actually been launched several months prior to the Lahore Summit and may or may not have been designed to scuttle a peace process that was already beginning to take shape.

53 *abolishing the Eighth Amendment*: Talbot, *Pakistan*, p. 360.

53 *the Lawyers' Movement*: Rana Tanveer, "A Chronology of the Lawyers' Movement," *Daily Times*, November 3, 2008.

54 *long sojourn*: Milam, *Bangladesh and Pakistan*, p. 248.

3: Religion, Zia, and the Anti-Soviet Jihad in Afghanistan

56 *carnival atmosphere*: See the description in Lyon, "Power and Patronage," pp. 210–11.

57 *conceived of as direct*: See Metcalf, *Islamic Revival*, pp. 265–67. See also Haqqani, "Weeding Out the Heretics," p. 76.

57 *rural religion of the region*: Metcalf, *Islamic Revival*, p. 265.

57 *assimilated Hindu rituals*: Lyon, "Power and Patronage," pp. 209–11.

58 *Quran and the Hadith*: The Hadith are a collection of narratives that convey the words, teachings, and deeds of the Prophet Mohammed as passed down to subsequent generations by those who lived and worked with him.

58 *back-to-the-basics*: See Metcalf, "'Traditionalist' Islamic Activism," for a discussion of the roots and tenets of Deobandism and its relationship to contemporary radical Deobandi groups such as the Taliban. A more comprehensive account of the founding and teachings of the original Deoband school can be found in Metcalf's *Islamic Revival*.

58 *regarded as heretical*: Metcalf, *Islamic Revival*, p. 152.

58 *finding particular resonance*: See Waseem, "Origins and Growth Patterns of Islamic Organizations in Pakistan," p. 25.

58 *lower middle classes in Punjab*: Ibid.

58 *in the Seraiki belt*: The Seraiki belt refers to the region of southern Punjab, centered on Bahawalpur, populated in large part by the Seraikis, a distinct ethnic group that speaks its own language.

58 *Tablighi Jamaat*: See the discussion of the Tablighi Jamaat in Metcalf, "'Traditionalist' Islamic Activism."

58 *run by the Deobandi sect*: Cohen, *Idea of Pakistan*, p. 180.

58 *smaller Ahle Hadith*: Haqqani, "Weeding Out the Heretics," p. 77.

58 *even more literalist*: For a good brief discussion of the differences between the Ahle Hadith and Deobandi on matters of Islamic jurisprudence, see the Indian

Islamic scholar Yoginder Sikand, "Wahabi/Ahle Hadith, Deobandi and Saudi Connection," Sunninews.co.cc, April 14, 2010.

59 *defend the traditional religion*: See the account of the founding of the Barelvi school by Ahmad Riza Khan in Jones, *Socio-Religious Reform Movements*, pp. 70–72. See also the shorter account in Metcalf, *Islamic Revival*, p. 265.

59 *25 percent*: Jones, *Socio-Religious Reform Movements*, p. 76.

59 *Bhutto were Shiites*: Nasr, *The Shia Revival*, pp. 88–90.

59 *religious tolerance*: There is one Barelvi group in Pakistan that can fairly be described as militant. This is the Sunni Tehrik, based in Karachi, which has engaged in often violent struggles with Deobandi groups for control of mosques in the Sindh capital.

59 *Jamiat Ulema-e-Islam*: Talbot, *Pakistan*, p. 451.

59 *Maulana Diesel*: See the profile of Fazlur Rehman at the website for the 2008 Pakistani parliamentary elections, www.elections.com.pk/candidatedetails.php?id= 2509.

60 *most influential religious party*: See Stephen Cohen's excellent profile of the Jamaat-e-Islami in *Idea of Pakistan*, pp. 175–80. Vali Nasr, the preeminent Western scholar of the Jamaat, has written two books on the subject, *The Vanguard of the Islamic Revolution* and *Mawdudi & the Making of Islamic Revivalism*.

60 *establish sharia rule*: For a good short account of sharia, see H.A.R. Gibb, formerly director of the Center for Middle Eastern Studies at Harvard University, *Mohammedanism*, pp. 60–72.

60 *vanguard party*: Explained to me by party officials during a visit to Jamaat-e-Islami headquarters in the Lahore suburb of Mansoora in 1999.

61 *street power*: Waseem, *Politics and the State*, p. 23.

62 *obsequious behavior*: Ardeshir Cowasjee, "The General's General," *Dawn*, June 25, 1995.

62 *a pious general*: Haqqani, *Pakistan*, p. 112.

62 *finally had its man*: Ibid., p. 123.

62 *admired the Jamaat*: Ibid., pp. 139–40.

62 *fundamentalist Sunni lines*: See the excellent and comprehensive discussion of Zia's Islamization campaign in Talbot, *Pakistan*, pp. 270–79, from which much of my account is drawn. Also see Lau, "Twenty-Five Years of Hudood Ordinances," pp. 1305–307. Lau focuses primarily on the Zina Ordinance on rape and adultery.

63 *sexual intercourse*: Lau, "Twenty-Five Years of Hudood Ordinances," p. 1297.

63 *Tehrik-e-Nifaz-e-Fiqh-e-Jafaria Pakistan*: Talbot, *Pakistan*, p. 271.

63 *major confrontation*: Ibid., p. 251.

64 *the establishment* of *madrassas*: Cohen, *Idea of Pakistan*, pp. 183–84.

64 *removing rape*: Lau, "Twenty-Five Years of Hudood Ordinances," p. 1311.

65 *retreat from Kabul*: Allen, *Soldier Sahibs*, pp. 40–42.

65 *separated politically*: Ibid., pp. 30–31.

65 *known as the NWFP*: Renamed Khyber Pakhtunkhwa in April 2010. I will use NWFP until the events described in this book reach that date.

65 *willingly signed off*: See Omrani, "The Durand Line," pp. 183–85.

66 *voted overwhelmingly*: Haqqani, *Pakistan*, pp. 161–62.

66 *similarly named Afghan cousin*: Ibid., pp. 171–72.

67 *ignominiously crushed*: Roy, *Islam and Resistance in Afghanistan*, pp. 75–76.

67 *moved against Daoud*: Haqqani, *Pakistan*, p. 176.

67 *trusted rival*: Ibid., pp. 183–84.

68 *writings of Syed Qutb*: See the brief account of Qutb's influence in Bergen, *The Osama bin Laden I Know*, pp. 18–20. Qutb was not the first Muslim thinker to reject Western influence. Thomas W. Simons, Jr., who was my first ambassador in Islamabad and has taught courses on Islam in South and Central Asia at Harvard, pointed out to me that the philosophical roots of radical Islam's rejection of the West go back at least as far as Jamal al-Din al-Afghani in the late nineteenth century.

68 *reduced to charred ruins*: Steve Coll includes a brilliantly rendered account of these events in *Ghost Wars*, pp. 21–34.

68 *leisurely bicycle tour*: Talbot, *Pakistan*, p. 249.

69 *signal U.S. displeasure*: Ibid.

70 *pay for it*: Coll, *Ghost Wars*, p. 62.

70 *dollar for dollar*: Ibid., pp. 81–82.

70 *Inter-Services Intelligence Directorate*: Haqqani, *Pakistan*, pp. 188–89.

70 *completely relinquish*: Cohen, *Idea of Pakistan*, p. 100.

71 *also referred to as mujahideen*: See the discussion in chapter 1. Talbot also uses the term *mujahideen* in referring to the irregular Pakistani forces that infiltrated into Kashmir as part of Operation Gibraltar during the 1965 war with India, *Pakistan*, p. 177.

71 *religious pedigree*: Not all the mujahideen groups had a Jamaat pedigree. A good example was the National Islamic Front of Afghanistan, headed by Ahmed Ghailani, who was a Sufi pir. But ISI directed most of its support to the Jamaat-affiliated groups.

71 *followers of Sufi Islam*: Farangis Najibullah, "Can Sufis Bring Peace to Afghanistan?" Radio Free Europe/Radio Liberty Pressroom, March 5, 2009.

72 *three million Afghans eventually fled*: Haqqani, *Pakistan*, p. 189.

72 *the ISI favorite*: Coll, *Ghost Wars*, p. 165.

72 *"Defense of the Muslim Lands"*: Available in English at www.religioscope.com/info/doc/jihad/azzam_defence_2_intro.htm.

72 *Saudi construction magnate*: Haqqani, *Pakistan*, pp. 191–92.

72 *radical Egyptian physician*: Coll, *Ghost Wars*, p. 154.

73 *look favorably*: Ibid., p. 155.

73 *established the Harakat*: Jamal, "Growth of the Deobandi," pp. 8–9.

73 *flowed into the coffers*: See the discussion of Saudi funding for Pakistani madrassas in Kaushik Kapisthalam, "Learning from Pakistan's Madrassas," *Asia Times*, June 23, 2004. Also Cohen, *Idea of Pakistan*, pp. 183–84.

74 *redress the imbalance*: Rashid, *Taliban*, p. 89.

74 *4,000 HUJI recruits*: Jamal, "Growth of the Deobandi," p. 9.

74 *force of 150,000*: Roy, *Islam and Resistance*, p. 172. This figure refers to full-time fighters in the field.

74 *Kalashnikov culture*: For an account of the phenomenon published seven years after the Soviets left Afghanistan, see Kenneth J. Cooper, "A Kalashnikov Culture: Pervasive Assault Weapons Make Daily Life in Pakistan Deadly," *Washington Post*, March 14, 1996, p. A17.

75 *along Sunni lines*: For a relatively brief but authoritative account and analysis of the origins of sectarian competition and violence in Pakistan, see Zaman, "Sectarianism in Pakistan."

75 *visited on the Ahmadi*: Ibid., pp. 701–702.

75 *local businessmen*: Ibid., pp. 705–706.

75 *toiled for Shiite masters*: Ibid., p. 711.

75 *their Shiite orientation*: Ibid., p. 698.

76 *The Lashkar-e-Jhangvi*: Haqqani, "Weeding Out the Heretics," pp. 84–85.

4: Kashmir, India, and the Institutionalization of Jihad

78 *snatching dramatic victory*: Unlike in American baseball, where balls and strikes are called by the umpire, and a batter can keep fouling off pitches, in "limited over cricket," which was what India and Pakistan were playing, there are no balls and strikes. Each team gets a chance to swing at only a specific, limited number of deliveries. In limited over cricket, there are a specified number of overs— usually ranging from twenty to fifty—each of which consists of six deliveries. The team scoring more runs by the end is the winner. Miandad was down to the last delivery of the last over of the match. He had to hit the ball for a six on that delivery or Pakistan would lose the match. It was as sensational an outcome as is possible in the game of cricket.

78 Curfewed Night: Peer, *Curfewed Night*, pp. 12–13.

79 *in February 1975*: See Bose, *Kashmir*, pp. 88–89. This is the definitive book on the history of Kashmir and development of the insurrection.

80 *returned to office*: Ibid., pp. 90–92.

80 *carted off to jail*: Ibid., pp. 47–49.

80 *put down the protests*: See Peer, *Curfewed Night*, p. 15, and Bose, *Kashmir*, p. 109.

80 *sudden disappearance*: Bose, *Kashmir*, p. 95.

80 *formed in 1977*: Jamal, *Shadow War*, p. 101.

80 *into Pakistani-held territory*: Peer, *Curfewed Night*, pp. 34–35.

81 *as early as 1984*: Jamal, *Shadow War*, p. 123.

81 *an independent Kashmiri state*: Bose, *Kashmir*, p. 126.

82 *the nom de guerre*: Ibid., p. 50.

82 *dominant insurgent group*: Ibid., pp. 128–31.

83 *under a new name*: Jamal, "Growth of the Deobandi Jihad," p. 9. See also Zahab and Roy, *Islamist Networks*, pp. 27–28.

83 *senior HUA ideologue*: Zahab and Roy, *Islamist Networks*, p. 29.

83 *appeared on the scene*: See Qandeel Siddique, "What Is Lashkar-e-Taiba?" paper

presented at the Norwegian Defense Research Establishment, FFI, December 10, 2008, p. 1. See also Jamal, "A Guide to Militant Groups in Kashmir," p. 10. Other authors give a 1989 start date. See Haqqani, "Ideologies of South Asian Jihadi Groups," p. 24.

83 *Abdullah Azzam*: Zahab and Roy, *Islamist Networks*, p. 32.

83 *primary objective*: Ibid., p. 35.

84 *reported in 1993*: "Lashkar-e-Toiba: Army of the Pure," listed under "India, Jammu and Kashmir, Terrorist Groups," South Asia Terrorism Portal, www.satp .org/satporgtp/countries/india/states/jandk/terrorist_outfits/lashkar_e_toiba.htm.

84 *special interrogation facilities*: See Peer, *Curfewed Night*, pp. 46–54, in which he recounts his personal experience in being caught up in a crackdown by Indian security forces. Pages 140–42 detail the goings-on at a notorious interrogation and torture center. Bose discusses crackdowns and interrogation centers on pp. 113–14 in *Kashmir*.

85 *ISI turned increasingly*: Bose, *Kashmir*, pp. 135–40. See also Jamal, "Growth of the Deobandi Jihad," p 9.

85 *1995 kidnapping*: Bose, *Kashmir*, p. 135.

85 *perform charitable works*: Zahab and Roy, *Islamist Networks*, p. 35.

85 *headquarters complex at Muridke*: Siddique, "What is Lashkar-e-Taiba?" p. 4.

85 *university graduates*: Zahab and Roy, *Islamist Networks*, p. 36.

86 *charitable activities*: Siddique, "What Is Lashkar-e-Taiba?" pp. 3–4.

86 *broader geographical area*: Ibid., p. 4.

86 *"composite dialogue"*: See Kux, *India-Pakistan Negotiations*, pp. 39–40.

86 *highest war zone*: For a good short synopsis of the Siachen fighting, see Global Security.org, "Siachen Glacier/Operation Meghdoot," www.globalsecurity.org/ military/world/war/siachen.htm. See also Kux, *India-Pakistan Negotiations*, pp. 37–38.

86 *most fateful decision*: Kux, *India-Pakistan Negotiations*, p. 37.

87 *a bit disingenuous*: The text of the Simla agreement can be found Ibid., pp. 77–79.

87 *talks went nowhere*: A description of these talks and the Indian reaction to them can be found Ibid., pp. 26–29.

88 *pressuring the Pakistanis*: Riedel, *American Diplomacy and the 1999 Kargil Summit*, p. 3.

88 *July 4 meeting*: Ibid., p. 13.

93 *HUM payback*: We did not learn who the perpetrators were until a year later when an informant fingered them to the Pakistani authorities. They turned out to be a group of Shiite amateurs, acting on their own but hoping to curry favor with Iran, whose ringleader and his wife were killed in a subsequent shoot-out with the Pakistani security forces.

94 *its final destination*: See the contemporary account by Anthony Spaeth, "A Risky Precedent" *Time Asia*, January 1, 2000.

94 *new jihadist group*: Zahab and Roy, *Islamist Networks*, pp. 28–30.

94 *HUM with him*: Ibid., p. 28.

94 *ISI played a part*: For example, Ibid., p. 43, and Cohen, *Idea of Pakistan*, p. 181.

95 *it clearly recruited*: Zahab and Roy, *Islamist Networks*, pp. 30–31.

95 *with guns blazing*: Bose, *Kashmir*, p. 141.

95 *adopted similar tactics*: Ibid., pp. 141–42.

95 fidayeen, *or life daring*: Zahab and Roy, *Islamist Networks*, p. 40.

96 *attacked the Red Fort*: John Cherian, "Raid on the Red Fort," *Frontline*, January 6–18, 2001.

96 *Srinagar airport*: "Lashkar Bid to Storm Srinagar Airport, 10 Killed," *Times of India*, January 17, 2001.

96 *brink of war*: Nayak and Krepon, "US Crisis Management in South Asia's Twin Peaks Crisis," p. 16.

96 *had a bracing effect*: Ibid., p. 34.

96 *permanently cut off*: Ibid., pp. 35–38.

97 *Opinions differ*: Ibid., p. 35.

5: The Taliban, bin Laden, and the Road to 9/11

100 *Dostam joined*: Coll, *Ghost Wars*, p. 234.

101 *Masood had offered*: Ibid., pp. 236–37.

101 *rape, pillage, and burn*: Rashid, *Taliban*, pp. 21–22.

102 *his own tanks*: Ibid., p. 25.

102 *rough frontier justice*: See the excellent account of Pashtunwali and its influence on Taliban behavior and practices in Johnson and Mason, "No Sign Until the Burst of Fire," pp. 58–64. Much of the Taliban's behavior is better explained by unvarnished rural Pashtunwali than it is by religious fanaticism, although in the case of the Taliban they go hand in hand.

102 *Robin Hood figure*: Rashid, *Taliban*, p. 25.

102 *educated urban Pashtuns*: Ibid., p. 19.

102 *foreign affairs committee*: Ibid., p. 90.

103 *open up trade routes*: Coll, *Ghost Wars*, pp. 290–91.

103 *gravitate toward India*: Ibid., p. 290.

103 *capturing Kandahar itself*: See Rashid, *Taliban*, pp. 28–29, and Coll, *Ghost Wars*, p. 291.

104 *swept into Kabul*: Benazir Bhutto told Steve Coll in an interview (*Ghost Wars*, p. 331) that she had grown to oppose the idea of the Taliban taking over Kabul and supported a UN-brokered agreement on Afghanistan that would have included Masood. She claims that this time she was overruled by ISI, which was reluctant to pull back with Taliban victory within its grasp. She told Coll she believed that the army chief, Jehangir Karamat, supported her position but suggested that ISI may have evaded his orders. This latter suggestion strikes me as extremely improbable for the reasons I cited in chapter 3. If ISI was pushing to get the Taliban into Kabul, it was because those were its orders. Coll cites no corroboratory evidence that Bhutto had, in fact, changed her position on the Taliban, so we apparently have only her word. It seems unlikely, although not impossible, that she would have changed her mind about the Taliban, who, after

all, owed their current position primarily to her, and to do so just as they were on the verge of their greatest victory. Her justification—that she feared they might extend their militancy into Central Asia—rings hollow considering that Taliban forces at the time had not yet even taken Kabul. Given the problems the Taliban eventually caused through its harboring of Osama bin Laden, it is not surprising she would embrace a revisionist account of her own position. As for what Karamat really believed, Tom Simons, the U.S. ambassador at the time, probably got it right when he told Coll that by this point in time the army felt it had no realistic alternative to supporting the Taliban.

104 *finally hanged him*: Rashid, *Taliban*, pp. 49–50, and Coll, *Ghost Wars*, p. 332.

105 *leaving the kingdom*: Coll, *Ghost Wars*, p. 231.

105 *would feel welcome*: Ibid., p. 325.

105 *anti-U.S. fatwas*: Rashid, *Taliban*, p. 133.

105 *home base in Kandahar*: Coll, *Ghost Wars*, p. 351.

105 *prepare its foot soldiers*: Rashid, *Taliban*, p. 134.

106 *promulgate such a decree*: Coll, *Ghost Wars*, p. 386.

106 *members of the HUM*: Rashid, *Taliban*, p. 134.

106 *left the area*: Coll, *Ghost Wars*, p. 411.

106 *never deemed reliable enough*: Ibid., pp. 422–23.

107 *dropped its neutrality*: Ibid., pp. 519–20. As events after 9/11 demonstrated, with massive U.S. air support the Northern Alliance did have sufficient manpower to defeat the Taliban. Once again, this was not considered a reasonable policy option in the run-up to 9/11 because it would have meant an open declaration of war, something the United States was not prepared to contemplate until Al Qaeda dramatically raised the stakes on 9/11.

110 *commando unit*: Ibid., p. 481.

110 *Thomas Pickering*: Ibid., pp. 482, 513–14.

111 The Sullivans: Ibid., pp. 486–87.

112 *ten thousand madrassas*: International Crisis Group, "The State of Sectarianism in Pakistan," p. 6.

112 *fourteen thousand*: Hasan-Askari Rizvi, "Madrassas and Militancy," *Daily Times*, October 25, 2009.

112 *estimates considerably higher*: Ibid. See also Cohen, *Idea of Pakistan*, p. 182, who posits a possible upper limit of forty-five thousand, the highest figure I have seen.

112 *Ten to fifteen percent*: This is the percentage that Cohen uses, p. 182.

113 *began to target*: Nasr, *Shia Revival*, p. 166.

114 *alongside the Taliban*: Zahab and Roy, *Islamist Networks*, pp. 24–25.

114 *secured a ministerial post*: Ibid., p. 24.

114 *as false encounters*: Ibid., p. 26.

114 *kill police officers*: Jamal, "A Profile of Pakistan's Lashkar-e-Jhangvi," p. 12.

114 *finally tracked down*: Zahab and Roy, *Islamist Networks*, p. 24.

116 *buy off Sufi Mohammed*: Abbas, "The Black-Turbaned Brigade."

6: The Tribal Areas, 9/11, and the Rise of the Pakistani Taliban

121 *porous as a sieve*: Johnson and Mason, "No Sign Until the Burst of Fire," p. 44.

122 *Armitage told Mahmud*: Rashid, *Descent Into Chaos*, pp. 24–27.

122 *the Stone Age*: Musharraf, *In the Line of Fire*, p. 201.

123 *Indian military bases*: Rajiv Chandrasekaran, "India to Allow U.S. to Use Bases for Staging Ground," *Washington Post*, September 17, 2001.

123 *weighed heavily*: Musharraf, *In the Line of Fire*, p. 202.

124 *United States readily accepted*: Ibid., pp. 204–206. See also Rashid, *Descent into Chaos*, p. 28.

124 *a good deal to lose*: Rashid, *Descent into Chaos*, p. 77.

124 *Mazar-e-Sharif had fallen*: Ismail Khan, "Mazar Falls to Alliance: Taliban Say They're Regrouping," *Dawn*, November 10, 2001.

124 *Kandahar surrendered*: Jonathan Aiken et al., "Celebrations, Confusion as Kandahar Falls," CNN, December 7, 2001.

124 *on a motorbike*: "Mullah Omar Flees on Motorbike," BBC News, January 5, 2002.

124 *C-130 cargo plane*: "Tora Bora Revisited: How We Failed to Get Bin Laden and Why It Matters Today." Report to the Members of the Committee on Foreign Relations, U.S. Senate, November 30, 2009, p. 2.

125 *nowhere to be found*: Ibid., p. 14.

125 *guard the border*: Fair and Jones, "Pakistan's War Within," p. 167.

125 *number deployed vary*: See, for example, Yusufzai, "Fall of the Last Frontier?" Yusufzai, the preeminent Pashtun journalist in Pakistan, cites a range from eight thousand up to sixty thousand. A big part of the problem in assessing how many forces were actually involved during this period is that the Pakistan army has not revealed the information, so it tends to be based on hearsay or speculation.

125 *border unguarded*: Rashid, *Descent into Chaos*, pp. 147–48.

125 *saw fit to praise*: Fair, *Counterterror Coalitions*, pp. 27–28.

125 Marine Corps Gazette: Khan, "Pakistan—An Enduring Friend," pp. 34–38.

125 *escape from Tora Bora*: Philip Smucker, "How bin Laden Got Away," *Christian Science Monitor*, March 4, 2002.

125 *into North Waziristan*: Rashid, *Descent into Chaos*, p. 99.

126 *rousted from his bed*: Ibid., pp. 224–25.

126 *"blessed right hand"*: Mark Mazzetti and Margot Williams, "In Tribunal Statement, Confessed 9/11 Plotter Burnishes His Image as a Soldier," *Washington Post*, March 16, 2007.

127 *also a Jaish member*: Musharraf, *In the Line of Fire*, pp. 225–28. See also Rashid, *Descent into Chaos*, pp. 151–53.

127 *Protestant church*: "Hunt for Pakistan Church Bombers," CNN, March 18, 2002.

127 *French naval workers*: "Karachi Bus Blast Kills Fifteen," BBC News, May 8, 2002.

127 *Pakistani bystanders*: Zaffar Abbas, "Analysis: Pakistan Searches for Blast Leads," BBC News, June 14, 2002.

127 *missionary school*: "Gunmen Attack Pakistan School," BBC News, August 5, 2002.

127 *government blamed*: Zahab and Roy, *Islamist Networks*, p. 63. See also Jamal, "Profile of Lashkar-e-Jhangvi," p. 11.

128 *allowed to run*: Zahab and Roy, *Islamist Networks*, p. 25.

128 *militants affiliated with*: Musharraf, *In the Line of Fire*, p. 248.

128 *chief collaborator*: Ibid., pp. 255–61.

128 *called itself Jundullah*: Zahid Hussain, "Al Qaeda's New Face," *Newsline*, August 2004. See also Musharraf, *In the Line of Fire*, p. 234.

128 *Shaukat Aziz*: Musharraf, *In the Line of Fire*, p. 235.

129 *even expressed understanding*: Khan, "Pakistan," p. 36.

130 *a landslide victory*: Ismail Khan, "MMA Takes Convincing Lead in Frontier PA," *Dawn*, October 11, 2002.

130 *World Food Programme*: C. R. Bijoy, "India: Transiting to a Global Donor," in *South-South Cooperation 2010*, Reality of Aid, pp. 69–70.

130 *new parliament building*: Peter Wonacott, "India Befriends Afghanistan, Irking Pakistan," *Wall Street Journal*, August 19, 2009.

131 *uneasy exile in Pakistan*: Rashid, *Descent into Chaos*, p. 12.

131 *would have to leave*: Ibid., pp. 3–4.

132 *every instrument of governance*: Dodge, "The Causes of US Failure in Iraq," pp. 85–106. This is the best account I have read of the complete—and totally unanticipated—collapse of state power in Iraq caused by the U.S. invasion.

132 *fifteen thousand soldiers*: Belasco, *Troop Levels in the Afghan and Iraq Wars*, p. 9.

132 *reestablish themselves*: Scott Baldauf, "Taliban Appears to Be Regrouped and Well-Funded," *Christian Science Monitor*, May 8, 2003.

133 *eventually switched sides*: See excerpted transcripts of interviews with Steve Coll and the former U.S. special envoy to Afghanistan Peter Tomsen taken from the *Frontline* documentary "Return of the Taliban" on PBS, October 3, 2006, www.pbs.org/wgbh/pages/frontline/taliban/militants/haqqani.html.

133 *persuaded to cooperate*: Rashid, *Descent into Chaos*, pp. 242–44.

134 *ratchet up the pressure*: Ibid., p. 270.

134 *economic and military aid*: "Background Notes: Pakistan," Bureau of Public Affairs, U.S. Department of State, March 31, 2009.

134 *Colin Powell*: Rashid, *Descent into Chaos*, p. 270.

134 *"search-and-cordon"*: Ismail Khan, "Operation in S. Waziristan," *Dawn*, February 19, 2004.

135 *swelled to seven thousand*: Fair and Jones "Pakistan's War Within," p. 169.

135 *reluctant to fight*: Rashid, *Descent into Chaos*, p. 270.

135 *his compound*: Rahimullah Yusufzai, "Profile: Nek Mohammed," BBC News, June 18, 2004.

135 *pledged to halt*: Fair and Jones, "Pakistan's War Within," p. 171.

135 *one of their aircraft*: Rahimullah Yusufzai and Steve Coll, "Frontline: Return of the Taliban: Nek Mohammed," PBS, October 3, 2006.

136 *stop harboring foreign fighters*: "Pakistan's Most Wanted: Baitullah Mehsud," *Jane's*, February, 12, 2008.

136 *resuming his attacks*: Carlotta Gall and Ismail Khan, "In Pakistan, Doubts Over the Fight in the Tribal Areas," *New York Times*, February 12, 2008.

137 *considerable time in Swat*: Wadhams and Cookman, "Faces of Pakistan's Militant Leaders."

137 *they had resisted*: Abbas, "A Profile of Tehrik-i-Taliban Pakistan," pp. 1–4.

137 *disaffected members*: A former senior army officer who follows such matters emphasized to me in the summer of 2010 that many members of what is now called the Punjabi Taliban—many of whom were drawn from Punjabi jihadist and sectarian organizations—had gone to the tribal areas to support the Pakistani Taliban early on. They were precisely the same kind of people and, in some cases, no doubt, the very same people who had collaborated with Al Qaeda in its attacks on Western and government targets in Pakistan after 9/11. Some, presumably, had trained in Afghanistan before 9/11 and even fought alongside the Taliban.

138 *David Rohde*: David Rohde, "A Rope and a Prayer," *New York Times*, October 21, 2009.

139 *Hafiz Gul Bahadur*: Sulaiman and Bukhari, "Hafiz Gul Bahadur," p. 5.

139 *issued a proclamation*: Ismail Khan, "Forces, Militants Heading for Truce," *Dawn*, June 23, 2006.

139 *finalized in September*: Pazir Gul, "Waziristan Accord Signed," *Dawn*, September 6, 2006.

139 *an out clause*: "Return of the Taliban," *Frontline*, October 3, 2006.

140 *similar agreement with Fakir Mohammed*: Bill Roggio, "Pakistan Signs the Bajaur Accord," *Long War Journal*, March 17, 2007.

140 *Bush personally endorsed*: Rashid, *Descent into Chaos*, p. 277. See also the text of the Bush-Musharraf news conference, "President Bush and President Musharraf of Pakistan Participate in Press Availability," Office of the Press Secretary, the White House, September 22, 2006, http://merln.ndu.edu/archivepdf/pakistan/WH/20060922.pdf.

141 *obliged to condemn it*: Imtiaz Ali and Massoud Ansari, "Pakistan Fury as CIA Airstrike on Village Kills 18," *Daily Telegraph*, January 15, 2006. See also Ismail Khan, "Two Senior Al Qaeda Men Killed in Bajaur Raid," *Dawn*, January 19, 2006.

141 *denials of involvement*: See, for example, David Ignatius, "A Quiet Deal with Pakistan," *Washington Post*, November 4, 2008. Ignatius's article was written three years after the events depicted in this chapter, but it describes the same process of collaboration between the United States and Pakistan on the Predator attacks that undoubtedly existed from the outset. Ignatius describes a negotiation in which the United States gained Pakistani approval for a wider range of targets and greater number of attacks. This, as we will see, has been the general trend with drone strikes over time. The contention that the Pakistanis approved Predator strikes on their territory was subsequently also borne out by Embassy Islamabad reporting cables made public by WikiLeaks in late 2010 in which Pakistani officials were quoted as approving the strikes.

141 *had to be involved*: Carol Grisanti and Mushtaq Yusufzai, "Pakistanis Outraged over Continued Drone Attacks," MSNBC, January 26, 2009.

142 *under their control*: "Afghanistan Five Years Later: The Return of the Taliban," *Senlis Afghanistan*, September 2006, p. xi.

142 *reached six hundred*: Riedel, "Afghanistan."

142 *no longer winning*: Neumann, *The Other War*, p. 109.

142 *their daytime patrols*: Rashid, *Descent into Chaos*, p. 354.

144 *near Mir Ali*: Hazi Pazir Gul and Zulfiqar Ali, "Suicide Bomber Kills 5 in North Waziristan," *Dawn*, January 22, 2007.

144 *town of Tank*: Iqbal Khattack, "26 Killed in Tank Fighting," *Daily Times*, March 29, 2007.

7: Lal Masjid, Army Failures, and the Domestic Terrorism Campaign

145 *Musharraf a traitor*: Abbas, "Road to Lal Masjid."

145 *embarrassment to the government*: Zaffar Abbas, "The Creeping Coup," *Dawn*, March 31, 2007.

146 *tearing down two*: Shahzad Malik, "Two Mosques Demolished in Islamabad over Security Threat," *Daily Times*, January 21, 2007.

146 *government library*: Abbas, "Road to Lal Masjid."

146 "The Creeping Coup": Zaffar Abbas, "The Creeping Coup," *Dawn*, March 31, 2007.

146 *suffer the consequences*: Mohammed Imran, "Cleric Gives Government a Week to Impose Sharia," *Daily Times*, March 31, 2007.

146 *kidnapped four local policemen*: "Hostage Policemen: Case Filed Against Lal Masjid Admin," *Daily Times*, May 19, 2007.

146 *massage parlor*: "Lal Masjid Frees Hostages," *Daily Times*, June 24, 2007.

147 *very best ally*: "Editorial: Lal Masjid's Damage to Pak-China Relations," *Daily Times*, June 29, 2007.

147 *number of female students*: Iqbal Khattak, "Musharraf Ready to Raid Lal Masjid But . . . ," *Daily Times*, June 30, 2007.

147 *a firefight*: Syed Irfan Raza and Munawar Azeem, "Fierce Gunbattles Rock Capital: Army Troops Deployed Around Lal Masjid; Curfew Imposed in Area; Rangers Man, Journalist Among 10 Killed; Govt Buildings Torched," *Dawn*, July 4, 2007.

147 *disguised in a burqa*: "1200 Surrender at Lal Masjid," *Daily Times*, July 5, 2007.

147 *commando assault*: "It's All Over as Ghazi Is Killed," *Dawn*, July 11, 2007.

147 *The death toll*: Syed Irfan Raza, "Lal Masjid Women, Children also Killed: G-6 Curfew to Be Lifted Today," *Dawn*, July 14, 2007.

147 *human shields*: "Pakistani Solders Storm Mosque," BBC News, July 10, 2007.

147 *ten foreign fighters*: "Bodies of 10 Foreigners Recovered from Mosque," *Dawn*, July 15, 2007.

147 *letter of encouragement*: Dean Nelson and Ghulam Hasnain, "Bin Laden's Deputy Behind the Red Mosque Bloodbath," *Sunday Times* (London), July 15, 2007.

148 *Western culture*: See Sahi, "The Punjab Connection," for a brief survey of Talibanization in the Seraiki belt.

148 *reached Lahore*: Salman Masood, "Fear of Taliban Reaches Lahore," *International Herald Tribune*, November 3, 2008.

148 *mass burning of CDs*: Aamir Latif, "Taliban Fear Burns Lahore Porn CDs," Islam Online.net, October 13, 2008.

148 *Musharraf talked tough*: Rana Qaisar, "Lal Masjids Never Again: Musharraf," *Daily Times*, July 13, 2007.

148 *public backlash*: "Editorial: Feeling Insecure in Islamabad," *Daily Times*, September 4, 2009.

148 *London exile*: "Nawaz Demands Judicial Probe into Lal Masjid Incident," *Daily Times*, July 19, 2007.

148 *seventy new mosques*: Editorial, *Daily Times*, September 4, 2009.

148 *"implement Islamic law"*: Declan Walsh, "Red Mosque Siege Leader Walks Free to Hero's Welcome," *Guardian*, April 17, 2009.

149 *released a videotape*: "Al Qaeda Issues Pakistan Threat," BBC News, July 11, 2007.

149 *disavowed the cease-fire*: "Two Days of Homicide Attacks Kill 70 in Pakistan," Fox News, July 15, 2007.

149 *killed six soldiers*: Haji Mujtaba, "6 Soldiers Killed in North Waziristan Suicide Attack," *Daily Times*, July 5, 2007.

149 *tried to shoot down*: Isambard Wilkinson, "Gen Musharraf Survives Gun Attack on Plane," *Telegraph*, July 7, 2007.

149 *four soldiers at Dir*: "Dir Suicide Attack Kills 4 Troops," *Daily Times*, July 7, 2007.

149 *seven people*: "7 Including 3 Cops Killed in NWFP Attacks, Blasts," *Daily Times*, July 13, 2007.

149 *Frontier Corps troops*: "Suicide Bomber Kills 23 FC Troops," *Daily Times*, July 15, 2007.

149 *forty-nine army*: Ismail Khan, "At Least 49 Are Killed by Suicide Bombers in Pakistan," *New York Times*, July 15, 2007.

149 *killing seventeen*: Baqir Sajjad Syed, "Another Carnage Visits Capital: 17 Killed in Suicide Bombing; PPP Reception Camp Targeted at CJ Rally Venue," *Dawn*, July 18, 2007.

149 *several Chinese workers*: "Scores Killed in Pakistan Attacks," BBC News, July 19, 2007.

149 *town of Bannu*: Manzoor Ali Shah, "9 Civilians Die in Bannu Attacks," *Daily Times*, July 26, 2007.

149 *Aabpara Market*: Sadaqat John, "Bombing, Mosque Riot Rock Islamabad," *Washington Post*, July 28, 2007.

149 *U.S. diplomat*: "Pakistan Bomb Kills US Diplomat," BBC News, March 2, 2006.

149 *interior minister*: Ismail Khan and Gulzar Khan, "Sherpao Survives Suicide Attack," *Dawn*, April 29, 2007.

150 *building up its forces*: "2 More Brigades Deployed in Tribal Region," *Daily Times*, July 4, 2007.

150 *additional two divisions*: Najam Sethi, "No Emergency, Elections on Time, Media Must Not Sympathize with Religious Extremists," *Daily Times*, July 19, 2007.

150 *six infantry divisions*: Nawaz, "FATA," p. 9.

150 *without a shot being fired*: Ahmed Rashid, "Pakistan Crisis 'Hits Army Morale,'" BBC News, September 13, 2007.

151 *his own peace agreement*: Iqbal Khattak, "Polio Vaccination, Girls Education in Swat: Govt Signs Peace Deal with TNSM," *Daily Times*, May 23, 2007.

151 *separate governing institutions*: Khattak, "Battle for Pakistan," p. 8.

151 *driving the TNSM out*: "Pakistan Hunting Swat Militants," BBC News, December 8, 2007.

151 *mountain hideouts*: Khattak, "Battle for Pakistan," p. 8.

152 *National Reconciliation Ordinance*: Shakil Shaikh, "Corrupt Politicians Given a Clean Slate," *The News*, October 6, 2007.

153 *140 people*: "Attack on Bhutto Convoy Kills 130," BBC News, October 19, 2007. See also Carlotta Gall and Salman Masood, "After Bombing, Bhutto Assails Officials' Ties," *New York Times*, October 19, 2007.

153 *obliged to acquiesce*: Carlotta Gall, "Former Prime Minister Nawaz Sharif Returns to Pakistan," *New York Times*, November 25, 2007.

153 *slammed her head*: Eric Schmitt and Salman Masood, "Head Injury Killed Bhutto, Report Said to Find," *New York Times*, February 8, 2008. See also the UN report on the assassination, "Report of the United Nations Commission of Inquiry into the Facts and Circumstance of the Assassination of Former Pakistani Prime Minister Mohtarma Benazir Bhutto." The report criticizes the government for failing to provide adequate security as her SUV was leaving the rally. There is no doubt the security could have been better; this is a chronic problem in Pakistan. But it is very hard to protect politicians who love to connect in public with their followers and who stand in open hatches to wave to cheering crowds. The wonder is that there have not been more such assassinations.

153 *CIA director*: Joby Warrick, "CIA Places Blame for Bhutto Assassination," *Washington Post*, January 18, 2008.

153 *her condemnation*: "Benazir Backs Government," *Dawn*, July 11, 2007. See also M. Ziauddin, "Rising Extremism Threatens Pakistan's Existence: Benazir," *Dawn*, July 12, 2007.

154 *Mehsud was elected*: Hassan Abbas, "Profile of Tehrik-i-Taliban," p. 2.

154 *go his own way*: Sulaiman and Bukhari, "Hafiz Gul Bahadur," pp. 5–6.

154 *was being formed*: Abbas, "Profile," p. 3.

154 *Haqqani network neighbors*: Syed Saleem Shahzad, "Taliban Wield the Ax Ahead of New Battle," *Asia Times Online*, January 24, 2008.

154 *Uzbek fighters*: Abbas, "South Waziristan's Maulvi Nazir."

155 *Qari Hussain*: Tahir Ali, "Qari Hussain Ahmed Mehsud," *Australia News*, January 28, 2010, www.australia.to. See also Brian Wolfe, "The Pakistani Taliban's Suicide Bomber Trainer: A Profile of Qari Hussain Mehsud," *Critical Threats*, May 25, 2010.

155 *in Sararogha*: Noor Alam, "Taliban Over Run South Waziristan FC Fort," *Daily Times*, January 17, 2008. See also Fair and Jones, "Pakistan's War Within," p. 173.

155 *knockout blow*: Fair and Jones, "Pakistan's War Within," pp. 173–74. See also the account in Mahsud, "Battle for Pakistan," p. 16.

156 *Four thousand homes*: Fair and Jones, "Pakistan's War Within," p. 174.

156 *began pulling out*: Ibid.

156 *deal with Mullah Fazlullah*: Mahsud, "Battle for Pakistan," pp. 8–9.

156 *The army responded*: Ibid., p. 9.

156 *only ski resort*: Ibid.

157 *hunkered down*: Hussain, "Paradise Lost."

157 *major staging area*: Jane Perlez and Pir Zubair Shah, "Pakistani Taliban Repel Government Offensive," *New York Times*, August 10, 2008.

158 *destroyed in Bajaur*: Rahmanullah, "Battle for Pakistan," pp. 8–10.

158 *first really significant*: Ismail Khan and Amarullah Khan, "Bajaur Tribe Promises to End Militancy, Respect Govt Writ," *Dawn*, March 10, 2009.

158 *cave system*: "Key Taliban Complex Captured in Bajaur," *Dawn*, March 2, 2010.

158 *reluctant to fight*: Mahsud, "Battle for Pakistan," p. 16.

159 *publicly warn*: Jane Perlez, "Pakistan's Military Chief Criticizes the U.S. Over a Raid," *New York Times*, September 10, 2008.

160 *retired ISI officers*: Rashid, *Descent into Chaos*, pp. 221–22.

160 New York Times: Mark Mazzetti and Eric Schmitt, "Pakistanis Aided Attack in Kabul, U.S. Officials Say," *New York Times*, August 1, 2008.

160 *"planning guidance"*: Mark Mazzetti and Eric Schmitt, "Afghan Strikes by Taliban Get Pakistan Help, U.S. Aides Say," *New York Times*, March 25, 2009.

160 *Matt Waldman*: Waldman, "The Sun in the Sky." The study also quotes a source who claimed that the Pakistani president, Asif Zardari, met with a group of fifty Afghan Taliban prisoners in the spring of 2010. Zardari is alleged to have told them they had been arrested due to U.S. pressure but would be released soon because Pakistan was on their side (pp. 8–9). This report, which is based on hearsay, is impossible to believe. Not only is there no evidence I am aware of suggesting that the Pakistanis have actually detained such a large number of Afghan Taliban, but it defies credulity that the president of the country would have met with them. The Afghan Taliban number two, Mullah Baradar, was arrested in February 2010 but, as we shall see later, this was an exception and most likely intended to ensure that he not negotiate with the United States or Afghan government behind Pakistan's back. I doubt Asif Zardari would have met with him. Unfortunately, by including such a transparently unbelievable report in his study, Waldman casts doubt on his product as a whole.

161 *container cargo*: Nawaz, "FATA," p. 10.

162 *Factory at Wah*: "Death Toll in Wah Blasts Climbs to 70," *The News*, August 21, 2008.

162 *ANP election rally*: Daud Khattak and Manzoor Ali Shah, "25 Killed in Suicide Attack on ANP Rally in Charsadda," *Daily Times*, February 10, 2008.

162 *Asfandyar Wali*: Isambard Wilkinson, "Suicide Bomber Attacks Pakistan Politician's Home," *Telegraph* (London), October 2, 2008.

162 *ANP provincial assemblyman*: "ANP Legislator Killed in Bomb Attack," *Daily Times*, February 12, 2009.

162 *Marriott Hotel*: Syed Shoaib Hasan, "Islamabad's 'Message from Hell,'" BBC News, September 20, 2008. See also Salman Masood, "More Bodies Pulled from Hotel Rubble in Pakistan," *New York Times*, September 21, 2008.

162 *Sri Lankan cricketers*: Jane Perlez, "For Pakistan, Attack Exposes Security Flaws," *New York Times*, March 3, 2009.

163 *Punjabi Taliban*: "Sri Lanka Team Attack Suspect Held," *Dawn*, June 17, 2009.

163 *joint statement*: "Editorial: Taliban's Unity and Our Disunity," *Daily Times*, February 24, 2009.

164 *drove a hard bargain*: "Sufi's 10-point Swat Peace Plan," *Daily Times*, February 24, 2009.

164 *endorsed by the army*: "Army Has Ceased Swat Operations," *Daily Times*, February 24, 2009.

164 *considerable pressure*: "Swat Deal Hard to Understand: U.S.," *Daily Times*, February 29, 2009.

165 *ratify the agreement*: Zulfiqar Ghuman and Irfan Ghauri, "President Signs Nizam-e-Adl after NA Nod," *Daily Times*, April 14, 2009. The MQM, which had begun to have its own problems with Pakistani Taliban taking root in Karachi, but which was allied with the PPP government, abstained from the vote.

165 *forces into Buner*: "Swat's Taliban Expand Operations," *Daily Times*, April 22, 2009.

165 *Fazlullah spokesman*: "TTP Says Osama Welcome in Swat: Taliban Reject Peace Accord," *Daily Times*, April 22, 2009.

8: Mumbai, the Buner Moment, and Troubles with the United States

166 *Taj Mahal Hotel*: Motlagh, "Sixty Hours of Terror." This is by far the most detailed and best-written account of the Mumbai attacks.

167 *Ajmal Kasab*: Saeed Shah, "Revealed: Home of Mumbai's Gunman in Pakistani Village," *Observer*, December 7, 2008.

167 *casualty statistics*: South Asia Terrorism Portal, "Fatalities in Terrorist Violence 1988–2010," *Jammu and Kashmir Data Sheets*, www.satp.org/satporgtp/countries/india/states/jandk/data_sheets/annual_casualties.htm. This India-based website keeps a running log of terrorist violence in Kashmir as well as encounters between jihadist groups and Indian security forces.

168 *Siachen Glacier*: "Guns to Fall Silent on Indo-Pak Borders, *Daily Times*, November 26, 2003. For an Indian account, see Amit Baruah and Sandeep Dikshit, "India-Pak Ceasefire Comes Into Being," *Hindu*, November 25, 2003.

168 *composite dialogue*: Qudssia Akhlaque, "Dialogue to Start Next Month: Joint Statement at Musharraf-Vajpayee Meeting," *Dawn*, January 7, 2004. See also

Amit Baruah and B. Muralidhar Reddy, "India, Pakistan to Start Dialogue in February," *Hindu*, January 7, 2004.

168 *bus service*: Amit Baruah and B. Muralidhar Reddy, "India, Pakistan Seal Deal on Srinagar-Muzaffarabad Bus Link," *Hindu*, February 17, 2005. See also Qudssia Akhlaque, "Kashmir Bus Service to Start from April: Travel Across LOC by Permit; India Ready to Look at Gas Project and Open Khokhrapar Rail Link; Agreement on Lahore-Amritsar Route," *Dawn*, February 17, 2005.

169 *Steve Coll*: Steve Coll, "The Back Channel," *New Yorker*, March 2, 2009.

169 *Khurshid Kasuri*: Babar Dogar, "'Interim Pact' on Kashmir Was for 15 Years: Kasuri," *The News*, April 28, 2010.

169 *similar assertion*: Coll, "Back Channel," p. 40.

170 *Geelani steadfastly refused*: Dogar, "'Interim Pact'."

171 *Jamaat-ud-Dawa*: M. Ilyas Khan, "Profile: Hafiz Mohammed Saeed," BBC News, June 2, 2009.

171 *far outstripped*: See the vivid account of the Lashkar effort following the Kashmir earthquake in Coll, "Letter from Kashmir."

172 *Afghan theater*: Tankel, "Lashkar-e-Taiba in Perspective."

172 *two hundred people*: "Pakistan 'Role in Mumbai Attacks,'" BBC News, September 30, 2006. The Indians also blamed ISI and the local radical Indian Islamic group Students Islamic Movement.

172 *threats of retaliation*: Omar Waraich, "Pakistan Continues to Resist Indian Pressure on Mumbai," *Time*, January 7, 2009.

172 *conceded the point*: Ibid.

172 *Zaki-ur-Rehman Lakhvi*: Syed Irfan Raza, "Thaw at Last: Mastermind Lakhvi in Custody; Eight Named in FIR; 30 Questions Given to India," *Dawn*, February 13, 2009.

172 *formally charged*: "Seven Indicted for Mumbai Attacks," *The News*, November 26, 2009.

172 *order his release*: Zahid Hussain and Matthew Rosenberg, "India Slams Pakistan's Release of Cleric, *Wall Street Journal*, June 3, 2009. The decision by the Lahore High Court to release Saeed was later upheld by the Pakistani Supreme Court. See "Government Fails in Bid to Keep Hafiz Saeed in Detention," *Dawn*, May 26, 2010.

172 *carried out raids*: Tariq Naqash and Syed Irfan Raza, "Army Raids LeT Compound in Kashmir, Say Witnesses," *Dawn*, December 8, 2008.

172 *told Indian investigators*: Diwakar and Vishwa Mohan, "ISI Guided LeT at Every Step for 26/11," *Times of India*, June 10, 2010.

173 *prevent the Lashkar*: Jason Burke, "Pakistan Intelligence Services 'Aided Mumbai Attack,'" *Guardian*, October 18, 2010.

174 *"up in flames"*: Jane Perlez and Salman Masood, "Terror Ties Run Deep in Pakistan, Mumbai Shows," *New York Times*, July 26, 2009.

175 *savagely whipped*: Declan Walsh, "Video of Girl's Flogging as Taliban Hand Out Justice," *Guardian*, April 2, 2009. The video is widely available on the Internet and can also be accessed with the Walsh article.

175 *moved into Buner*: Muhammad Anis, "Troops Regain Control of Buner District HQ," *The News*, April 30, 2009.

175 *Right Path*: Khattak, "Battle for Pakistan," p. 10.

175 *army began urging*: Declan Walsh, "Pakistan Urges Evacuation of Taliban-Controlled Town," *Guardian*, May 5, 2009.

175 *refugee camps*: Khattak, "Battle for Pakistan," p. 10.

175 *three million people*: Fair and Jones, "Pakistan's War Within," p. 177.

176 *out of Mingora*: Iftikhar A. Khan, "Army Takes Mingora," *Dawn*, May 31, 2009.

176 *elude capture*: Hai Kakar, "Taliban Leader 'Flees Pakistan,'" BBC News, November 17, 2009.

176 *entire valley*: Khattak, "Battle for Pakistan," p. 10.

176 *began returning*: Howard LaFranchi, "Pakistan Begins Returning Swat Valley Refugees Home," *Christian Science Monitor*, July 14, 2009.

176 *back into jail*: Zulfiqar Ali, "Sufi Mohammed, Two Sons Held in Peshawar," *Dawn*, July 27, 2009.

176 *commanding general*: Matthew Rosenberg, "Pakistan Army Faces Test Beyond Swat," *Wall Street Journal*, June 12, 2009.

176 *stay in Swat*: "Troops to Stay in Swat til Normality Returns: Kayani," *Dawn*, November 22, 2009.

176 *follow up its efforts*: Zulfiqar Guhman, "Govt Orders Operation Against Baitullah Mehsud," *Daily Times*, June 15, 2009.

177 *abandoned their alliance*: Szrom, "The Survivalist of North Waziristan."

177 *candidate Obama*: Barack Obama, "Remarks of Senator Obama: The War We Need to Win," BarackObama.com, August 1, 2007.

177 *expanded target set*: David Ignatius, "A Quiet Deal with Pakistan," *Washington Post*, November 4, 2008.

177 *final four months*: This information comes from a very useful running tally, "Year of the Drone," maintained by Peter Bergen and Katherine Tiedemann of the New America Foundation. They obtain most of their information from newspaper accounts in the Pakistani and international press. There is also a similar, and similarly useful, running tally maintained by anonymous contributors on Wikipedia under the title "Drone Attacks in Pakistan." Specific entries on each site contain links to the original press reports. Both sets of tallies track fairly closely, but there are differences. In many instances, the information available is insufficient to determine who the actual targets were.

177 *survey of Predator strikes*: Bergen and Tiedemann, "Year of the Drone 2009."

178 *their sovereignty*: Dean Nelson, "Pakistan Warns United States Against Drone Attacks," *Telegraph*, October 1, 2009.

178 *killing the newlyweds*: Christina Lamb, "High-Profile Victories in the Battle Against Terror," *Sunday Times*, August 9, 2009. This report highlights the glucose drip aspect. Other reports center on the massage. See, for example, "Baitullah Mehsud 'Killed by CIA While Receiving a Leg Massage,'" *Telegraph*, August 11, 2009, and Declan Walsh, "US Airstrike Kills Wife of Pakistan Taliban Leader," *Guardian*, August 5, 2009.

178 *reports of dissension*: Zahid Hussein, "Hakimullah Mehsud Named as New Pakistan Taliban Leader," *The Times*, August 23, 2009.

178 *ruffled feathers*: Fishman, "Pakistan's Failing War on Terrorism." See also Ismail Khan, "Battle for Waziristan Looms," *Dawn*, October 2, 2009.

179 *residents fled*: "Thousands Flee S Waziristan Ahead of Offensive," *Dawn*, October 15, 2009.

179 *Path to Salvation*: Mahsud, "Battle for Pakistan," p. 16.

179 *thirty thousand troops*: Ibid.

179 *possession of the Mehsud lands*: Ibid. See also Bill Roggio, "Taliban Escape South Waziristan Operation," *Long War Journal*, November 26, 2009.

179 *upsurge in terrorist spectaculars*: An entry in Wikipedia titled "List of Terrorist Incidents in Pakistan since 2001" carries a running tally of terrorist incidents in Pakistan since 9/11. Each entry has one or more links to contemporary press reports concerning the incident in question. Using this data it is possible to run down additional press accounts of the incidents in question. The Wikipedia entry does not attempt to distinguish between purely sectarian attacks, which predated 9/11, and those instigated by Al Qaeda, their Pakistani jihadist and sectarian allies, and the Pakistani Taliban against nonsectarian targets in the aftermath of 9/11. Nor does it distinguish between attacks against military and police targets outside the battlefield arena and attacks against civilian targets. But generally sufficient information is provided to determine the intended target of each attack. The entry is quite comprehensive, particularly for following trends, such as the uptick in attacks following both Lal Masjid and the 2009 Swat and South Waziristan operations. http:// en.wikipedia.org/wiki/List_of_terrorist_incidents_in_Pakistan_since_2001.

179 *headquarters of ISI*: "Pakistani Taliban Claim Bombing," BBC News, May 28, 2009.

179 *Pearl Continental*: Daud Khattak, "Pakistan: Massive Hotel Bomb Further Erodes Security," *Christian Science Monitor*, June 10, 2009.

179 *crowded bazaar*: "Death Toll from Peshawar Suicide Blast Rises to 52," *Dawn*, October 10, 2009.

179 *training academies*: Salman Aslam, "Lahore Rocked by Three Terror Attacks," *The News*, October 16, 2009.

180 *Mohammed Aqeel*: There are several good real-time sources on this, arguably the most audacious of all terrorist attacks inside the Pakistani heartland. See, inter alia, Amir Mir, "Militants Flow in to Negotiate with GHQ Attackers," *The News*, October 16, 2009; Tahir Niaz, "Who Is Dr. Osman?" *Daily Times*, October 12, 2009; Editorial, "Interpreting the GHQ Attack," *Daily Times*, October 12, 2009. See also Bill Roggio, "Rawalpindi Attack Mastermind Previously Arrested and Released," *Long War Journal*, October 12, 2009.

180 *joined up with*: Abbas, "Defining the Punjabi Taliban Network." This is an excellent overview of the origins and makeup of the Punjabi Taliban. It was written following the attack on the Sri Lankan cricket team, almost six months before the attack on army headquarters.

180 *variously described*: See, for example, Niaz, "Who Is Dr. Osman?" and Roggio, "Rawalpindi Attack Mastermind."

181 *has disappeared*: "Pakistan Denies Militant Arrested," BBC News, December 18, 2008.

181 *headquarters in Bahawalpur*: Saeed Shah, "Al-Qaeda Allies Build Huge Pakistan Base," *Telegraph on Sunday*, September 13, 2009.

182 *late October 2009*: Ali Hazrat Bacha, "At Least 101 Killed, 150 Injured; Fire Destroys Several Buildings; Many Trapped in Debris; Peshawar Bomb Targets Women, Children," *Dawn*, October 29, 2009.

182 *bank in Rawalpindi*: Mohammad Asghar, "Terrorists Target 35 Senior Citizens in Rawalpindi," *Dawn*, November 3, 2009.

182 *Rawalpindi mosque*: Mohammed Asghar, "Carnage in Pindi Army Mosque as Taliban Breach Security," *Dawn*, December 4, 2009.

182 *volleyball match*: "Pakistan Suicide Bomb Kills Scores at Volleyball Match," BBC News, January 1, 2010.

182 *Ashura procession*: Salis Bin Perwaiz, "Karachi Burns After Attack on Ashura Procession," *The News*, December 30, 2009.

182 *refugee camp*: Syed Yasir Shah, "41 Killed in Twin Kohat Suicide Bombings," *The News*, April 18, 2010.

182 *Ahmadi mosques*: Waqar Gillani and Jane Perlez, "Attackers Hit Mosques of Islamic Sect in Pakistan," *New York Times*, May 28, 2010.

182 *killing five more*: "Lahore Hospital Comes Under Attack from Gunmen," BBC News, June 1, 2010.

183 *Data Durbar shrine*: "Explosions at Famous Shrine in Pakistan Kill Dozens," CNN, July 2, 2010. See also Issam Ahmed, "Attack on Lahore Shrine Raises Concern About Sectarian Violence in Pakistan," *Christian Science Monitor*, July 2, 2010, and Sabrina Tavernise and Waqar Gillani, "Suicide Bombers Strike Sufi Shrine in Pakistan," *New York Times*, July 2, 2010.

183 *a Barelvi ceremony*: "Bomb Carnage at Karachi Prayers," BBC News, April 11, 2006.

183 *shrine in Peshawar*: Ali Hazrat Bacha, "Terrorists Turn on Sufi Saint's Shrine," *Dawn*, March 6, 2009.

183 *shrine in Karachi*: Shoaib Hasan, "Deadly Blast Hits Sufi Shrine in Pakistani City Karachi," BBC News, October 7, 2010.

183 *Baba Farid*: "Seven Killed in Blast at Baba Farid Shrine," *The News*, October 26, 2010.

183 *shrine in Lahore*: "3 Killed, 27 Injured in Lahore Shrine Blast," *Daily Times*, February 4, 2011.

183 *an urs celebration*: "DG Khan Shrine Bombing: Death Toll Reaches 50," *Express Tribune*, April 4, 2011.

183 *praised the attack*: Salman Siddiqui, "Hardline Stance: Religious Bloc Condones Murder," *Express Tribune*, January 5, 2011.

184 *interior minister conceded*: Jane Perlez, "Official Admits Militancy Has Deep Roots in Pakistan," *New York Times*, June 2, 2010.

184 *stop targeting Punjab*: "Shahbaz Asks Taliban Not to Attack Punjab," *The News*, March 15, 2010. For an idea of the reaction his comments caused, see the edito-

rial that appeared the next day in the *Daily Times*, titled "The Existentialist Threat." Shahbaz was particularly criticized for taking a narrow Punjab-centric view. He did not admit that the terrorist problem in Punjab was rooted in Punjab itself. His suggestion, rather, seemed to be that the PML-N and, therefore, its provincial Punjab government, were not adversarial toward the Taliban and that Punjab should, therefore, not be targeted. His comments fell on deaf Punjabi Taliban ears.

184 *announced plans*: Perlez, "Official Admits Militancy Has Deep Roots."

185 *pockets of resistance*: "Six Pakistani Troops Killed by Landmine," BBC News, October 22, 2010.

185 *Mohmand tribal area*: Shah Nawaz Mohmand, "Exodus Starts as Forces Intensify Mohmand Operation," *The News*, February 2, 2011.

185 *granted them safe haven*: Roggio, "Taliban Escape South Waziristan Operation."

185 *not moving against the Haqqanis*: Kim Ghattas, "Clinton Raises Pressure on Pakistan to Fight Militants," BBC News, July 18, 2010.

186 *list of terrorist organizations*: Anwar Iqbal, "US Acts against Haqqani Network," *Dawn*, July 23, 2010.

187 *battlefield casualties*: "Global War on Terror Claims 30,000 Pakistani Casualties," Ummid.com, February 18, 2010. The high-ranking army officer who provided the statistics on the number of army troops engaged in the fighting in South Waziristan and Swat cited this same figure in discussing army casualties.

187 *ISI officers*: This statistic also comes from the officer cited above.

188 *Twelve months*: See, for example, Jane Perlez, "Rebuffing U.S., Pakistan Balks at Crackdown," *New York Times*, December 14, 2009.

189 *first and foremost*: Jane Perlez, Eric Schmitt, and Carlotta Gall, "Pakistan Is Said to Pursue Foothold in Afghanistan," *New York Times*, June 24, 2010. See also Baqir Sajjad Syed, "Pakistan Trying to Broker Afghan Deal," *Dawn*, June 16, 2010.

189 *base of operations*: Dressler, "The Haqqani Network," pp. 6 and 9.

189 *collaborated with ISI*: Sarah Davison and Jonathan S. Landay, "Pakistan-based Group Suspected in Indian Embassy Bombing," *McClatchy Newspapers*, October 8, 2009.

190 *arrested Baradar*: Dexter Filkins, "Pakistanis Tell of Motive in Taliban Leader's Arrest," *New York Times*, August 22, 2010.

190 *high level joint commission*: Shumaila Andleeb, "Pakistan, Afghanistan Set Up Joint Commission to Pursue Peace," *Dawn*, April 17, 2011.

190 *a Turkish proposal*: "Pakistan Would Back Taliban Office in Turkey: Official," *Express Tribune*, April 14, 2011.

190 *convince the Haqqanis*: Perlez, Schmitt, and Gall, "Pakistan Is Said to Pursue Foothold."

190 *tempo of drone attacks*: Scott Shane, "C.I.A. to Expand Use of Drones in Pakistan," *New York Times*, December 3, 2009.

190 *overwhelming majority*: See "Year of the Drone, 2010," the running tally maintained by Bergen and Tiedemann. The great majority of the attacks are against targets in North Waziristan. Not all the attacks were necessarily against Haqqani

network targets. Some were reportedly aimed at members of the Hafiz Gul Bahadur Pakistani Taliban and others at Al Qaeda.

190 *Mohammed Haqqani*: "Jalaluddin Haqqani's Son Killed in Drone Attack," *Dawn*, February 20, 2010.

190 *test Pakistani limits*: Chris Brummitt and Deb Riechmann, "Pakistan Cuts NATO Supply Line After Border Firing," Associated Press, September 30, 2010.

191 *interior Sindh*: "Militants Set Fire to NATO Tankers in Pakistan," Reuters, October 1, 2010. See also Sarfaraz Memon and Shehzad Baloch, "Terrorists Torch 27 NATO Tankers," *Express Tribune*, October 1, 2010.

191 *public apology*: Helene Cooper and Eric Schmitt, "U.S. Tries to Calm Pakistan Over Airstrikes," *New York Times*, October 6, 2010.

191 *into Kurram agency*: "Haqqani's Two Sons Mediating in Kurram," *Dawn*, October 21, 2010.

191 *offensive in North Waziristan*: See the speculation by the Middle East Media Research Institute, "Pakistani Army Allows Taliban to Move to New Sanctuary in Kurram Agency While Finally Agreeing to Carry Out Operation Against Militant Commanders in North Waziristan," October 25, 2010.

192 *remote base*: Jeremy Page, "Google Earth Reveals Secret History of US Base in Pakistan," *The Times*, February 19, 2009. Google Earth imaging of Shamsi air base in Baluchistan reportedly revealed three drone aircraft parked there. Senator Dianne Feinstein, chair of the Senate Intelligence Committee, also inadvertently admitted their presence in Pakistan in a Senate hearing. See "Editorial: The Drones Are Here," *Daily Times*, February 15, 2009.

192 *exasperated Secretary of State*: "Pakistan 'Hard to Believe" on Al Qaeda: Clinton," *Dawn*, October 30, 2009.

192 *non-NATO ally*: "Bush Names Pakistan 'Major Ally,'" BBC News, June 17, 2004.

192 *annual security assistance*: K. Alan Kronstadt, "Direct Overt U.S. Aid and Military Reimbursements to Pakistan, FY2002–FY2011," Congressional Research Service, June 7, 2010, www.fas.org/sgp/crs/row/pakaid.pdf.

192 *F-16 aircraft*: Yochi J. Dreazen, "U.S. to Offer Smart-Bomb Kits, Drones to Pakistan," *Wall Street Journal*, March 2, 2010.

192 *"strategic dialogue"*: U.S.-Pakistan Strategic Dialogue at the Ministerial Level March 24–25, 2010," Office of the Spokesman, U.S. Department of State.

192 *$1.5 billion*: Kronstadt, "Direct Overt U.S. Aid."

193 *firestorm of protest*: Saeed Shah, "Pakistan Army Anger over $1.5Bn U.S. Aid Deal," *Telegraph*, October 7, 2009.

193 *"judicial processes"*: The full text of the Kerry-Lugar Bill can be found at www.govtrack.us/congress/billtext.xpd?bill=s111-1707. The offending part is section 203 on Limitations on Certain Assistance.

193 *wild rumors*: Karen DeYoung and Pamela Constable, "Anti-U.S. Wave Imperiling Efforts in Pakistan, Officials Say," *Washington Post*, September 25, 2009. See also "US Marines Not Coming to Pakistan: US Embassy," *Geo News*, September 8, 2009.

193 *Pew Research poll*: "Most Pakistanis See US as an Enemy," *Express Tribune*, July 30, 2010.

193 *harassing U.S. diplomats*: Jane Perlez and Eric Schmitt, "Pakistan Reported to Be Harassing U.S. Diplomats," *New York Times*, December 16, 2009.

193 *Kashmir mandate*: Emily Wax, "U.S. Removes Kashmir from Envoy's Mandate; India Exults," *Washington Post*, January 30, 2009.

193 *praise the Indian role*: Sandeep Dikshit, "India Has a Major Role in Afghanistan: U.S.," *Hindu*, July 23, 2010.

194 *CIA withdrew*: Mark Mazzetti and Salman Mehsud, "Pakistani Role Is Suspected in Revealing U.S. Spy's Name," *New York Times*, December 17, 2010.

194 *surveilling the activities*: Mark Mazzetti, Ashley Parker, Jane Perlez, and Eric Schmitt, "American Held in Pakistan Worked with CIA," *New York Times*, February 21, 2011.

194 *were not robbers*: Omar Waraich, "U.S. Diplomat Could Bring Down Pakistan Government," *Time*, February 9, 2011.

194 *a CIA commitment*: Carlotta Gall and Mark Mazzetti, "Hushed Deal Frees CIA Contractor in Pakistan," *New York Times*, March 16, 2011.

195 *claimed forty-eight lives*: Salmon Masood and Pir Zubair Shah, "CIA Drones Kill Civilians in Pakistan," *New York Times*, March 17, 2011.

195 *senior Peshawar journalist*: Rahimullah Yusufzai, "Deadliest Drone Strike, But Not the Last," *News*, March 22, 2011.

195 *shrill Pakistani protests*: Eric Schmitt, "New CIA Drone Attack Draws Rebuke from Pakistan," *New York Times*, April 13, 2011.

195 *kill Osama bin Laden*: Peter Baker, Helene Cooper, and Mark Mazzetti, "Bin Laden Is Dead, Obama Says," *New York Times*, May 1, 2011.

195 *Hilary Clinton declared*: "Clinton: Pakistan Helped Lead U.S. to Bin Laden," ABC News, May 2, 2011.

9. The Shape of Things to Come

201 *precipitate a mutiny*: See Lieven, "How Pakistan Works," pp. 10–11.

203 *extend the term*: Shuja Nawaz, "Kayani, a Man for Many Seasons," the AfPak Channel, *Foreign Policy*, July 23, 2010.

204 *in sufficient strength*: Ahmed Rashid, "Pakistan Faces Taliban Resurgence," BBC News, May 9, 2010. See also Jane Perlez and Eric Schmitt, "Pakistan Army Finds Taliban Tough to Root Out," *New York Times*, July 4, 2010.

204 *seven CIA operatives*: Spencer S. Hsu and Greg Miller, "U.S. Government Charges Pakistani Taliban Leader Hakimullah Mehsud in CIA Attack," *Washington Post*, September 1, 2010.

204 *Faisal Shahzad*: See the profile of Faisal Shahzad and background to the Times Square car bombing attempt in the Time Topics People section of the online edition of *The New York Times*.

205 *more than fifty thousand*: Jayshree Bajoria cites a figure of thirty to thirty-five

thousand. See "Pakistan's New Generation of Terrorists," Council on Foreign Relations, May 6, 2010. Caroline Wadhams and Colin Cookman in "Faces of Pakistan's Militant Leaders" have estimated the number of forces commanded by each major Pakistani Taliban leader. The total amounts to more than fifty thousand.

205 *ten and twenty thousand*: Wadhams and Cookman, "Faces of Pakistan's Militant Leaders." See also Omar Waraich, "Pakistan Takes on Taliban Leader Mehsud," *Time*, June 16, 2009.

205 *Lashkar-e-Jhangvi*: Department of State, *Country Reports on Terrorism 2009*, "Lashkar i Jhangvi," chapter 6.

205 *two thousand Punjabis*: Aamir Latif, "Punjabi Taliban Rise in Waziristan," Islam Online.net, April 22, 2007.

205 *729 militants*: "Malik Sees Terror Roots in South Punjab," *Daily Times*, May 31, 2010.

206 *contest local elections*: Jane Perlez, "Official Admits Militancy's Deep Roots in Pakistan," *New York Times*, June 2, 2010.

207 *two guesthouses*: Karin Brulliard, "Afghan Intelligence Ties Pakistani Group Lashkar-e-Taiba to Recent Kabul Attack," *Washington Post*, March 3, 2010.

207 *Lashkar fighters*: Alissa J. Rubin, "Militant Group Expands Attacks in Afghanistan," *New York Times*, June 15, 2010.

207 *massive protests erupted*: Jyoti Thottam, "Valley of Tears," *Time*, September 4, 2008.

207 *half million people*: George Arney, "Non-Violent Protest in Kashmir," BBC World Service, October 14, 2008.

207 *two Kashmiri women*: Lydia Polgreen, "Women's Deaths, and Inquiry's Findings, Enrage Kashmir," *New York Times*, December 14, 2009.

207 *stone-throwing youths*: "Kashmir Protests Erupt into Violence After Government Troops Kill Four," *Guardian*, August 13, 2010. See also Amit Baruah, "Why Kashmir Is Again on a Knife Edge," BBC News, August 10, 2010, and Jim Yardley and Hari Kamir, "India Calls for Easing of Security in Kashmir," *New York Times*, September 25, 2010.

208 *Chatham House poll*: Bradnock, "Kashmir: Paths to Peace," p 16.

208 *The other interesting result*: Ibid., p. 17.

208 *militant violence*: Ibid., p. 14.

210 *Dennis Blair*: Jeremy Khan, "The Next Al Qaeda?" *Newsweek*, February 26, 2010. For analysis suggesting the Lashkar may be embracing a more global agenda, see Tankel, "Lashkar-e-Taiba in Perspective" and "Lashkar-e-Taiba: From 9/11 to Mumbai." See also Chalk, "Lashkar-e-Taiba's Growing International Focus," pp. 6–9.

212 *singled out ISI*: "27 Killed, Nearly 326 Injured; ISI Agents, 11 Policemen Among the Dead: ISI, Police Attacked," *Daily Times*, May 28, 2009.

212 *offices in Multan*: "12 Killed as Taliban Target ISI in Multan," *Daily Times*, December 9, 2009.

212 *interior minister admitted*: "Malik Sees Terror Roots in South Punjab," *Daily Times*, May 31, 2010.

213 *become Talibanized*: "Editorial: Feeling Insecure in Islamabad," *Daily Times*, September 4, 2009.

213 *Pakistan watcher Anatol Lieven*: Lieven, *Pakistan: A Hard Country*, p. 300.

10. The Final Unraveling

218 *one hundred warheads*: Karen De Young, "New Estimates Put Pakistan's Nuclear Arsenal at More Than 100," *Washington Post*, January 31, 2011. Also see Norris and Kristensen, "Nuclear Notebook," p. 83.

218 *ballistic missiles*: Ibid., pp. 86–87.

219 *National Resources Defense Council*: "The Consequences of Nuclear Conflict Between India and Pakistan." In the ground burst scenario, the actual targets were eight Pakistani and seven Indian cities. Twelve warheads were dropped on the Indian cities and twelve on the Pakistani, with fifteen million people at risk on each side. The actual projection was that a total of twenty-two million people combined would die from radiation alone, presumably with equivalent fatalities on each side.

220 *Hamid Gul*: The one time I met Gul was at a small reception hosted by the Jamaat at the Holiday Inn in Islamabad, probably in 2000. So far as I could tell, he was the only former army officer there. Other than me, he was the only one wearing a business suit.

221 *training Special Operations*: Christina Lamb, "Elite US Troops Ready to Combat Pakistani Nuclear Hijacks," *Sunday Times*, January 17, 2010.

221 *sympathetic army officers*: Gregory, "The Terrorist Threat to Pakistan's Nuclear Weapons." See also David Sanger, "Pakistan Strife Raises U.S. Doubt on Nuclear Arms," *New York Times*, May 3, 2009, and Hersh, "Defending the Arsenal."

221 *based on speculation*: See the report by Nick Schifrin of ABC News, "Have Pakistan's Nuclear Installations Already Been Attacked?" August 12, 2009. His Pakistani interlocutors vehemently denied that nuclear weapons had been located at any site previously attacked by terrorists. One of them, retired Lieutenant General Talat Masood, called the speculation absurd. Masood, whom I know well, was formerly secretary for defense production and is now a respected security analyst. He knows what he is talking about.

Bibliography

Abbas, Hassan. "The Black-Turbaned Brigade: The Rise of TNSM in Pakistan." *Terrorism Monitor* 4 (2006): 1–4.

———. "South Waziristan's Maulvi Nazir: The New Face of the Taliban." *Terrorism Monitor* 5 (2007), www.jamestown.org/programs/gta/single/?tx_ttnews[tt_news]=4147&tx_ttnews[backPid]=182&no_cache=1.

———. "The Road to Lal Masjid." *Terrorism Monitor* 5 (2007), www.jamestown.org/programs/gta/single/?tx_ttnews[tt_news]=4322&tx_ttnews[backPid]=182&no_cache=1.

———. "A Profile of Tehrik-i-Taliban Pakistan." *CTC Sentinel* 1 (2008): 1–4.

———. "Defining the Punjabi Taliban Network." *CTC Sentinel* 2 (2009): 1–4.

Allen, Charles. *Soldier Sahibs.* New York: Carroll & Graf, 2000.

Belasco, Amy. *Troop Levels in the Afghan and Iraq Wars FY2001–FY2012: Cost and Other Potential Issues.* Congressional Research Service, 2009.

Bergen, Peter. *The Osama bin Laden I Know: An Oral History of Al Qaeda's Leader.* New York: Simon and Schuster, 2006.

Bergen, Peter, and Katherine Tiedemann. "Year of the Drone." New America Foundation, 2010, http://counterterrorism.newamerica.net/drones.

Bose, Sumantra. *Kashmir: Roots of Conflict, Paths to Peace.* Cambridge, MA: Harvard University Press, 2002.

Bradnock, Robert W. "Kashmir: Paths to Peace," Chatham House, Royal Institute for International Affairs, 2010, www.chathamhouse.org.uk/files/16664_0510pp_kashmir.pdf.

Chalk, Peter. "Lashkar-e-Taiba's Growing International Focus and Its Links with Al Qaeda." *Terrorism Monitor* 8 (2010): 6–9.

Cohen, Stephen. *The Idea of Pakistan*. Washington, D.C.: Brookings Institution Press, 2004.

Coll, Steve. *Ghost Wars: The Secret History of the CIA, Afghanistan, and Bin Laden, from the Soviet Invasion to September 10, 2001*. New York: Penguin Press, 2004.

———. "Letter from Kashmir: Fault Lines: After the Earthquake." *New Yorker*, November 21, 2005.

———. "The Back Channel." *New Yorker*, March 2, 2009, pp. 38–51.

Dodge, Toby. "The Causes of US Failure in Iraq." *Survival* 49 (2007): 85–106.

Dressler, Jeffrey A. "The Haqqani Network: From Pakistan to Afghanistan." *Afghanistan Report* 6, Institute for the Study of War, 2010, www.understandingwar.org/files/Haqqani_Network.pdf.

Dressler, Jeffrey A., and Carl Forsberg. "The Quetta Shura Taliban in Southern Afghanistan: Organization, Operations and Shadow Governance." Institute for the Study of War, 2009, www.understandingwar.org/report/quetta-shura-taliban-southern-afghanistan.

Fair, C. Christine. *The Counterterror Coalitions: Cooperation with Pakistan and India*. Santa Monica: Rand Corporation, 2004.

Fair, C. Christine, and Seth G. Jones. "Pakistan's War Within," *Survival* 51 (2009–10): 161–88.

Fair, C. Christine, and Shuja Nawaz. "The Changing Pakistan Army Officer Corps." *Journal of Strategic Studies*, forthcoming. Available online at http://papers.ssm.com/sol3/papers.cfm?abstract_id=1615842.

Farooq, Omer. "Education." *Economic Survey of Pakistan, 2009–2010*, Ministry of Finance, Government of Pakistan, 2010.

Federation of American Scientists. "Pakistan Nuclear Weapons: A Brief History of Pakistan's Nuclear Weapons Program," 2002, www.fas.org/nuke/guide/pakistan/nuke.

Filipe, Jesus, and Juan Miranda. "A Plea to Pakistan: Fix Your Economy." *Far Eastern Economic Review* 172 (2009): 41–44.

Fishman, Brian. "Pakistan's Failing War on Terrorism." *Foreign Policy*, December 1, 2009, www.foreignpolicy.com/articles/2009/12/01/pakistans_failing_war_on_terror.

Gibb, H.A.R. *Mohammedanism: An Historical Survey*. New York: Oxford University Press, 1978.

Gilmore, David. *The Ruling Caste: Imperial Lives in the Victorian Raj*. New York: Farrar, Straus and Giroux, 2005.

Gregory, Shaun. "The Terrorist Threat to Pakistan's Nuclear Weapons." *CTC Sentinel* 2 (2009): 1–4.

Haqqani, Husain. *Pakistan: Between Mosque and Military*. Washington, D.C.: Carnegie Endowment for International Peace, 2005.

———. "The Ideologies of South Asian Jihadi Groups." *Current Trends in Islamist Ideology* 1 (2005): 12–26.

———. "Weeding Out the Heretics: Sectarianism in Pakistan." *Current Trends in Islamist Ideology* 4 (2006): 73–88.

Hersh, Seymour. "Defending the Arsenal." *New Yorker*, November 16, 2009, pp. 28–35.

Hopkirk, Peter. *The Great Game: The Struggle for Empire in Central Asia*. New York: Kodansha Globe, 1992.

Hussain, Zahid. "Paradise Lost." *Newsline*, February 8, 2009, www.newslinemagazine .com/2009/02/paradise-lost/.

International Crisis Group. "The State of Sectarianism in Pakistan," *Asia Report* 95 (2005), www.crisisgroup.org/~/media/Files/asia/south-asia/pakistan/095_the_state_ of_sectarianism_in_pakistan.ashx.

Jalal, Ayesha. *The Sole Spokesman*. New York: Cambridge University Press, 1985.

———. *The State of Martial Rule*. New York: Cambridge University Press, 1990.

———. *Democracy and Authoritarianism in South Asia*. New York: Cambridge University Press, 1995.

Jamal, Arif. *Shadow War: The Untold Story of the Jihad in Kashmir*. Brooklyn: Melville House, 2009.

———. "A Profile of Pakistan's Lashkar-e-Jhangvi." *CTC Sentinel* 2 (2009): 11–14.

———. "A Guide to Militant Groups in Kashmir." *Terrorism Monitor* 8 (2010): 8–11.

———. "The Growth of the Deobandi Jihad in Afghanistan." *Terrorism Monitor* 8 (2010): 8–11.

Johnson, Thomas H., and M. Chris Mason. "No Sign Until the Burst of Fire: Understanding the Pakistan-Afghanistan Frontier." *International Security* 32 (2008): 41–77.

Jones, Kenneth W. *The New Cambridge History of India, Part 3, Vol. 1: Socio-Religious Reform Movements in British India*. New York: Cambridge University Press, 1989.

Khan, Asad. "Pakistan—An Enduring Friend." *Marine Corps Gazette* 86 (2002): 34–38.

Khattak, Daud Khan. "The Battle for Pakistan: Militancy and Conflict in the Swat Valley." New America Foundation, 2010, http://counterterrorism.newamerica.net/ sites/newamerica.net/files/policydocs/swat.pdf.

Kux, Dennis. *India-Pakistan Negotiations: Is Past Still Prologue?* Washington, D.C.: United States Institute for Peace, 2006.

Lau, Martin. "Twenty-Five Years of Hudood Ordinances—A Review." *Washington and Lee Legal Review* 64 (2007): 1292–1314.

Lieven, Anatol. "How Pakistan Works." Lecture at Chatham House, Royal Institute of International Affairs, December 5, 2007, www.chathamhouse.org.uk/files/10669 _051207lieven.pdf.

———. *Pakistan: A Hard Country*. New York: Public Affairs, 2011.

Luce, Edward. *In Spite of the Gods: The Rise of Modern India*. New York: Anchor Books, 2009.

Lyon, Stephen. "Power and Patronage in Pakistan." Doctoral thesis in social anthropology, University of Kent, 2002. Available online at http://sapir.ukc.ac.uk/SLyon/ Lyon.pdf.

Mahsud, Mansur Khan. "The Battle for Pakistan: Militancy and Conflict in South Waziristan." New America Foundation, 2010, http://counterterrorism.newamerica .net/sites/newamerica.net/files/policydocs/southwaziristan.pdf.

Metcalf, Barbara. *Islamic Revival in British India: Deoband, 1860–1900*. Princeton: Princeton University Press, 1982.

————. "'Traditionalist' Islamic Activism: Deoband, Tablighis, and Talibs." In *After 9/11*. Social Science Research Council, 2002, http://essays.ssrc.org/sept11/essays/metcalf.htm.

Milam, William. *Bangladesh and Pakistan*. New York: Columbia University Press, 2009.

Motlagh, Jason. "Sixty Hours of Terror." *Virginia Quarterly Review*, 2009, www.vqronline.org/webexclusive/2009/11/19/motlagh-mumbai-attacks/.

Musharraf, Pervez. *In the Line of Fire: A Memoir*. New York: Free Press, 2006.

Nasr, Vali. *The Vanguard of the Islamic Revolution: The Jama'at-i Islami of Pakistan*. Berkeley: University of California Press, 1994.

————. *Mawdudi & the Making of Islamic Revivalism*. New York: Oxford University Press, 1996.

————. *The Shia Revival: How Conflicts Within Islam Will Shape the Future*. New York: Norton, 2006.

National Resources Defense Council. "The Consequences of Nuclear Conflict Between India and Pakistan," 2002, www.nrdc.org/nuclear/southasia.asp.

Nawaz, Shuja. *Crossed Swords: Pakistan, Its Army, and the Wars Within*. New York: Oxford University Press, 2008.

————. "FATA—A Most Dangerous Place: Meeting the Challenge of Militancy and Terror in the Federally Administered Tribal Areas of Pakistan." Center for Strategic and International Studies, 2009, www.scribd.com/doc/14663311/FATA-a-Most-Dangerous-Place.

Nayak, Polly, and Michael Krepon. "US Crisis Management in South Asia's Twin Peaks Crisis." Report 57, Henry L. Stimson Center, 2006.

Nayyar, Abdul Hameed. "Pakistan and Islamism." *Noref Policy Brief*. Norwegian Peacebuilding Centre, 2009.

Neumann, Ronald E. *The Other War: Winning and Losing in Afghanistan*. Washington, D.C.: Potomac Books, 2009.

Norris, Robert S., and Hans Kristensen. "Nuclear Notebook: Pakistani Nuclear Forces, 2009." *Bulletin of the Atomic Scientists* 65 (2009): 82–89.

Omrani, Bijan. "The Durand Line: History and Problems of the Afghan-Pakistan Border." *Asian Affairs* 40 (2009): 177–95.

Peer, Basharat. *Curfewed Night: One Kashmiri Journalist's Frontline Account of Life, Love, and War in His Homeland*. New York: Scribner, 2010.

Rahmanullah. "The Battle for Pakistan: Militancy and Conflict in Bajaur." New America Foundation, 2010, http://counterterrorism.newamerica.net/sites/newamerica.net/files/policydocs/bajaur.pdf.

Rashid, Ahmed. *Taliban: Islam, Oil and the New Great Game in Central Asia*. New York: I. B. Tauris, 2000.

————. *Descent into Chaos: The United States and the Failure of Nation Building in Pakistan, Afghanistan, and Central Asia*. New York: Viking, 2008.

Riedel, Bruce. *American Diplomacy and the 1999 Kargil Summit at Blair House*. Center for the Advanced Study of India, University of Pennsylvania, 2002.

―――. "Afghanistan: The Taliban Resurgent and NATO." Brookings Institution, 2006, www.brookings.edu/opinions/2006/1128globalgovernance_riedel.aspx.

Roy, Olivier. *Islam and Resistance in Afghanistan*. New York: Cambridge University Press, 1990.

―――. *Globalized Islam: The Search for a New Ummah*. New York: Columbia University Press, 2004.

Sahi, Aoun Abbas. "The Punjab Connection." *Newsline*, October 15, 2008, www .newslinemagazine.com/2008/10/the-punjab-connection/.

Schmidle, Nicholas. *To Live or Perish Forever: Two Tumultuous Years in Pakistan*. New York: Henry Holt, 2009.

Schmidt, John R. "The Unravelling of Pakistan." *Survival* 51 (2009): 29–54.

Siddiqa, Ayesha. *Military Inc*. London: Pluto Press, 2007.

―――. "Terror's Training Ground." *Newsline*, September 9, 2009, www.newsline magazine.com/2009/09/terror%E2%80%99s-training-ground/.

Simons, Thomas W., Jr. *Islam in a Globalizing World*. Stanford: Stanford University Press, 2003.

Sisson, Richard, and Leo Rose. *War and Secession: Pakistan, India, and the Creation of Bangladesh*. Berkeley: University of California Press, 1991.

Sulaiman, Sadia, and Syed Adnan Ali Shah Bukhari. "Hafiz Gul Bahadur." *Terrorism Monitor* 7 (2009): 4–6.

Szrom, Charlie. "The Survivalist of North Waziristan: Hafiz Gul Bahadur Biography and Analysis." American Enterprise Institute, 2009, www.criticalthreats.org/pakistan/ survivalist-north-waziristan-hafiz-gul-bahadur-biography-and-analysis.

Talbot, Ian. *Pakistan: A Modern History*. New York: Palgrave Macmillan, 2005.

Tankel, Stephen. "Lashkar-e-Taiba: From 9/11 to Mumbai." International Centre for the Study of Radicalisation and Political Violence, 2009, www.icsr.info/news/ attachments/1240846916ICSRTankelReport.pdf.

―――. "Lashkar-e-Taiba in Perspective: An Evolving Threat." New America Foundation, 2010, www.newamerica.net/sites/newamerica.net/files/policydocs/tankel.pdf.

Wadhams, Caroline, and Colin Cookman. "Faces of Pakistan's Militant Leaders: In-Depth Profiles of Major Militant Commanders." Center for American Progress, 2009, www.americanprogress.org/issues/2009/07/talibanleaders.html.

Waldman, Matt. "The Sun in the Sky: The Relationship Between Pakistan's ISI and Afghan Insurgents." Crisis States Research Centre, London School of Economics, 2010, www.crisisstates.com/download/dp/DP%2018.pdf.

Waseem, Mohammad. *Politics and the State in Pakistan*. Lahore: Progressive Publishers, 1989.

―――. "Causes of Democratic Downslide." *Economic and Political Weekly* 37 (2002): 4532–538.

―――. "Origins and Growth Patterns of Islamic Organizations in Pakistan." In *Religious Radicalism and Security in South Asia*, pp. 17–34. Honolulu: Asia-Pacific Center for Security Studies, 2004.

Woodward, Bob. *Obama's Wars*. New York: Simon and Schuster, 2010.

Yusufzai, Rahimullah. "Fall of the Last Frontier?" *Newsline*, June 7, 2002, www .newslinemagazine.com/2002/06/fall-of-the-last-frontier/.

Zahab, Mariam Abou, and Olivier Roy. *Islamist Networks: The Afghan-Pakistan Connection*. New York: Columbia University Press, 2004.

Zaidi, S. Akbar. "Pakistan's Roller-Coaster Economy: Tax Evasion Stifles Growth." Policy Brief 88, Carnegie Endowment for International Peace, September 2010.

Zaman, Muhammad Qasim. "Sectarianism in Pakistan: The Radicalization of Shi'i and Sunni Identities." *Modern Asian Studies* 32 (1998): 689–716.

———. *The Ulama in Contemporary Islam: Custodians of Change*. Princeton: Princeton University Press, 2002.

Acknowledgments

I have many people to thank for their help in writing this book. At the top of the list is Thomas W. Simons, Jr., who was my first ambassador in Pakistan and was responsible for my getting a position there. Despite his own busy work schedule at Harvard, he found the time to carefully read through my manuscript and provide many invaluable suggestions based on his own profound knowledge of Pakistan and the Islamic tradition in South Asia. When Tom finally says it's okay, you know it's okay.

There would be no book were it not for Scott Moyers at the Wylie Agency. He saw my original article in *Survival* and contacted me out of the blue to suggest it could be expanded into a valuable and timely book. Eric Chinski, my editor at Farrar, Straus and Giroux, helped enormously in shaping the final product. He was able to see clearly where it needed work, and his suggestions have made the book much better. I also thank Karl Inderfurth, who was assistant secretary for South Asia at the State Department when I served in Islamabad and later asked me to teach a graduate seminar on "Pakistan and the Radical Islamic Threat" at the Elliott School of International Affairs at George Washington University. He also read through the manuscript and provided many helpful comments.

I am grateful to Thomas Pickering, who was under secretary of state for political affairs when I was in Pakistan. He, too, was kind enough to read through the entire manuscript, and I greatly benefited from his many insights, born of his unparalleled career in diplomacy, including as U.S. ambassador to India. But I suppose he had no choice since he also happens to be my father-in-law. I also thank my other ambassador in Islamabad, William Milam, who proved to be an ideal sounding board and purveyor of many excellent ideas during our many conversations over dinner during the writing of this book. Many thanks as well to Rachel LoCurto, who dug up a wealth of extremely useful information while serving as my research assistant before heading off to India to study Urdu.

Special thanks to the many Pakistanis who contributed to my understanding of their country and its policies during my time there and in the years since. At the head of this list comes Mahmud Durrani, who helped me to understand the Pakistan army and much else besides. Nishat Ahmed and Talat Masood are two other former generals who greatly added to my understanding of their organization and their country. I was also fortunate enough to get to know a lot of senior politicians during my three years in Pakistan. They were invariably kind and gracious to me. I liked them all a lot and learned a great deal about Pakistani politics and culture from them. They include Chaudhry Shujaat, Gohar Ayub, Chaudhry Pervez Elahi, Ijaz ul-Haq, Ghulam Sarwar Cheema, Sheikh Rashid, Abida Hussain, Fakir Imam, Amin Fahim, Qazi Hussain Ahmed, Aitzaz Ahsan, Majid Malik, Elahi Bux Soomro, Raja Zafar ul-Haq, Daniel Aziz, and Asfandyar Wali. I am particularly grateful to Mohammad Waseem, whose academic work on the Pakistani political process is unequaled and who provided my first real insights into that unique political culture. Many Pakistani journalists also contributed to my understanding of their country. These include Maleeha Lodhi, who has also enjoyed a brilliant diplomatic career, Najam Sethi, Talat Hussain, M. Ziauddin, Ayesha Siddiqa, and Arif Jamal.

Finally, I thank Amanullah (Aman) Khan, who was my senior Pakistani political assistant in Islamabad. He knew everybody in Pakistan worth knowing and managed to introduce me to most of them. He was also the person who first taught me, patiently and with great skill, most of what I still pretend to know about Pakistan, a country that I have grown both to care for and despair over. Thank you, Aman.

Index